Writing from Experience

REVISED EDITION

*With Grammar and Language
Skills for ESL/EFL Students*

by Marcella Frank
American Language Institute, New York University

D1297010

The University of Michigan Press
Ann Arbor

Copyright © by the University of Michigan 2004
All rights reserved
ISBN 0-472-08809-2
Published in the United States of America by
The University of Michigan Press
Manufactured in the United States of America

2007   2006   2005   2004   4   3   2   1

Acknowledgments

Grateful acknowledgment is made to the following authors and publishers for permission to reprint previously published materials.

Bantam Dell Publishing Group for "Potato and Vegetable" recipe from *The Complete Book of Vegetable Cookery,* by Myra Waldo, copyright © 1962 Bantam Dell Publishing Group Division of Random House Inc.

Gerri Barr for home repair photograph.

Columbia University Press for the selection from "Carnival" from *Columbia Encyclopedia,* 5th ed. Copyright © 1993, Columbia University Press. Reprinted with the permission of the publisher.

CultureGrams for adaption of "Customs and Courtesies." Abridged from the 2002 *CultureGrams Standard Edition: United States of America,* "Customs and Courtesies." Reprinted with permission from CultureGrams a division of Millennial Star Network and Brigham Young University, Provo, UT.

European Travel Commission for Map of Europe, "Your Invitation to Europe," October 1997.

Grolier Incorporated for adaptions of map of Great Britain and Ireland from *The Encyclopedia Americana,* 1978 Edition, copyright © 1978 by Grolier Incorporated, and adaption of "Etiquette," from *The Encyclopedia International,* 1967 Edition, copyright © 1967 by Grolier Incorporated. Reprinted by permission.

Kerri Kijewski for Halloween photograph.

Library of Congress, Prints and Photographs Division, for the following photos: Albert Einstein (LC-USZ62-60242), Mahatma Gandhi (LC-US762-97285), William Shakespeare (LC-USZ62-119825).

Little, Brown and Company for adaption from *Mythology* by Edith Hamilton. Copyright 1942 by Edith Hamilton; © renewed 1969 by Dorian Fielding Reid and Doris Fielding Reid. By permission of Little, Brown and Company.

New York Times for adaptions of the Western and Oriental Animal (horoscope) Cycles by Frank V. Rubens, New York Times Pictures. Copyright © 1976.

New York University students for their collaborative composition "The Celebration of Loy-Krathong in Thailand" in Unit 5.

Pearson Computer Publishing for "North America" from *The Complete Idiot's Guide to Geography* and adaption from *The Complete Idiot's Guide to Etiquette,* 2d ed. Reprinted with the permission of Alpha Books, as represented by Pearson Computer Publishing, a Division of Pearson Education, from *Complete Idiot's Guide to Geography* by Thomas E. Sherer, Jr., and *Complete Idiot's Guide to Etiquette,* 2d ed., by Mary Mitchell. Copyright 1997 by Alpha Books and Copyright 2000 by Alpha Books.

Random House for adaption of "The Old Lady in the Cave" from *Favorite Folktales from around the World* by Jane Yolen, editor. Introduction copyright © 1986 by Jane Yolen. Reprinted by permission of Pantheon Books, a division of Random House, Inc.

Pete Sickman-Garner for illustration.

Simon & Schuster for adaption from *Amulets, Talismans and Fetishes*. Reprinted with the permission of Atheneum Books for Young Readers, an imprint of Simon & Schuster Children's Publishing Division from *Amulets, Talismans and Fetishes* by Arthur S. Gregor. Copyright © 1975 Arthur S. Gregor.

Teachers College Press for material from "Reading Hygiene" and "Taking an Examination" from *Study Types of Reading Exercises* by R. Strang. Reprinted by permission of the publisher from Strang, R., *Study Types of Reading Exercises* (New York: Teachers College Press, © 1951 by Teachers College, Columbia University. All rights reserved), pp. 74, 145–146.

Tribune Media Services for "The Good Old Days? Think Again" by Ed Perkins from the *San Diego Tribune*, July 27, 1997, copyright © 1997. © Tribune Media Services, Inc. All Rights Reserved. Reprinted with permission.

Xavier Urquieta for select illustrations.

Don Ward for photograph of the Washington Monument.

World Book Publishing for adaption of "Etiquette" and excerpt from "Superstition" from *The World Book Encyclopedia*. Excerpted from *The World Book Encyclopedia* © 2000 World Book, Inc. By permission of the publisher. www.worldbook.com.

Every effort has been made to trace the ownership of all copyrighted material in this book and to obtain permission for its use. We regret any oversights that have occurred and will rectify them in future printings of this book.

Contents

CONTENTS

Introduction

Writing from Experience, Revised Edition, is a writing workbook for adults. Such students are at a transitional stage in which they need to continue their mastery of the basic language skills while they gradually develop the rhetorical skills necessary to write effective compositions in today's high schools, community colleges, and universities.

This workbook is the result of many years of classroom testing, both in the United States and abroad. During this time I have constantly modified my approach to make the text more useful in the classroom. I have also benefited from the suggestions made by teachers at New York University and elsewhere who have tested the materials.

Like the first edition, this revision is content oriented. It also uses the same kind of guided approach to teaching composition through an outline-discussion procedure. However, some new features, in particular, peer review of compositions, journal writing, and summary writing, have been added to enrich the language learning experiences.

Writing from Experience has great flexibility of use. It may be the only text in a writing class or it may be a supplementary text in a grammar class or a class for combined language skills. Because of the great amount of controlled practice in the text, it may also be used in a writing workshop or in a tutorial program staffed by teaching assistants. The wide variety of language practice in *Writing from Experience*—speaking, writing, reading, listening, grammatical structure—represents a careful integration of the language skills and is designed to maintain student interest.

Because *Writing from Experience* is intended for students who are still challenged by problems on the sentence level, the workbook does not require them to explore a composition in depth. Students can write from their own knowledge and experience, without much support from readings or lengthy instructions. The composition topics involve mainly rhetorical patterns that are relatively easy to handle, such as description, narrative, and explanation.

The text contains nine units, each dealing with one particular subject. The topics in these units become progressively more comprehensive, and the level of difficulty increases.

Unique Features

1. Rhetorical Control (of the organization and development of compositions)

Rhetorical control comes essentially from an outline given for the main composition in each unit. This outline guides the two stages that are preliminary to the writing of the composition. The first stage provides for a discussion of each item in the outline. The second stage, introduced in Unit 4 after students have gotten used to working from an outline, requires the completion of an organizational work sheet based on the outline. This work sheet, which offers students the opportunity to make preliminary notes, serves as the basis for the final draft of the composition.

Constant use of such outlines makes students aware of the need for an organic structure to their compositions, a structure required by the rhetorical rules of English, but not necessarily by the writing conventions of other languages. The repeated use of outlines also gives students an awareness of paragraph development within the context of the composition, so students get a better feeling for writing effective paragraphs than if they wrote them in isolation.

While the control offered by the outline serves as a loose model for the main composition of each unit, a later practice activity contains a full model. Also, some contextualized exercises offer partial models.

2. Grammatical Control (of the structures needed to write about a particular subject)

The text sets up the preliminary discussion stage in such a way that the teacher can help the students with any of the grammatical structures needed to discuss the subject of the composition. In addition, the text provides many reinforcement exercises for oral and written practice in these structures.

3. Semantic Control (of the vocabulary needed to write about a particular subject)

The discussion stage also offers an opportunity for the teacher to supply needed vocabulary. Furthermore, vocabulary related to the subject is found throughout the exercises, much of it recycled many times.

In addition, many units give students the opportunity to enlarge the vocabulary needed for describing (geography and scenic views, personal characteristics), giving instructions (including recipes), and writing letters.

4. Communicative Control (of the subject matter)

Each unit consists of a concrete topic that lends itself to discussion. Thus, students can talk and write about subjects that come from their own knowledge and experience. What they want to say is merely channeled through an outline. Each unit helps the students expand their thinking on the subject and increases the range of vocabulary needed to discuss the subject.

The discussion of the subject matter in each unit offers the opportunity for cross-cultural exchanges between student and student as well as between students and teacher. Also, the practice materials throughout the text provide the teacher with information that can help in conveying many aspects of American culture.

Organization of the Units

Each of the nine units is divided into six sections:

    1. Discussion and Composition
    2. Grammar Practice
    3. Extra Speaking and Writing Practice

4. Listening-Writing Practice

5. Reading-Writing Practice (summary)

6. For Your Information (not in every unit)

Discussion and Composition

While each unit is about the subject in general, most of the compositions are specifically geared to the student's own culture. Obviously, for all students of ESL who do not remember much about their native country or who have spent most of their lives in the United States, these compositions can be about the country in which they are presently living.

This section is set up in two parts.

1. Discussion: Preliminary outline for the composition (prewriting stage)

The guidance for this stage is presented in two columns. The left column is the outline. The right column suggests guidance that the teacher can give as the students discuss the items on the outline. This guidance includes ideas, grammar and usage, and vocabulary, as well as elements of composition building.

This outline-discussion format facilitates the integration of all the levels of writing—sentence, paragraph, and full composition—in one process.

2. Composition (to be done before or after the grammar practice)

A. Organizing the Composition

From Unit 4 on, each unit includes an organizational work sheet, which is based on the discussion outline and which requires students to set up the structural framework of their compositions.

The work sheet requires students to indicate the contents of their introductions and conclusions, to write many of the opening sentences of paragraphs, and to list supporting details in each paragraph. Textual notes for each point on the outline guide the students in the use of their paragraphs. Thus, much of the guidance in rhetorical control that was first given orally during the discussion is noted at the appropriate place on the work sheet.

B. Writing the Composition

In this stage, instructions are given for writing the composition based on the notes made on the organizational work sheet. Also, instructions for the composition's format are included as needed as a reminder of the form that is to be followed.

C. Correcting/Rewriting the Composition

The text sets up a procedure for students to correct their own compositions and to learn from their corrections. A Symbol Chart for Correction for Compositions for use by both the teacher and the student appears in the Appendix.

For Units 1–3, students are asked merely to make the corrections indicated by the symbols. From Unit 4 on, students first exchange compositions before they turn in their compositions to the teacher. In this peer review, students use a guideline to check for the rhetorical control of the composition and then for editing problems. All compositions will then need to be revised before being turned in.

Grammar Practice

This section includes a variety of oral and written drills on structure and vocabulary, many of which are on the sentence level. The choice of grammatical structures has been determined by the need to communicate about a particular subject matter. (Examples of such structures are: In Biography: prepositions of time; In Instructions: passive for a process, conditions for precautions; In Telling Stories: direct and indirect speech.) For this reason, the structures are not graded for degree of difficulty, nor do they cover all problems of grammatical usage. However, an effort has been made to include as many of the basic structures as possible, as a kind of review (and in some cases, an expansion) of structures students have previously learned. An effort has also been made to keep the explanations short and clear, with a minimum of grammatical terminology but with abundant examples.

The contents of the drills are all related to the subject matter of the unit. The vocabulary represents a mixture of formal and conversational styles appropriate for writing. As in the grammatical structures, the vocabulary is not graded.

Among the types of exercises are two of special note that appear in each of the units. One is on word forms. This type has been included because even advanced students continue to have difficulties with the use of the proper part-of-speech suffixes. The other type of exercise contains strings of lexical items that must be made into full sentences. This exercise serves both as a review of sentence structures already practiced in the unit and as further practice in using the appropriate verb forms and structure words such as articles and prepositions.

Extra Speaking and Writing Practice

The exercises in this section provide a variety of language activities that offer speaking and writing practice, or both. Many of them can be done by pairs of students or in larger groups. Some of these exercises begin with oral work based on visual material such as a map, a chart, or a diagram. Other oral practice, often leading to writing, may take the form of dialogues, role playing, or interviews.

This section also contains a provision for journal writing. However, most units require students to carry this work with freely written entries a step further. They are asked to use their journal entries as first drafts for a more carefully written work, often a letter to a teacher, a friend, or a family member.

Listening-Writing Practice

Each unit has one selection for **dictation** and one for a **dicto-comp** (dictation-composition), all based on the subject matter of the unit. Dicto-comps are longer selections than dictations; students write summaries from the dicto-comps that their teacher reads to them. Most of the dicto-comps serve as models for the main composition of the unit.

Reading-Writing Practice (summary)

Each unit contains a short selection to be summarized. Students are given instructions on how to write a summary, and model summaries are provided on the Web site.

For Your Information

Different materials are given in this section for students' information and enjoyment. Some examples are: a poem, a recipe, a student composition, a story, and a letter.

Appendix

- Symbol Chart for Correction of Compositions
- Punctuation Rules
- Spelling Rules
- Irregular Verbs
- Answers to all the reinforcement drills in each unit. These answers are particularly useful for students who are doing any of the exercises on their own.

Additional material helpful to students and teachers can be found on the Web site that accompanies this textbook: www.press.umich.edu/esl/writingfromexp. The following material is available:

- Specific suggestions to teachers for handling the work in each of the units.
- Two forms of a structure test that can be administered before and after the practice work with the text, not only to determine student progress, but also to pinpoint areas for student improvement.
- Model summaries for students.

To the Student

The method of writing compositions that you are going to follow in this book may be quite different from the way you have been taught before. In this book you will write compositions that are controlled by an outline. The use of such an outline will enable you to construct well-developed compositions. In order for you to concentrate on these techniques of composition building, you will be asked to write only about subjects that you know from your own experience.

Units 1 through 3 will help you get accustomed to following an outline. Beginning with Unit 4, you will be writing compositions that have three basic parts: an introduction, a body, and a conclusion. Such an organization may not be required in all types of writing, but it is the one most commonly used for formal papers and reports of the kind you might need for academic work. The introduction prepares the reader for what you are going to concentrate on, the body contains the main points that you are going to make, and the conclusion rounds out in some satisfying way what you have just said.

The following sections give a brief explanation of the use of introductions and conclusions, as well as of other elements of composition building. The examples are taken from Unit 7, Superstitious Beliefs.

1. Introductions

An introduction often makes general statements that lead into the specific subject (or the body) of your composition. There are a number of ways of making such general statements. One way that is suggested in this book is to give a definition of the broad term which you will treat in a narrower sense in the composition. For example, in the composition on "Superstitious Beliefs in (*name of country*)," you will be asked to begin the composition with a general definition of superstition. The text suggests that such a definition might include references to the fact that superstition:

- is an unreasonable belief that supernatural forces can cause good or bad things to happen
- results from ignorance and fear of the unknown
- often involves magic and witchcraft
- may have a religious origin

2. Transitional Lead-ins

A transitional lead-in helps you move from the general comments of the introduction to the body of your composition. This transition indicates how you are going to narrow down the general statements in your introduction to the specific subject of your composition. Also, the transition may actually mention the main points on your outline so that the reader can anticipate the way you are organizing your composition. For example, a transitional lead-in suggested for the composition on "Superstitious Beliefs in (*name of country*)" is: "Superstitions are often attached to numbers, animals and birds, and things." This transition tells the reader that you are going to organize your composition about superstitions under the headings of:

I. Superstitions about numbers
II. Superstitions about animals and birds
III. Superstitions about things

3. Paragraphing

The outline is very important in guiding you in the construction of your paragraphs. Each item on the outline is generally developed in a separate paragraph. The opening sentence of each paragraph (often called a *topic sentence*) includes a reference to the point on the outline. For example, the opening sentence of point I, superstitions about numbers, might be: "There are several superstitions about numbers in (*name of country*)."

The sentences that follow this opening sentence should be only about the topic from the outline—in this example, superstitions about numbers. Also, the sentences that follow the opening sentence of a paragraph should be connected properly. Suggested connectives that might link sentences after the opening sentence of that paragraph about numbers are:

For example, we have *one* about number 13.
or
The most common *one* concerns number 13.

4. Conclusions

The conclusion gives the composition a sense of completion by opening up from the main part of the composition to more general comments about the subject. Thus, the composition begins and ends with general statements about the subject.

For the conclusion of the composition on superstitions, this book suggests that general statements might consist of your own belief about superstition.

A conclusion need not be long, and it can sometimes be omitted if the main part of the composition ends on an important point or if a story merely comes to an end.

The general statements of introductions and conclusions given in this book are only suggestions. You might want to use your own ideas instead. However, introductions and conclusions should be kept short so that you can concentrate on the main part of your composition, which comes from the other points on the outline.

This kind of tight control through the use of an outline with an introduction and a conclusion may seem artificial to you, and in fact this control is not always so strict as that recommended in this book. However, it is useful for you to practice such control at first so that you may have the rules for composition building firmly in mind. Remember that your reader expects some guidance to the main points on your outline. Your awareness of these principles of writing is important not only for writing but also for reading textbooks. In the introduction and conclusion of the entire book, and often in each chapter, the writer of a text will guide the reader to the main ideas. Also, the writer will frequently use headings to draw attention to the main points from the outline.

5. Format of the Composition

Use 8½- by 11-inch white paper, with lines for handwritten compositions and without lines for computer-printed compositions. Double-space papers prepared on a computer, and skip alternate lines on handwritten compositions. Write on the front of the paper only and leave wide margins on *both the left and the right sides* of the paper. Indent the beginning of each paragraph. The first page of your composition should include your name, the date, your teacher's name, and the name of your class.

Procedures for the Teacher

Since the outline-discussion approach for teaching composition is basically different from other approaches, and since the success of this approach is partly dependent on the procedures for guiding the composition, it is especially important for the teacher to have some general guidelines.

First, a word about when the compositions should be written. Although each unit begins with the discussion and composition section, the decision of whether students should write the composition before or after the grammar exercises is up to the teacher. However, regardless of when the composition is to be written, it is highly desirable to begin the work of the unit with the discussion of the composition. There are several reasons for doing so.

This discussion requires students right from the start to face many of the semantic, structural, and rhetorical problems involved in writing about a particular subject. The oral guidance given by the teacher for points on the outline helps students to begin to overcome these problems. This guidance not only forestalls the possible number of mistakes in student compositions, but also helps students retain longer those structural and lexical items that they struggled for in the discussion and that they will also need when they write about the subject.

Furthermore, after students talk about the composition topic, they often realize that their mastery of some of the structures they have already studied is not as secure as they had thought. They are therefore more receptive to doing the grammar exercises and can gain more from them.

Another advantage of beginning with the discussion stage is that the cross-cultural exchange that is involved puts students at ease immediately. Communicating freely and meaningfully with each other creates a friendly and relaxed atmosphere in which the students and the teacher can learn from each other.

While the ultimate purpose of *Writing from Experience* is to develop the writing and composing skills of intermediate students, the text also provides for the development of other language skills to reinforce the writing. Many of the language skills are acquired through the medium of cultural experiences.

The text provides the customs found in American culture and gives the opportunity for students to compare cultures. Thus while students are learning to improve their language skills, they are also expanding their vision of American culture and broadening their acquaintance with other cultures through student exchange.

A few words of explanation are needed about the book's treatment of customs. While the text concentrates on customs in American culture, it takes into account changing customs and lifestyles. Also, for holidays that have a religious origin, the text includes only the festive activities that *most* Americans enjoy regardless of their religion. Students are exposed to these activities, and they are interested in learning about them and taking part in them.

For ESL students who have been in the United States for some time, the text indicates that the teacher can adapt some of the subjects of the compositions; for example, "My Trip to the United States" can be changed to a trip to another country. Also, if students are unfamiliar with traditional customs in their native country, they are told they can write about modern customs in the United States.

Although it is not necessary to follow the same order as in the book, it would be desirable to do so, since the work in the units gets progressively more difficult. And, obviously, not all of the work in the book needs to be done in class. Since the answers to the exercises are included in the book, some of the exercises can be assigned to students with individual needs. Also, the teacher will find that many students like to do some exercises on their own because of the answers in the book.

Procedures for the Discussion Stage

Because of the importance of the discussion stage for the work to be done in each unit, specific steps are suggested below for handling this stage. These suggestions are based on the use of the outline page(s) at the beginning of the Discussion and Composition section.

First, write on the board the title and the outline given in the left column. (Some subpoints can be omitted from the outline at first and then added as the discussion proceeds.) *Students' books should be closed,* in order to allow them to get the most benefit out of the oral work.

For the steps that are to follow, use the information from the right-hand column to help students with the content and expression of the composition. Include elements of the rhetorical development if the composition is to be written immediately after the discussion. Elicit as much of this information as possible from the students.

1. Call on individual students to give a full sentence for each point on the outline.

2. As a student makes a mistake or searches for a word, get the correct information from the class and place it on the board. Have students copy this information in their notebooks.

3. Continue calling on students until they give enough sentences for each point on the outline to enable you to place all the needed structures and vocabulary on the board. Encourage student exchange of information. In some units the discussion column has information on American culture that can be shared with the students.

4. If much student interaction has been generated during the class discussion, you might form student groups to continue discussing the points on the outline with each other.

5. From Unit 4 on, when introductions and conclusions are added to the composition, see how much of the suggested contents for these paragraphs you can get from the students themselves before you give the information from the discussion column (and of course additional suggestions of your own). The suggested contents of instructions and conclusions are especially important for the less proficient or less reflective students. Such students will follow the suggestions closely, while the others will be able to express their own ideas more freely. You might also ask the class for alternate transitions and opening sentences of paragraphs.

Procedures for the Writing Stage

If some time has elapsed between the preliminary discussion and the writing of the composition, it would be desirable to repeat the discussion based on the outline, especially for the handling of the introduction, conclusion, and transitions. Stress the use of opening sentences of paragraphs in order to start building an awareness of topic sentences.

Have the students fill out the organizational work sheet, which requires them to stay within the structural framework set up by the outline. Suggest that they check against the discussion outline for additional help.

For the first few compositions it is advisable to have students fill out the work sheet in class. Once this is done, the composition can be written (or at least started) in class, or it can be assigned for homework. The compositions in Units 8 and 9, which are rather long, may be broken into two parts, both for the discussion and the composition. The two parts, however, should hold together as one composition.

Advise students of the importance of revising their compositions several times so that what they hand in is the best work they can do.

Procedures for the Correcting/Rewriting Stage

In going over the compositions, mark mistakes with the symbols from the correction chart (see the Appendix) so that students can correct their papers themselves. An error may be marked by underlining it and placing the correction symbol directly above it, or better still, in the margin.

If you feel that this symbol system is too complicated for your students, you might at first select only the starred symbols, which cover the more basic problems in English, and then gradually introduce other correction symbols. Also, in some cases you might find it advisable to use some subsymbols—for example, V(tense), P(run-on).

Once students have been made sufficiently aware of a particular usage, mistakes in this usage might be merely underlined or circled instead of being labeled.

Encourage students to keep a list of corrections in a special section of their notebooks and to review these from time to time so they will avoid such mistakes in the future.

For the first three units, before collecting the compositions, give students some time to look over their compositions to try to correct any errors they find. From Unit 4 on, have students exchange compositions to check first for their rhetorical development and then for problems in grammar and usage. Then collect these compositions, write further comments on them, and mark the remaining mistakes with the correction symbols. Return the compositions for revision and for inclusion in writing portfolios.

From each set of compositions, you might reproduce sentences with errors for students to correct, especially sentences containing structures that have been studied recently. Also, it would be good to reproduce a student composition for the whole class to analyze for rhetorical development. For this purpose it's better not to include the mistakes in grammar and usage. Occasionally, you might reproduce some student compositions as examples of well-written compositions.

Procedures for the Grammar Practice

Although some of the Grammar Practice is specifically designated in the text as group work, actually almost all of the exercises can be done in groups. Division of students into pairs provides the most individual practice, but for some activities, larger groups might get the benefit of greater cross-cultural exchange.

Whether students are to do the exercises in class or at home, the explanations should be gone over first, and answers for the first few sentences should be made available to make sure that the students understand what is required in each exercise.

Procedures for the Extra Speaking and Writing Practice

These speaking and writing exercises, which provide a variety of short activities, have varying degrees of control. It would be best to work with these exercises after the composition has been corrected or rewritten.

Procedures for the Listening-Writing Practice

The Listening-Writing Practice consists of dictations and dicto-comps. These can be interspersed with the grammar exercises in order to give more variety to the classroom practice. A dictation or dicto-comp can be assigned for study beforehand or it can be done without previous preparation. In the latter case, it is advisable at the first reading to let students look at the selection in the book and to explain any difficult structures and vocabulary.

Dictations

For the dictations, the standard procedure is recommended:

1. Read the entire selection once at normal speed while students listen.
2. Read the selection again, more slowly but in natural phrases, for students to write.
3. Read the selection a third time at normal speed for students to check what they have written.

After the dictations are collected, have the students refer to the selection in the book immediately, while their interest is still keen on seeing what they got right or wrong. Other possible procedures are to let students correct their own dictations or to have them exchange papers for correction.

Dicto-comps

Dicto-comps are written summaries of selections that are read to the class by the teacher. Students get the most benefit from a dicto-comp if they have not seen it before they listen to it. However, if the selection is difficult for students, it might be assigned beforehand. The danger here, of course, is that students may merely memorize it, which defeats the purpose of the dicto-comp as listening-writing practice (although the memorization is helpful for internalizing certain structural and lexical items).

The dicto-comp, like the dictation, is read three times, but each time at normal speed. It is advisable to have students take notes of what they hear at each reading. After the last reading, to make sure that students have not missed the main points, you might ask a series of questions about the content in chronological order so that they can check their notes, and you might put key words on the board to guide the writing. Also, if there is time, you might form small groups for students to exchange their information with each other before they write their dicto-comps.

After students turn in what they have written, it is useful to have them look at the reading selections to get immediate feedback on problems they had in writing the dicto-comp.

Procedures for the Reading-Writing Practice (summary)

Be sure that students understand what a summary is. It would be wise to review in class the first few selections for summary writing to determine what information might go into each summary and to check for the development of the reading selection (comparison, contrast, time, etc.).

When student summaries are returned, reproduce and distribute the model summary from the Web site so that students can get some idea of what is expected. (Emphasize that this model is only one of several ways that the summary might have been written.)

Procedures for the For Your Information Section

The materials in this section, although given purely for student information and enjoyment, can lead to much discussion. For example, the poem in Unit 3 can lead to a general discussion about poetry. The recipe in Unit 4 can lead to an exchange of recipes from other cultures. (Not every unit contains a For Your Information section.)

Many possibilities for collaborative learning can result from the use of *Writing from Experience*. The subject matter in this text lends itself to multiple opportunities for students to work together. For example, students can videotape the role plays or produce puppet shows of their stories. They can also get together to edit and produce anthologies of some of their writing, especially compositions on holidays and superstitions or collections of stories and recipes.

Traveling to Another Country

Discussion and Composition

1. Discussion: Preliminary Outline for the Composition (prewriting stage)

Subject: *My Trip to the United States* (or to another country)

Outline (To be placed on the board. Books are closed.)	Discussion (Ideas, Grammar and Usage, Vocabulary, Elements of Composition Building)

I. Decision to travel to the country	Purpose:
	With *to:*
	    to continue my studies
	    to specialize in a particular field
	    to visit the country only
	    to get some practical experience
	    to immigrate
	With *for:*
	    for a visit
	    for business
	    for pleasure
	    for further education
	Problems:
	    overcoming my parents' objections
	    getting the money to live in the new
	      country

II. Preparations for the trip
  A. Getting the necessary documents
  B. Taking care of medical
     requirements
  C. Making the financial arrangements
  D. Buying clothes
  E. Purchasing the ticket for the trip
 	
  F. Packing bags
	
	Documents: passport, visa, I-20 for students
	Shots: injections; vaccination, inoculation;
	    immunization—for smallpox, cholera
	
	One way or round trip, tourist class,
	    business class, first class
	Plane fare
	Suitcases, luggage, baggage, carry-on
	Shipping trunk ahead

III. The trip itself
  A. Saying good-bye to family, friends
  B. Plane ride
	
	Tearful, crying
	Checking in, boarding pass, going through
	    security checks
	Long trip, nonstop
	Delays, plane trouble
	Comfortable, airsick
	Service, food

Plane ride (continued)	Flight attendants Feelings: sad, homesick, lonesome, worried, anxious, happy, excited Experiences, other passengers Views from the plane

IV. Arrival in the new country
    A. Experiences at the airport
	Impression of the airport
	Difficulty with the language
	Claiming bags from the baggage
	    (luggage) area
	Going through customs

B. First impressions of the new country	Ride from the airport to your destination

2. Composition (to be done before or after the grammar practice)

A. Writing a 400/500-Word Composition

Place the title of the composition at the top of the page:

My Trip to the United States
(or to another country)

Do not use quotation marks or a period for a title at the top of the page. Use initial capital letters for the first word of the title and for all other words except articles, prepositions, and coordinate conjunctions *(and, or, but)*. (Some style books use lower case letters for all prepositions and conjunctions.)

Write the composition "My Trip to the United States" (or to another country) following the outline that has been discussed. The right column of the outline pages can be of help to you.

Place each of the four main points in a separate paragraph. If any of these paragraphs is quite long, you may break it in two. Be sure to follow chronological order.

Refer to the student section for tips on producing your composition (whether on a computer or by hand). Use the *past tense*.

B. Correcting/Rewriting the Composition

Before you give your composition to your teacher, look it over carefully to correct any grammar, spelling, or punctuation mistakes.

When your teacher returns your composition, it will be marked with the symbols from the correction chart in the Appendix. Make the necessary corrections clearly on the composition and hand it back to your teacher. If you have made many mistakes, you will need to rewrite the composition before turning it in.

 **Grammar Practice**

Exercise 1: *very, too,* and *so* with Adjectives or Adverbs

> *Very, too,* and *so* are used with adjectives or adverbs to express degree (how much).
>
> *Very* expresses a large degree.
>> I was *very* nervous on the plane.
>
> *Too* expresses an excessive degree, more than is acceptable.
>> I was *too* nervous on the plane to eat the food.
>
> Sometimes the speaker determines how much is excessive.
>> It was *very* noisy at the airport.
>> It was *too* noisy at the airport.
>
> *So* is often an informal equivalent of *very*.
>> I was *so* nervous on the plane.
>
> This use of *so* for *very* should be avoided in compositions. *So* is appropriately used before adjectives or adverbs that are followed by *that*.
>> I was *so* nervous on the plane *that* I couldn't eat anything.

Supply *very, too,* or *so*. Do not use *so* for *very*.

1. At the Consulate, I had to wait in a __very__ long line.

2. There were __so__ many things I had to do that I thought I would never be ready to leave for my trip.

3. The night before I left, I was __too__ excited to sleep.

4. My trip was _____ nice and comfortable, but I couldn't sleep.

5. During the trip I felt _____ depressed.

6. The food on the plane was _____ bad that I couldn't eat it.

7. The plane arrived at the airport _____ late. It was _____ late for anyone to meet me.

8. There were _____ many people at the airport that I was _____ surprised.

9. I was carrying _____ many packages that I was afraid I would lose something.

10. The line at the customs checkout was _____ long that I thought I would never get out of the airport.

11. My suitcases were _____ heavy for me to carry. A _____ nice porter helped me take them to a taxi.

12. There were _____ few taxis at this time of the night that I was afraid I might not find one.

13. I was _____ happy when I was finally able to get a taxi.

14. The taxi was _____ expensive, but I was _____ tired to worry about money.

Exercise 2: Irregular Verbs—Past Tense and Past Participle

A. Supply the *past tense* or the *past participle* of the irregular verbs in these sentences. (The past participle is the third principal part of an irregular verb *[wear, wore, **worn**]* and comes after a form of the auxiliary *be* or *have*.) See the irregular verbs in the Appendix if you need help with this exercise.

1. Last month I (fly) _flew_ to Seattle in a 747 plane. I had never (fly) _flown_ in such a large airplane before.

2. Before I (leave) _____ my country, I (get) _____ a passport and a visa. I (put) _____ them in my wallet right away.

3. Soon after I had (leave) _____ my country, I started to feel homesick. I (begin) _____ to wish I had never (go) _____ away.

4. I (feel) _____ depressed in the plane, and I have (feel) _____ depressed many times since.

5. I hardly (eat) _____ or (drink) _____ anything on the plane. I should have (eat) _____ or (drink) _____ a little more.

6. I have often (think) _____ about the easy life I (have) _____ in my country.

7. I (know) _____ that I would have to work hard to learn the new language, and I wondered whether I would be (understand) _____.

8. Since I (come) _____ here, I have (come) _____ to the conclusion that life here is difficult but interesting.

9. I have (write) _____ many letters home about my experiences here, but I haven't (tell) _____ my family everything.

10. I haven't (say) _____ that I was almost (hit) _____ by a car and that some of my money was (steal) _____.

11. I did tell my family about the wonderful plays I've (see) _____ and the concerts I've (hear) _____.

B. Change the following sentences with irregular verbs to the *passive voice*. Keep in mind that:

> **(1) A passive sentence begins with the original object of the verb.**
> **(2) The verb consists of a form of *be* plus the past participle.**
> **(3) The original subject usually is placed in a *by* phrase.**
>
> | | Subject | Verb | Object | |
> |---------|--------------|-----------|-----------|--|
> | *Active* | My friends | gave | a party | for me before I left. |
> | *Passive* | A party | was given | | for me *by my friends* before I left. |
>
> *Note:* **The original subject may be omitted if it is not important.**

1. I lost my wallet at the airport a few weeks ago. (omit *I*)
   My wallet was lost at the airport a few weeks ago.

2. My girlfriend had made it for me.

   _____

3. I cannot buy such a wallet in this country. (omit *I*)

   _____

4. A customs inspector found it.

   _____

5. He gave it back to me.

   _____

6. He told me to be very careful with money.

   _____

7. I have already spent all my money. (omit *I*)

   _____

8. My mother will send me more money right away.

   _____

9. I'll pay some bills with this money. (omit *I*)

_____

10. I'll put the rest in the bank. (omit *I*)

_____

Exercise 3: Infinitives vs. Gerunds

Verbs that come after other verbs may be in infinitive form *(to do)* or in gerund form *(doing).*

Verbs Followed by Infinitives		*Verbs Followed by Gerunds*	
allow (someone)		anticipate	
help* (someone)		appreciate	
refuse	*to do* something	avoid	*doing* something
persuade (someone)		enjoy	
used		stop	

A few verbs are followed by the infinitive without *to.*

> have
> let   } someone *do* something
> make

After some words, *to* is regarded as a preposition and requires the *-ing* form.

> be used to
> object to } *doing* something

After certain expressions, the *-ing* form is required.

> be busy
> spend time } *doing* something

_____

* *help* may also be followed by a verb without *too* (<u>help</u> {someone} <u>do</u> something)

Use the correct form of the verb in parentheses.

1. At first my parents wouldn't let me (leave) _leave_ the country.

2. They objected to my (go) _going_ away because I wasn't used to (live) _living_ alone.

3. I couldn't understand why they refused (give) _to give_ me permission to go away.

4. But nothing could make me (change) _____ my mind.

5. Finally I persuaded my parents (allow) _____ me (take) _____ the trip.

6. I spent many days (prepare) _____ for the trip.

7. I was busy (buy) _____ the clothes I needed and (get) _____ the necessary documents.

8. I had my tailor (make) _____ some new clothes for me.

9. I made all my friends (gather) _____ information about the country I was going to.

10. My whole family helped me (pack) _____ my suitcases.

11. I had the airline (check) _____ my baggage.

12. I enjoyed (look) _____ at the land from the plane.

13. I used (think) _____ I knew English well, but when I arrived at the airport, I didn't understand everything.

14. My heart almost stopped (beat) _____ from fear and excitement.

15. Would I ever get used to (be) _____ in a strange country?

16. I anticipated (have) _____ lots of problems.

17. I couldn't avoid (think) _____ of the many friends I had left behind.

18. However, I knew I would appreciate (make) _____ new friends.

Exercise 4: Time—Structures with *before, after*

Before or *after* may introduce:

A subject plus a predicate

After *I finished* high school, I decided to come to the United States.

Before *I left* my country, I withdrew money from the bank.

The *-ing* form of the verb

After *finishing* high school, I decided to come to the United States.

Before *leaving* my country, I withdrew money from the bank.

Structures beginning with *before* or *after* may also be used at the end of the sentence, with no commas before them.

I decided to come to the United States *after* I finished high school.

I withdrew money from the bank *before* leaving my country.

A. Change each sentence by using *before* or *after* as indicated. Make the change in two ways: (1) use a subject plus a verb, and (2) use the *-ing* form of the verb. For this exercise, place each *before* or *after* structure at the beginning of the sentence and use a comma after the structure.

1. I got my passport; then I applied for my visa.   *after*

   After I got my passport, I applied for my visa.

   After getting my passport, I applied for my visa.

2. I had to overcome my parents' objections; afterward(s) I was able to come to the United States.   *before*

   Before I was able to come to the United States, I had to overcome my parents' objections.

   Before being able to come to the United States, I had to overcome my parents' objections.

3. I made a reservation for my plane flight; then I picked up my ticket.   *after*

   _____

   _____

   _____

4. I purchased my plane ticket; after that I bought some clothes.   *after*

   _____

   _____

   _____

5. I received my flu shot; after that I felt ill for a few days.   *after*

   _____

   _____

   _____

6. I was given a big party; afterward(s) I left for the United States.   *before*

   _____

   _____

   _____

7. I checked my luggage; then I boarded the plane for New York.   *before*

_____

_____

_____

8. The flight attendants served the beverages; then they served the food.   *after*

_____

_____

_____

9. I arrived at the airport; then I claimed my luggage.   *after*

_____

_____

_____

10. I had to go through customs; afterward(s) I was able to join my friends who were waiting for me.   *before*

_____

_____

_____

B. Write *true sentences* about a trip you made.

    1. Use five sentences containing *after* + the *-ing* form of the verb.

    2. Use five sentences containing *before* + the *-ing* form of the verb.

Exercise 5: Purpose—Structures with *to* or *for*

> **Purpose may be expressed with *to* or *for*.**
>
> *to* + a verb   **I went to the travel agency *to pick up my ticket.***
>   **(or *in order to pick up my ticket.*)**
>
> *for* + a noun   **I went to the travel agency *for my ticket.***

A. Change the information in parentheses to a phrase expressing purpose. Begin the phrase with:

> *to* (or *in order to*) + a verb
>
> or   *for* + a noun

See if both types of phrases of purpose are possible.

1. I argued for a long time (so that I might overcome my parents' objections to my leaving the country).

   I argued for a long time to (or in order to) overcome my parents' objections to my leaving the country.

2. I worked hard (in order that I might earn the money to come to this country).

   I worked hard (in order) to earn the money to come to this country.
   I worked hard for the money to come to this country.

3. I came to this country (so that I might learn about American culture).

   _____

4. I went to the bank (so that I might withdraw money to pay for my ticket).

   _____

5. I went to the travel agency (so that I might pick up my plane ticket).

   _____

6. I went to the doctor (so that I might get a shot).

   _____

7. I went to bed early (so that I wouldn't be tired on the day of the trip) (use *in order not to*)

   _____

8. I ate a big meal on the trip (so that I wouldn't be hungry when I arrived). (use *in order not to*)

   _____

9. I went to the baggage area (in order that I might claim my suitcases).

   _____

10. I had shipped a trunk ahead (so that I might have it when I arrived in the United States).

    _____

B. The words in parentheses express purpose. Use *to* or *in order to* with the verbs and *for* with the nouns.

1. I came to this country (_to, in order to_ to study medicine).

2. I came to this country (_for_ business reasons).

3. I came to this country (_____ a visit).

4. I came to this country (_____ get some practical experience in my field).

5. I came to this country (_____ study economics).

6. I wrote to an American university (_____ admission to their school).

7. I went to the American Consulate (_____ apply for a visa).

8. I went to the hospital (_____ a shot).

9. I went to the bank (_____ money to pay for my trip).

10. I went to the travel agency (_____ pick up my airline ticket).

Exercise 6: *it* vs. *there*

It and *there* are often used as "empty" words that merely fill subject position but have no meaning in themselves.

it with an adjective	*It* was very *noisy* at the airport. (*Noisy* is an adjective.)
there with a noun	*There* was a lot of *noise* at the airport. (*Noise* is a noun.)

Usually an "empty" *it* or *there* occurs with the verb *be*. In the case of *there,* the verb agrees with the following noun, which is the true subject of the sentence.

There *was* a bad *storm* during my trip. (The singular subject *storm* requires the singular verb *was*.)

There *were* several *storms* during my trip. (The plural subject *storms* requires the plural verb *were*.)

In the following sentences, use *it was, there was,* or *there were.*

1. _____*There were*_____ many people at the travel agency. (*people* is a noun)

2. _____*It was*_____ very crowded at the travel agency. (*crowded* is an adjective)

3. _____ a nonstop flight leaving for Seattle in the morning.

4. _____ many things I had to do before I could leave.

5. _____ a little painful to get my shots.

6. _____ a bad rainstorm the day before I was to take my flight.

7. _____ a lot of excitement at the airport because the president was arriving.

8. _____ exciting to feel the plane take off.

9. _____ a pretty girl sitting next to me.

10. _____ a choice of entrées for dinner on the plane.

11. _____ very cold and windy the day I arrived at Sea-Tac Airport.

12. _____ so many terminals at Sea-Tac Airport that I became confused.

Exercise 7: Word Forms (1)

Use the correct form of the word in parentheses.

1. I had made a (decide) _*decision*_ to come to the United States a long time ago.

2. My parents raised a few (object) _____ to my plan to go away for such a long time, but they finally gave me their (approve) _____.

3. I had to make many (prepare) _____ to go on my long trip.

4. I began to feel some (anxious) _____ as I went to the American embassy for some documents.

5. I made a (withdraw) _____ from the bank and then I (purchase) _____ my plane ticket.

6. When the day of (depart) _____ arrived, I bid a (tear) _____ good-bye to my family and friends.

7. The (fly)_____ was very (comfort) _____ during the first half of the trip; the flight attendants were (attend) _____ and (help) _____.

13

8. During the second half of the trip, a severe storm made many of the (passage) _____ airsick.

9. On my (arrive) _____ at Sea-Tac Airport, I had to pass through the customs office for the (inspect) _____ of my baggage.

10. Now that I was in my new country, I really felt (nerve) _____ and (fright) _____.

Exercise 8: Word Forms (2)

Add the word for either the profession or the person who follows the profession. Also add *a* or *an* for the person.

1. If you want to become ___*a*___ ___*dentist*___, you must study ___*dentistry*___.

2. If you want to become ___*a*___ ___*doctor*___, you must study ___Medicine___.

3. If you want to become ___*a*___ ___lawyer___, you must study ___*law*___.

4. If you want to become _____ _____, you must study ___*physics*___.

5. If you want to become ___*an*___ ___*economist*___, you must study ___economics___.

6. If you want to become ___*a*___ ___psychiatrist___, you must study ___*psychiatry*___.

7. If you want to become ___*an*___ ___*accountant*___, you must study _____.

8. If you want to become _____ _____, you must study ___*chemistry*___.

9. If you want to become ___*a*___ ___*financier*___, you must study ___finance___.

10. If you want to become _____ _____, you must study ___*mathematics*___.

11. If you want to become ___*a*___ ___*photographer*___, you must study _____.

12. If you want to become _____ _____, you must study ___*engineering*___.

13. If you want to become ___*a*___ ___psychologist___ you must study ___*psychology*___.

14. If you want to become ___*a*___ ___*nurse*___, you must study ___nursing___.

Exercise 9: Sentence Review

Make full sentences from the word groups below. Use the past tense for all verbs. Make whatever changes or additions are needed, but do not change the word order. Use commas, semicolons, or periods where necessary.

1. My wallet / lose / airport / few / weeks ago.

   My wallet was lost at the airport a few weeks ago.

2. Last month / I / fly / New York / I never / fly / such / large airplane / before.

   _____

3. My parents / object / me / go away / because / I / not / use / live / alone.

   _____

4. I / have / my tailor / make / some new clothes.

   _____

5. My heart / almost / stop / beat / from / fear / excitement.

   _____

6. I / apply / visa / after / get / my passport.

   _____

7. I / check / my luggage / then / I / board / plane / New York.

   _____

8. I / go / doctor / get / shot.

   _____

9. I / work / hard / money / come / this country.

   _____

10. Be / many things / have / do / before / I / can / leave.

    _____

11. Be / very cold / windy / when / I / arrive / Kennedy Airport.

    _____

12. Be / pretty girl / sit / next / me.

    _____

13. I / make / withdraw- / bank / then / I / purchase / my plane ticket.

_____

14. When / day / depart- / arrive / I / bid / tear- / good-bye / my family / friends.

_____

15. The fli- / be / very comfort- / flight attendants / be / atten- / help-.

_____

▷ **Extra Speaking and Writing Practice**

Exercise 10: Spelling—Changing *y* to *i*

> **A.** A final *y* is changed to *i* before *-s* or *-ed*.
>
> > *study* + *-s* becomes *studies* (Note that *e* is added before *s*.)
> > *study* + *-ed* becomes *studied*
>
> There is no change, however, if a vowel appears before the final *y*.
> > plays, played
>
> The ending *-ing* is not changed after final *y*.
> > studying, playing

Rewrite the words, adding the required endings.

country + s _____*countries*_____   difficulty + s ___difficulties___

carry + ed ___carried___   study + ing ___studing___

fly + s ___flies___   worry + ed ___worried___

delay + ing ___delaying___   enjoy + ing ___enjoying___

journey + s _____   party + s ___partiny___

hurry + ed _____   annoy + ing ___annoying___

accompany + ed _____   delay + ed ___delayed___

travel agency + s _____   employ + ed ___employed___

B. A final *y* is also changed to *i* before other endings.

final *y* + a syllable beginning with a *vowel:*

carry + *-age* = *carriage*

final *y* + a syllable beginning with a *consonant:*

happy + *-ness* = *happiness*

But there is *no change if a vowel precedes the y.*

employer, enjoyment

Rewrite the words, adding the required endings.

dirty + est _____*dirtiest*_____   friendly + er _____

lonely + ness _____   employ + ment _____

employ + ee _____   vary + ety _____

enjoy + ment _____   beauty + ful _____

lucky + ly _____   mystery + ous _____

library + an _____   pay + ment _____

Exercise 11: Role Play—On the Plane to the United States

Work in groups of four to role-play the situation of being on the plane that is taking you from another country to the United States.

The characters in the play are the flight attendant, the captain, and two passengers.

Action and Dialogue

The flight attendant and the captain enter the plane first. The captain goes forward to the cockpit; the flight attendant stands near the entrance to the seating area. The two passengers enter. The flight attendant directs them to their seats in tourist class. Both passengers sit in the same row next to each other.

The passengers put one piece of hand luggage in the overhead compartment and the other under the seat in front of them. They buckle their seat belts. The captain announces their departure from the ground.

Every now and then throughout the play the captain announces their location. He or she also announces when the passengers are to return to their seats and buckle up because of the turbulence in the air.

The passengers engage in conversation. Here are some questions they ask and answer.

Where are you from?

What are your plans in the United States?

Did you have any trouble getting your passport and visa?

How do you feel about leaving home?

What do you think Americans are like?

During their discussion the flight attendant comes by. First he or she offers the beverage service. He or she asks what the passengers would like to drink. The soft drinks (cola, ginger ale, etc.) and fruit juices are free. There is a charge for wine, beer, or cocktails.

Then the flight attendant comes by with the meal.

The passengers discuss the food. They say whether they like it. They ask each other what they like to eat in their country.

Later the flight attendant comes by to remove the meal trays.

Time passes.

The captain announces that flight attendants are to prepare for landing. He or she warns the passengers to fasten their seat belts.

The passengers look down and talk about what they can already see on the ground.

The plane lands and all the passengers leave with their hand luggage to claim the bags they checked and to go through customs.

Exercise 12: Journal Writing (dialogue with your teacher)

Write freely on *one* of the following subjects. Do not be concerned about mistakes in English.

1. Write about some of your impressions of the United States. Consider the city you are in, the school you are attending, and the appearance and the behavior of the people.

2. Write about some of the language problems you or someone you know had when you first arrived in the United States. Was the person new to this country able to understand what people were saying? Could the person express what he or she wanted to say?

Hand in this journal entry to your teacher for a response to the things you wrote.

◎ Listening-Writing Practice

Exercise 13: Dictation

Your teacher will dictate the paragraph three times. The first time is for listening only, the second time is for writing, and the third time is for checking.

Immediately after you give your teacher the dictation you have written, check the dictation in the book for any problems you had in writing it.

When I arrived in the United States, I had to do many things before I could leave the airport. First I had to have my health documents examined by the public health officials. Then I had to go to Immigration for the inspection of my passport, visa, and other documents. Finally, I had to go to the Customs area to have my bags inspected. Luckily everything was in order, and I was permitted to leave the airport. Now the problem was to get a taxi. I went to the taxi stand and told the driver where I wanted to go. He turned the meter on and took me to my destination. When I got out of the cab I paid him the amount on the meter plus a 15% tip.

Exercise 14: Dicto-comp

Take notes as your teacher reads the dicto-comp several times. Then reconstruct the dicto-comp from your notes. The dicto-comp does not need to be written exactly as you heard it, but it should be grammatically correct.

Before you write the dicto-comp, your teacher may ask the class to get together in groups to check with each other on what you heard. Immediately after you give your teacher the dicto-comp you have written, check the dicto-comp in the book for any problems you had in writing it.

My father had always promised me that when I finished high school, he would let me come to the United States to study business. I studied English privately for a few years so that I would know the language well when I went to the United States.

At last the day of my high school graduation came. It was a great day for me because I knew I would be leaving for the United States soon. But there were many things to do. I wrote to an American university for admission. After I received my I-20 form, I arranged to get a passport. Then I got the shots I needed. Finally, I applied to the American Consulate for an F-1 visa.

When I had all the necessary documents, I picked up my airline ticket at the travel agency, and I made all the financial arrangements for my stay abroad. Then I went shopping for clothes. My mother went with me to be sure I chose suitable clothes. My whole family helped me pack my trunk, which I sent ahead by air freight.

Finally the day of my departure arrived. My family accompanied me to the airport. They bid me a tearful good-bye when I boarded the plane.

Reading-Writing Practice (summary: "The Good Old Days? Think Again")

You are going to write a one to three paragraph summary of a reading selection. A summary is a restatement, in shortened form, of the main ideas of a selection.

In preparation for the summary, skim through the selection quickly to determine the way the ideas are developed (through comparison, contrast, listing, time, space, or example). Then reread the selection carefully, underlining the important points that should be included in the summary. (Do not underline too much.)

In writing the summary, use your own words as much as possible. You may include the important words from the reading selection, but use quotation marks around whole phrases taken directly from the selection.

Devote more attention to the main points than to their supporting details. Omit examples unless they are important to the development of the ideas. Do *not* give your own ideas in a summary.

The selection to be summarized appeared in the travel column of a newspaper. The writer develops his ideas through a contrast between air travel in the past and air travel today. The selection begins and ends with general statements.

The Good Old Days? Think Again

Quite a few travel writers of a certain age glorify the **"good old days"** of flying. Not me.

My first flight was about 50 years ago and most of the changes I've seen have been for the better: improvements in safety, speed and reliability, and the long-term decrease in constant-dollar cost. When writers **pine** for older, simpler times, they tend to forget some of the **quirks** of flying in the late '40s and '50s.

On those early flights, the "seat pocket in front of you" didn't have any of today's routine **stuff**—safety information card, in-flight magazine, airborne shopping catalog or frequent-flyer application form. Instead, only one object sat there: an empty cardboard container, about the size and shape of the cartons in which we buy premium ice cream today. It didn't provide for your being airsick, it invited you to be airsick.

If you've flown only on jets, you've probably experienced **turbulence** largely as a repetitive jolting sensation—similar to the feeling you get in a car on a very rough road. But in the old **piston** days, turbulence often resulted in swoops and dips, something like the sensation you get on a **roller coaster** or on a small boat on rough seas and far more likely to cause real distress than today's occasional roughness. Those airsickness containers saved many a traveler from a major mess.

If your concept of baggage claim is confined to the now **ubiquitous carousel,** you'd have a tough time comprehending the system in the late '40s. Then, bags were unloaded from the plane onto a cart, pushed to a claim area and transferred again to a rack behind a counter. You had to give your claim check to a skycap, who searched the rack for the corresponding bag and handed it to you in exchange for a tip (as I recall, 50 cents was the going rate).

The typical scene at the claim counter was a major **hassle:** dozens of travelers waving baggage checks, pointing to bags and shouting for the skycap's attention. Next time you have to wait at a carousel think about how long it would take if you had to wait for all the bags to be stacked, then for someone to find your bag and hand it to you.

Food service, too, has changed a lot. Planes in the '40s didn't have pull-down trays. Instead, the flight attendant handed you a pillow, on which you **precariously** balanced your meal tray. As I remember, the DC6 was the first plane to have a firm tray at each seat—not a convenient pull-down, but one that plugged into the armrest, sometimes with considerable difficulty.

Back in the late '40s and early '50s, could we have foreseen air travel as it is today? We correctly predicted steady gains in aircraft size, speed and range. As for jets, many of us wondered why it took so long to adapt proven military technology to civilian uses. On the other hand, I think none of us would have predicted the huge **divergence** of in-flight service and comfort—either the **opulence** of today's business and first class or the meanness of coach/economy.

No, I'm not about to **whine** for the "good old days." And if you're ever tempted, just think about those airsickness cartons, one-by-one baggage claims and a dinner tray **perched** on a pillow.

"The Good Old Days? Think Again" by Ed Perkins,
San Diego Union Tribune, July 27, 1997.

Vocabulary

1. **good old days**—an older time, when things were supposed to be better

2. **pine**—greatly long for, desire strongly

3. **quirk**—a peculiar action

4. **stuff**—(informal) things

5. **turbulence**—shakey movement

6. **piston**—a disk that fits into a cylinder and moves back and forth to produce motion, as in a car

7. **roller coaster**—in an amusement park, an elevated railway with open cars that go up and down hills

8. **ubiquitous**—found everywhere, especially at the same time

9. **carousel** (also carrousel)—a large, circular-shaped conveyor belt for baggage in an airport

10. **hassle**—an informal word for trouble or bother

11. **precariously**—dangerously, insecurely

12. **divergence**—difference

13. **opulence**—luxury

14. **whine**—complain

15. **perch**—rest on lightly, as a bird on a tree

FYI For Your Information
(Culturegram article on U.S.)

The following information about American customs and courtesies will be useful to students and travelers coming to the United States from overseas.

The selection comes from "Culturegram 2002: United States of America," published by Brigham Young University. (This Culturegram is one of a series covering most countries of the world.)

Note: More information about American customs regarding politeness is given in Unit 8, Rules of Etiquette.

Greetings

Both men and women usually smile and shake hands when greeting. The American handshake is often firm. Good friends and relatives may embrace when they meet, especially after a long absence. In casual situations, people may wave rather than shake hands. Americans may greet strangers on the street by saying *Hello* or *Good morning,* although they may pass without any greeting. Among the youth, verbal greetings or handslapping gestures (such as the "high five") are common. Except in formal situations, people who are acquainted address one another by given name. Combining a title (*Mr., Mrs., Miss, Dr.,* for example) with a family name shows respect. When greeting someone for the first time, Americans commonly say *Nice to meet you* or *How do you do?* A simple *Hello* or *Hi* is also common. There are regional variations, such as *Aloha* in Hawaii or *Howdy* in parts of the west. Friends often greet each other with *How are you?* and respond *Fine, thanks.* Americans do not really expect any further answer to the question.

Gestures

When conversing, Americans generally stand about two feet away from each other. However, they may spontaneously touch one another on the arm or shoulder during conversation. Members of the opposite sex may hold hands or show affection in public. To point, a person extends the index finger. One beckons by waving all fingers (or the index finger) with the palm facing up. Direct eye contact is not necessary for the duration of a conversation, but moments of eye contact are essential to ensure one's sincerity. Winking to children is a gesture of friendliness; when adults wink it usually means that they or someone else is kidding or joking.

Visiting

Although Americans are informal, they generally are conscious of time. Appointments are expected to begin promptly. Guests invited to a home for dinner should arrive on time because the meal is often served first. Hospitality takes many forms: a formal dinner served on fine dishes, an outdoor barbecue with paper plates, or a leisurely visit with no refreshments. Most events are casual. Guests are expected to feel comfortable, sit where they like, and enjoy themselves. It is not unusual for either guests or hosts to agree on a reasonable limit of time for the visit if schedules are pressing. Guests are not expected to bring gifts, but a small token such as wine, flowers, or a handicraft might be appreciated. Hosts inviting close friends to dinner may ask them to bring a food item to be served with the meal. Americans enjoy socializing; they gather in small and large groups for nearly any occasion, and they enjoy talking, watching television or a movie, eating, and relaxing together.

Eating

Eating styles and habits vary between people of different backgrounds, but Americans generally eat with a fork in the hand with which they write. They use a knife for cutting and spreading. Otherwise they lay it on the plate. When a knife is used for cutting, the fork is switched to the other hand. People eat some foods, such as french fries, fried chicken, hamburgers, pizza, and tacos, with the hands. They generally place napkins in the lap. Resting elbows on the table usually is considered impolite. Dessert, coffee, or other after-dinner refreshments are frequently served away from the dining table. Guests are expected to stay for a while after the meal to visit with the hosts. In restaurants, the bill usually does not include a service charge; leaving a tip of 15 percent is customary.

Adapted from "Customs and Courtesies" section,
CultureGrams Standard Edition: United States of America,
Millennial Star Network and Brigham Young University, 2002.

2

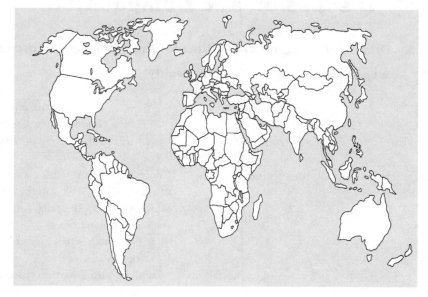

Geography

Grammar and Usage

Compass points used with geographic names—
   capital letters, adjective forms, prepositions
the with geographic names
Passive voice
Countable vs. noncountable nouns
Passive sentences (natural resources)
Reducing coordinate structures containing *and*
Comma faults (or run-on sentences)
Nonrestrictive adjectival phrases and clauses—
   punctuation
Combining sentences with phrases containing *of which*
Reversal of subject and verb after initial expressions
   of place

Rhetoric

Using an outline to guide the composition

Discussion and Composition

1. Discussion: Preliminary Outline for the Composition (prewriting stage)

Subject: *The Geography of* (name of country)

Outline *(To be placed on the board. Books are closed.)*	Discussion *(Ideas, Grammar and Usage, Vocabulary, Elements of Composition Building)*

I. Location on the continent	Names of the continents (seven large land masses): Africa, Asia, Europe, North America, South America, Australia, Antarctica
	the with place names:
	    with all bodies of water except lakes
	      or bays
	    with all plural names, especially
	      mountains
	    with all names that end in *of* phrases
	    with all names that include a word for a
	      political union (*the* Dominican Republic)
	Choices for position on the continent:
	    in the south of Europe
	    in the southern part of Europe
	off the continent: Japan is off the east coast
	    of Asia.
	Initial capitals with words for points of the compass that are part of the geographic name:
	    South Africa *vs.* in the south of Africa
	    the Middle East *vs.* east of Europe
	No quotation marks around geographic names
	Adjective forms of words for points of the
	    compass: eastern, western, etc.
	    Combinations: northeastern,
	    southwestern, north central
	Passive voice: the country is located
	    in _____.

II. Bordering areas	Only *it* (not *she*) is used to refer to a country
	    when discussing its geography.
	Prepositions of place and direction:
	    To the north of the country is _____.
	or The country is bordered on the north
	    by _____.

in the north is *inside* the country.
to the north is *outside* the country.
Passive voice: The country is surrounded
    by _____.
Additional vocabulary (if needed):
    peninsula, archipelago

III. Location of principal cities,
     rivers, mountains

The with place names (already given under I)
Initial capitals for *River, Mountains* when
    they are part of the name
Passive voice (for a location):
    The _____ River is located in
    _____.

Additional vocabulary (if needed):
    mountain range
    For a river:
        tributary, mouth, source, drain

IV. Location of principal industries

Passive voice:
    Coffee is grown in _____.
    Cattle are raised in _____.
    Gold is mined in _____.
Vocabulary items (if needed):

Product	*Industry*	*Place*
metals (gold, silver, aluminum, etc.), gemstones (diamonds, emeralds, etc.), and coal	mining	mine
crops (rice, cotton, tobacco, coffee, etc.)	agriculture (or farming)	farms (or plantations for very large farms in warm climates)
textiles (cloth: cotton, wool, etc.)	manufacturing	mills
automobiles	manufacturing	plants, or factories

| domestic animals, poultry (chicken, turkey, duck) | (cattle) raising | farms, ranches for larger animals like cattle, horses |
| fruit (apples, oranges, lemons) | agriculture | orchards |

2. Composition (to be done before or after the grammar practice)

A. Writing a 400/500-Word Composition

Place the title of the composition at the top of the page:

> ### *The Geography of* (name of country)

Do not use quotation marks or a period for a title at the top of the page. Use initial capital letters for the first word of the title and for all other words except articles, prepositions, and coordinate conjunctions *(and, or, but)*.

Write the composition "The Geography of *(name of country)*" following the outline that has been discussed. The right column of the outline pages can be of help to you.

Place items I and II in the same paragraph. Use separate paragraphs for items III and IV. You will thus have three paragraphs in the composition.

Since you are making general statements about this country, use the *present tense* of the verbs.

B. Correcting/Rewriting the Composition

Before you give your composition to your teacher, look it over carefully to correct any grammar, spelling, or punctuation mistakes.

When your teacher returns your composition, it will be marked with the symbols from the correction chart in the Appendix. Make the necessary corrections clearly on the composition and hand it back to your teacher. If you have made many mistakes, you will need to rewrite the composition before handing it in.

☑ Grammar Practice

**Exercise 1: Compass Points Used with Geographic Names—
Capital Letters, Adjective Forms, Prepositions**

Noun
the north
the east
the south
the west
the northwest
the southwest

Adjective
the northern part
the eastern part
the southern part
the western part
the northwestern part
the southwestern part
also:
the north-central part
the south-central part

the Middle East
(in Asia)
the Middle West
or the Midwest
(in the United
States)

[handwritten annotations: North written by the N, East by the E, West by the W, South by the S; "I live in the East Boston"; "North East west Soath"]

Note these differences in the use of initial capital letters.	
No Initial Capital	*Initial Capital*
He lives in the *south* of France.	He lives in the *South*.
The *south* is a geographic location, not a name.	The *South* is the name of a definite geographic area in the United States. Compare with *the Middle East, the West.*
He lives in *southern* France.	He lives in *South* America.
The term *southern* is the equivalent of *the south of*— a geographic location.	*South* in South America is part of the name of the geographic area.

A word for a point of the compass is not capitalized if it merely gives a direction.
   France is to the *south* of England.

Referring to the map that follows, write full sentences for all the information that is called for in this exercise. Remember to capitalize words for points of the compass when they are part of the name, but not when they indicate direction or simple location.

Western Europe
(Source: European Travel Commission, 1997)

1. Italy: Write sentences that tell what is (a) to the *east*, (b) to the *south*, (c) to the *west*, (d) to the *northwest* of Italy.

   (a) *To the east of Italy is the Adriatic Sea.*

   (b) to the east of the U S

   (c)

   (d)

2. France: Write sentences that tell what borders France (a) on the *north*, (b) on the *south*, (c) on the *west*.

   (a) *France is bordered on the north by the English Channel.*

   (b)

   (c)

3. Capital cities: Write sentences that give the location in their country of these capitals: (a) London, (b) Paris, (c) Lisbon, (d) Madrid, (e) Rome, (f) Berlin.

   (a) *London is located in the southeastern part of England.*
       Note that the noun *part* requires the adjective *southeastern*.

   (b)

   (c)

   (d)

   (e)

   (f)

Exercise 2: *the* with Geographic Names

The four most important rules regarding the use of *the* with geographic names are:

1. Use *the* with all bodies of water except lakes or bays: *the Atlantic Ocean, the Mediterranean Sea, the Mississippi River* (but *Lake Erie, Hudson Bay*).
2. Use *the* with all plural names, especially mountains: *the Rocky Mountains, the Philippines, the Finger Lakes.*
3. Use *the* with all names that end in *of* phrases: *the Gulf of Mexico.*
4. Use *the* with all names that end in a word for a political union: *the British Commonwealth, the Dominican Republic.*

(Note the use of capital letters for words like *River, Ocean, Mountains* when these are part of the name.)

Names of continents, countries, and cities are generally used without *the* unless one of these four rules applies.

To the above rules we might add the use of *the* with north, east, south, west when these words are names for geographic areas: *the Middle East, the West.*

The is also used with deserts, valleys, peninsulas, and archipelagos.

Supply *the* where needed.

1. _The_ Pacific Ocean is the largest ocean in the world.

2. _____ Lake Geneva is a beautiful lake in _____ Switzerland.

3. To the east of India is _____ Bay of Bengal.

4. _The_ Great Lakes separate _the_ United States from _Ø_ Canada.

5. Several of the world's highest mountains, including _Ø_ Mount Everest, are in _Ø_ southern Nepal.

6. _The_ Malay Archipelago, the world's largest group of islands, lies off the southeast coast of _Ø_ Asia.

7. _The_ Suez Canal separates _Ø_ Africa from _Ø_ Asia.

8. ___✗___ Turkey is bounded on the north by ___the___ Black Sea.

9. ___the___ Sahara Desert, which is in _____ North Africa, extends from _____ Atlantic Ocean to _____ Nile River.

10. _____ British Isles consist mainly of _____ Great Britain and _____ Ireland.

11. _____ Republic of Venezuela exports much of the oil it produces.

12. Many good wines are produced in _____ Rhine Valley.

Exercise 3: Passive Voice

The passive construction is often used in writing about geography. Use the required passive forms in the following sentences.

1. Portugal (locate) _is located_ in the southwestern part of Europe.

2. A peninsula (surround) _____ by water on three sides; it (attach) _____ to land on one side.

3. The Pyrenees Mountains (find) _____ in the northeastern part of Spain.

4. North America and South America (situate) _____ in the Western Hemisphere.

5. Various fruits (grow) _____ in California.

6. Several kinds of seafood (catch) _____ in the waters off the Atlantic Coast.

7. Chickens (raise) _____ on New Jersey farms.

8. Cloth (produce) _____ in textile mills in the eastern part of the United States.

9. Cars (manufacture) _____ in Detroit.

10. Tobacco and cotton crops (cultivate) _____ on large farms; cattle and other livestock (raise) _____ on ranches.

11. In Alaska, seals (trap) _____ for their fur by native people.

12. Dairy products (make) _____ from milk.

Exercise 4: Countable vs. Noncountable Nouns

> The names for some products are noncountable and therefore do not take the -s plural ending. Also, they require singular verbs when used as subjects.
>
> The *lumber* we need for our bookcase *is* very expensive.
>
> Sometimes words for foods are used in the plural to mean *kinds of, varieties of*.
>
> There are many fishes in the sea.
>
> The wines from France are well known.
>
> Several citrus fruits are grown in Florida.

In the following list, add -s to the names of products that are countable.

Products Grown in the Ground
- vegetable
- tobacco
- cotton
- beet
- potato
- grape

Products from Trees
- fruit
- coconut
- cocoa
- banana
- timber
- rubber

Grains
- wheat
- rye
- corn
- oat
- barley

Products from Mines
- coal
- iron
- silver
- copper

Products from the Sea
- oyster
- fish
- shrimp
- pearl

Dairy Products
- milk
- cheese
- butter
- cream
- yogurt

Products from Animals and Birds
- beef
- bacon
- liver
- egg
- wool
- leather
- feathers

Animals and Birds Raised for Food
- cattle (Cattle is always plural.)
- cow
- sheep (Countable; may be used with a plural verb, but it doesn't take an ending for plural: one sheep is; two sheep are.)
- poultry
- pig
- goat
- chicken (Plural refers to individual birds. As a food it's noncountable.)

Products Manufactured or Processed
- textile
- wine
- chemical
- paper
- handicraft
- pottery
- fertilizer
- machinery
- farm equipment

Natural resources in the continental United States

Exercise 5: Passive Sentences—Natural Resources

The resource map of the United States indicates where industries such as farming, mining, and fishing are located. Working in pairs, ask and answer questions (in full sentences) about where certain resources are found. Use the *passive voice*. Keep in mind that:

(1) *A particular crop* is produced (or raised, cultivated, grown).
Fruit is grown in the southwestern part of the United States.

(2) *Certain animals* are raised.
Hogs are raised in the north central part of the United States.

(3) *Certain fish* are caught.
Salmon are caught off the northwestern coast of the United States. (For the names of fish, the plural form is usually the same as the singular, although sometimes the -s is added.)

(4) *Certain minerals* are mined (or produced, found).
Oil is found off the southeastern (or south-central) coast of the United States.

Note: For variety in your questioning, after an answer is given about the location of an industry, you may also ask questions such as:
Where else are cattle raised? (or *in what other part* of the country are cattle raised?)

Exercise 6: Reducing Coordinate Structures Containing *and*

Short sentences that are joined by *and* should be avoided when only small amounts of information are given in each sentence. To improve such sentences, eliminate the *and* and grammatically reduce one of the sentences. Make whatever change is necessary in the other sentence.

Poor Use of *and*:   Brazil is the largest country in South America, and it is located in the east.

Improved: Brazil, which is the largest country in South America, is located in the east.

Better: Brazil, the largest country in South America, is located in the east.

Note that in the improved sentences, *Brazil* is the subject of the sentence, and *is located in the east* is its predicate.

Rewrite the following sentences by eliminating the word *and* and reducing the first or second part of each sentence as indicated. Keep the same word order.

1. *Japan is located off the east coast of Asia,* and it is an island country. (Reduce the *first* part.)

    Japan, which is located off the east coast of Asia, is an island country.
    or, *Japan, located off the east coast of Asia, is an island country.*
    (Note that the reduced information is put within commas.)

2. Japan consists of four main islands, *and they are Hokkaido, Honshu, Shikoku, and Kyushu.* (Reduce the *second* part.)

    Japan consists of four main islands, Hokkaido, Honshu, Shikoku, and Kyushu.
    (Note that a colon *[:]* may replace the comma before a list of items.)

3. *Mexico City is the biggest city in my country,* and it is located in the central part of the Republic. (Reduce the *first* part.)

    _____

    _____

4. Two other big rivers in Italy flow into the Adriatic Sea, *and they are the Adige and the Piave.* (Reduce the *second* part.)

    _____

    _____

5. *The Amazon is the largest river system in the world,* and it drains more than one third of South America. (Reduce the *first* part.)

_____

_____

6. *Africa is a great plateau,* and it is about 5,000 miles long from north to south. (Reduce the *first* part.)

_____

_____

7. *My country is Malaysia,* and it is a small country in Southeast Asia. (Reduce the *first* part.)

_____

_____

Exercise 7: Comma Faults (run-on sentences)

Short sentences joined by *and,* although often not effective, are grammatically correct because *and* permits two sentences to be joined into one. It is incorrect, however, to join two sentences with only a comma. This error is called a *comma fault* or *run-on sentence.*

The capital city is Madrid, it is located in the central part of the country.

Such a sentence can be made grammatically acceptable by using a period (or a semicolon) instead of the comma. However, when both sentences are short, it is better to reduce one part of the sentence.

The capital city, Madrid, is located in the central part of the country.

Correct the comma faults in these sentences by reducing the part of each sentence that is indicated. Use commas around the reduced structure.

1. *The Nile is the longest river in the world,* it travels 4,000 miles before reaching the Mediterranean. (Reduce the *first* part.)

    The Nile, the longest river in the world, travels 4,000 miles before reaching the Mediterranean.

2. Saudi Arabia has two capitals, *they are Riyadh and Mecca.* (Reduce the *second* part.)

_____

_____

3. *Europe is a huge peninsula,* it is subdivided into a number of lesser peninsulas. (Reduce the *first* part.)

_____

_____

4. *The islands of Japan rise from great depths of the sea,* they are mostly mountainous. (Reduce the *first* part; change *rise* to *rising.*)

_____

_____

5. In the northern part of Argentina is the Gran Chaco, *it is a land of forests, lakes, and swamps.* (Reduce the *second* part.)

_____

_____

6. *Peru was once famous for its precious metals,* today it produces other important minerals. (Reduce the *first* part.)

_____

_____

7. *Alaska is the largest of the fifty states,* it has a variety of climates ranging from temperate to frigid. (Reduce the *first* part.)

_____

_____

Exercise 8: Nonrestrictive Adjectival Phrases and Clauses—Punctuation

> Adjective structures that come after *proper nouns* (names that begin with capital letters) usually require commas.
>
> > Manhattan, (which is) surrounded on all sides by water, is a busy seaport.
>
> Compare with: Manhattan is a busy seaport (which is) surrounded on all sides by water. (no comma after *seaport*)
>
> Such adjective structures with proper nouns may also appear at the beginning of sentences.
>
> Surrounded on all sides by water, Manhattan is a busy seaport.
>
> In this position, the adjective structure must also be set off by a comma.

A. Reduce the *second sentence* to an adjective structure and place it after the proper noun in the first sentence. Use commas with each adjective structure. Also, see which structures can be moved to the beginning of the sentence.

1. The Andes Mountains _____
   form the longest mountain range in this continent.
   They run along almost the entire coast of South America. (reduce)

   > *The Andes Mountains, which run along (or, running along) almost the entire coast of South America, form the longest mountain range in this continent.*
   >
   > *Running along almost the entire coast of South America, the Andes Mountains form the longest mountain range in this continent.*

2. _____
   ... ... Sweden, and ... enmark.
   ... ... rthern ... of Europe. (reduce)

   _____

3. ... ... the ... ital of India. (reduce)

   _____

4. ... ... of sailors for ... turies.
   ... and lacks natural ... ... (reduce)

   _____

5. South America _____
   ... joined to North America by the Isthmus of Panama.
   South America is roughly triangular in shape. (reduce)

39

6. Chile _____
   stretches along the west coast of South America for 2,600 miles.
   Chile is sometimes called the "Shoestring Republic." (reduce)

7. Israel _____
   is a hot and arid land.
   Israel lies between Egypt and Jordan on the eastern shores of the
   Mediterranean. (reduce)

B. Write five sentences with *which* clauses after the name of a country or the name of a city, river, or mountain in a country. Use commas around each *which* clause.

   Example: *The United States, which lies between Canada and Mexico, has*
             a temperate climate.

   _____
   _____
   _____
   _____
   _____
   _____
   _____
   _____
   _____
   _____
   _____
   _____

C. See how many of the *which* clauses in your sentences can be reduced to *-ing* or *-ed* phrases. Then move the reduced phrase to the beginning of the sentence.

   Example: *The United States, lying between Canada and Mexico, has a*
             temperate climate.

             Lying between Canada and Mexico, the United States has a
             temperate climate.

_____

_____

_____

_____

_____

_____

_____

_____

_____

_____

_____

_____

_____

Exercise 9: Combining Sentences with Phrases Containing *of which*

A phrase containing *of which* permits two separate sentences to be joined into one.

Sentences: Columbia has twenty-four states.
All of them are important.

Combination: Columbia has twenty-four states, *all of which* are important.

In such a sentence, if *of which* is replaced by *of them,* an unacceptable combination is formed.

Comma Fault: Columbia has twenty-four states, *all of them* are important.

Rewrite the following sentences using *of which* to replace a phrase like *of them, of it.* Use a comma before the second part of the sentence. Note which of the sentences given in the exercise have comma faults.

1. There are several mountain ranges, the most important *of them* is the Andes range. (*comma fault*)

   There are several mountain ranges, the most important of which is the Andes range.

2. We already have small industries, one of the largest *of them* is the textile industry.

   _____

   _____

3. There are also many other small islands. Some *of them* are gathered in small archipelago fashion.

   _____

   _____

4. There are many rivers in Venezuela. The most important *of them* are the Orinoco River and the Apure River.

   _____

   _____

5. Most of Denmark is farmland, about half *of it* is used for grazing.

   _____

   _____

6. Island groups off the Asian mainland are Japan, the Philippines, and Indonesia. All *of these* have become as important as mainland countries.

   _____

   _____

7. Asia is very rich in natural resources, many *of them* have not been developed.

   _____

   _____

Exercise 10: Reversal of Subject and Verb after Initial Expressions of Place

Expressions of place at the beginning of sentences often require a reversal of subject and verb.

Usual Order: Canada is to the north of the United States.

Reversal: To the north of the United States *is* Canada. (*Canada* is the subject of the sentence.)

Usual Order: The Hawaiian Islands are located in the middle of the Pacific Ocean.

Reversal: Located in the middle of the Pacific Ocean *are* the Hawaiian Islands. (*The Hawaiian Islands* is the subject of the sentence. Note that in this reversal the participle *located* is separated from the auxiliary *are*.)

Move the expressions of place to the beginning of the sentence and use a reversal of subject and verb.

1. The island of Sicily is off the southern coast of Italy.

   Off the southern coast of Italy is the island of Sicily.

2. Gold and silver are among the many metals mined in this area of the continent.

   _____

3. The Strait of Gibraltar is at the northern shore of Morocco.

   _____

4. Iran's rich oil fields are situated near the Persian Gulf. (Start with *situated*.)

   _____

5. There are two broad plateaus in the eastern part of South America. (Omit *there*.)

   _____

6. Demavend, Iran's highest peak, is located in the Elburz Mountains. (Start with *located*.)

   _____

7. Micronesia, or "little islands," lies in the western Pacific. (Begin with *lying* and use *is* for the verb.)

   _____

Exercise 11: Word Forms

Use the correct form of the word in parentheses.

1. New York City is in the (northeast) _northeastern_ part of the United States.

2. Coal (mine) _____ is an important industry in the South.

3. People who own (farm) _____ are called (farm) _____.

4. The (cultivate) _____ of crops is very difficult in (rock)
   _____ regions.

5. The cost of cattle (raise) _____ is cheaper if good (graze)
   _____ land is readily available.

6. The (produce) _____ of coffee is an important industry in Brazil.

7. The Pyrenees Mountains form a natural (bound) _____ between
   Spain and France.

8. Texas is in the south (center) _____ part of the United States.

9. (Lie) _____ in the middle of the Pacific Ocean, Hawaii is considered a place where the East meets the West.

10. Both (agriculture) _____ crops and (manufacture)
    _____ goods are (produce) _____ in the eastern part
    of the United States.

11. Many of the (develop) _____ countries want to become (indus-
    try) _____ as rapidly as possible.

12. New York City is both a (commerce) _____ and an (industry
    _____ center.

13. Venezuela's (economic) _____ has greatly expanded because of
    the (develop) _____ of its oil industry, but the country continues
    to have some (economy) _____ problems.

Exercise 12: Sentence Review

Make full sentences from the word groups below and complete the unfinished words. Make whatever changes or additions are needed, but do not change the word order. Use commas, semicolons, periods, or capital letters wherever necessary.

1. Iberian peninsula / consist / Spain / Portugal.

   The Iberian Peninsula consists of Spain and Portugal.

2. United States / bound / north / Canada / and / Great Lakes.

   _____

3. London / locate / southeast- / part / England.

   _____

4. Suez canal / separate / Africa / from / Asia.

   _____

5. north America / south America / situate / West- / hemisphere.

   _____

6. Dairy products / make / from / milk.

   _____

7. Cultivat- / crops / be / very difficult / rock- / regions.

   _____

8. Manhattan / be / island / surround / all sides / water.

   _____

9. Lima / capital / Peru / situate / west coast.

   _____

10. Mexico city / biggest city / my country / locate / centr- / part / Republic of Mexico.

    _____

11. Pacific ocean / be / largest ocean / world.

    _____

12. Sahara desert / extend / Atlantic ocean / Nile river.

_____

13. My country / have / two important rivers / both / make / great contribution / economy / nation.

_____

▷ **Extra Speaking and Writing Practice**

Exercise 13: Composition—Great Britain

You are going to write a three-paragraph composition based on the two maps of Great Britain that appear with this exercise. Your teacher will ask you to get into pairs or groups first in order to discuss the information that will be required for the composition. Use full sentences in the composition.

A   B

Great Britain. (Adapted from The Encyclopedia Americana.
Copyright © 1978 Grolier Incorporated.)

46

(first paragraph)	I. Countries in Great Britain and the surrounding area (A)
	A. Tell which countries Great Britain consists of and give their location in Great Britain.
	B. Give the bodies of water surrounding Great Britain and give their location. (A)
	(B may begin with: Great Britain is surrounded on the _____ by _____, etc.)
(second paragraph)	II. Principal cities and rivers in Great Britain (A)
	Name the principal cities and rivers and give their location in each country.
	(Synonyms for *is located* for geographic areas are *is situated and lies*.)
(third paragraph)	III. Natural resources in Great Britain (B)
	Give the location in their country of some of the natural resources of Great Britain.
	(Keep in mind that: animals are raised; crops are produced, raised, grown; minerals are mined, produced, found; dairy products are produced.)

Exercise 14: Journal Writing

Write a journal entry on the following subject. Write freely since you are the only one who will see this entry.

Select a city in the United States and another city outside the United States. Compare the two cities to see how they are alike and how they are different. Consider some of the following: location, size, buildings, streets, traffic, transportation facilities.

Now use your journal entry as the basis for a more careful letter to your teacher that is to be handed in.

◎ Listening-Writing Practice

Exercise 15: Dictation

Your teacher will dictate the paragraph three times. The first time is for listening only, the second time is for writing, and the third time is for checking what you have written.

Immediately after you give your teacher the dictation you have written, check the dictation in the book for any problems you had in writing it.

Niagara Falls, one of the most popular attractions in North America, has 12 to 14 million visitors every year, and was once very popular with honeymooners. It is located partly in the United States and partly in Canada. It is on the Niagara River, which connects two of the five Great Lakes, Ontario and Erie. The name Niagara is derived from a native American word meaning "thundering water." Niagara Falls is the 49th highest falls in the world, but it is the third greatest in power and volume of water that flows through them. The sight of the falls is truly spectacular, especially Horseshoe Falls on the Canadian side. After dark the falls are made even more spectacular by the play of colored lights that change during the evening. The Canadian side also has many more tourist attractions than the U.S. side. It has the world's largest butterfly conservatory, a winery, and a 24-hour gambling casino.

Exercise 16: Dicto-comp

Take notes as your teacher reads the dicto-comp to you several times. Then reconstruct the dicto-comp from your notes. The dicto-comp does not need to be written exactly as you heard it, but it should be grammatically correct.

Before you write the dicto-comp, your teacher may ask the class to get together in groups to check with each other on what you heard.

Immediately after you give your teacher the dicto-comp you have written, check the dicto-comp in the book for any problems you had in writing it.

My country, the United States, is located mostly in the central part of North America. It is bordered on the north by Canada and the Great Lakes and on the south by Mexico and the Gulf of Mexico. To the east is the Atlantic Ocean and to the west is the Pacific Ocean. Two of the fifty states, Alaska and Hawaii, are not attached to the main part of the United States.

The United States has many large cities. Among the most important are New York, a center of commerce and industry on the East Coast; Chicago in the middle west, and New Orleans, which is located at the mouth of the Mississippi River in the southeast. Washington, D.C., the capital, is in the north-central part of the eastern seaboard, between the states of Virginia and Maryland.

The principal mountains are the Appalachian Mountains in the East and the Rocky Mountains in the West. The major river system is the Mississippi River with its tributary, the Missouri. This river system runs from north to south in the east-central part of the United States.

Reading-Writing Practice
(summary: "North America")

You are going to write a one to three paragraph summary of a reading selection. A summary is a restatement, in shortened form, of the main ideas of a selection.

In preparation for the summary, skim through the selection quickly to determine the way the ideas are developed (through comparison, contrast, listing, time, space, example). Then reread the selection carefully, underlining the important points that should be included in the summary. (Do not underline too much.)

In writing the summary, use your own words as much as possible. You may include the important words from the reading selection, but use quotation marks around whole phrases taken directly from the selection.

Devote more attention to the main points than to their supporting details. Omit examples unless they are important to the development of the ideas. Do *not* give your own ideas in a summary.

The selection to be summarized comes from a popular book on geography. It is divided into two related parts. Each part is developed according to space.

North America

North America stretches from near the **tropics** in the south to well within the Arctic Circle in the north, and these **latitudes** define the region's varied climate. The region is surrounded on three sides by oceans, which restrain the extreme climate in coastal areas. North America's location in the northern hemisphere leads to June–September summers and December–March winters.

The far north of Alaska and Canada have cold **polar** climates. These areas typically have short, cool summers and long, cold winters. The huge mass of North America experiences **humid** climates, cooler in the north and warmer in the south, with year-round **precipitation**. Southern Florida has a humid tropical climate, with typically dry winters. The southwestern United States and the south-central plains of Canada have a dry climate, with **arid** conditions prevailing in the far southwest.

North America's **vegetation** generally parallels its climatic areas (as happens worldwide). Tundra (a treeless expanse) in the extreme northern reaches of the region gives way to pine forests as you move south. As you move farther south, the pine forests yield to **deciduous** forests of broadleaf trees that seasonally lose their **foliage,** and in the southeast return to pine forests.

In the drier central areas, tallgrass **prairies** dominate. The prairies, which once supported vast herds of **bison** and the Plains Indian culture, are now primarily used for ranching. In the driest areas, desert vegetation with **cacti, shrubs, sage,** and **chaparral** growth is the norm.

Another type of vegetation that's specific to North America is found in the Pacific Northwest. There, in old-growth **temperate** rain forests, are the largest trees on earth. Redwoods, Douglas firs, sitka spruces, and giant sequoias reach more than 300 feet tall in this area. In California's Inyo National Forest, you can see the world's oldest living tree, a 4,600-year-old bristlecone pine.

From *The Complete Idiot's Guide to Geography*
by Thomas E. Sherer, Jr., Alpha Books, 1997, pages 71–72.

Vocabulary

1. **tropics**—the area south of the equator with a very hot climate
2. **latitude**—the distance, measured in degrees, north or south from the equator
3. **polar**—relating to one of the earth's poles (the North Pole or the South Pole)
4. **humid**—moist or damp; full of water vapor
5. **precipitation**—rain, snow, or hail
6. **arid**—extremely dry; without moisture
7. **vegetation**—plants
8. **deciduous**—shedding (getting rid of) leaves every year
9. **foliage**—leaves of a plant or tree
10. **prairie**—a large area of level or slightly rolling grassland, mostly treeless, with very fertile soil, especially in the Mississippi Valley
11. **bison**—a North American animal similar to an ox; more commonly called a buffalo
12. **cacti, shrubs, sage, and chaparral**—plants that grow in the desert
13. **temperate**—neither very hot nor very cold. The climate is warm in the summer, cold in the winter, and moderate in the spring and fall.

UNIT

3

*Mahatma Gandhi,
Albert Einstein, and
William Shakespeare.
(Courtesy of Library
of Congress, Prints
and Photographs
Division.)*

Biography

Grammar and Usage

Prepositions of time and place

Expressions of time—*since, for, ago*

Adjective clauses (restrictive)

Punctuation of adjective clauses
(restrictive and nonrestrictive)

Adjectival phrases

Questions and answers

Rhetoric

Using an outline to guide the composition

Discussion and Composition

1. Discussion: Preliminary Outline for the Composition (prewriting stage)

Subject: *My Autobiography*

Outline (To be placed on the board. Books are closed.)	Discussion (Ideas, Grammar and Usage, Vocabulary, Elements of Composition Building)

I. Childhood (0–11 years)
— A. When and where born
— B. Friends
— C. School
	Use of the *past* tense
	Verb form: I *was* born
	Prepositions:
	    time: *in*, with a month, year
	        on, with a day
	    place: *to*—go to elementary school
	        but: enter elementary school

II. Adolescence (12–18 years)
A. Where lived
B. Interests and hobbies
	Use of the *past* tense
	    place: *to*—go to high school
	        but: enter high school
	Transitional time expressions (especially to
	avoid beginning every sentence with *I*)
	    when I was _____ years old
	    at the age of _____ (years)
	    _____ years later
	    during my adolescence (for a period
	        of time)
	    then, after that, afterwards
	Hobbies: sports, photography, reading,
	    music, dancing, collecting stamps
	        or coins

III. Adulthood (from 18 years)
A. Age and marital status now
B. Present studies or work
C. Ambitions
	Use of the *present* tense
	    Verb form: I *am* _____ years old.
	    I *am* married (or single, or divorced).
	Prepositions:
	    from: to graduate from
	    of: to be a graduate (or alumnus,
	        alumna) of
	    to: go to college
	        but: go to the university

2. Composition (to be done before or after the grammar practice)

A. Writing a 400/500-Word Composition

Place the title of the composition at the top of the page:

My Autobiography

Do not use quotation marks or a period for a title at the top of the page. Use initial capital letters for the first word of the title and for all other words except articles, prepositions, and coordinate conjunctions *(and, or, but)*.

Write the composition on "My Autobiography" following the outline that has been discussed. The right column of the outline pages can be of help to you.

Place each of the three main points in a separate paragraph. If any of these paragraphs is quite long, you may break it in two. Be sure to follow chronological order. Use the *past tense* for points I and II and the *present tense* for point III.

B. Correcting/Rewriting the Composition

Before you give your composition to your teacher, look it over carefully to correct any grammar, spelling or punctuation mistakes.

When your teacher returns your composition, it will be marked with the symbols from the correction chart in the Appendix. Make the necessary corrections clearly on the composition and hand it back to your teacher. If you have made many mistakes, you will need to rewrite the composition before handing it in.

☑ **Grammar Practice**

Exercise 1: Prepositions of Time and Place

Time *in*		with a month: *in June*
		with a year: *in 1976*
on		with a day: *on June 1, 1976; on Sunday* (*on* is sometimes omitted)
during		with a period of time: *during the week, during his adolescence*
from–to/ until		the beginning or end point of a time: *from dawn to dusk*
Place *to*	*go to:*	elementary school
		high school
		college
		the university
		(but: enter high school, attend the university)
from		*graduate from* a school
on		with a street, avenue: *on Main Street, on Seventh Avenue*
at		with an address containing the street number: *at 500 Main Street*

(handwritten annotations in margin: "City, year, month" next to Time/in; "Days" next to on; "street avenue" next to on; "address" next to at)

Supply a preposition of time or place if necessary.

1. On December 1, 1955, Rosa Parks refused to give up her seat on a bus __*in*__ Birmingham, Alabama.

2. Abraham Lincoln was born _____ 1809 in Kentucky. He was assassinated in Washington, D.C. _____ April 15, 1865.

3. Nelson Mandela was the president of South Africa _____ 1994 _____ 1999.

4. The prime minister of England usually resides _____ 10 Downing Street.

5. Thoreau, the American writer, entered _____ Harvard College _____ 1833 and graduated _____ this college four years later.

6. Sir Winston Churchill was born _____ November 30, 1874.

7. Mark Twain, the author of *The Adventures of Tom Sawyer* and *The Adventures of Huckleberry Finn,* lived _____1835 _____ 1910.

8. The President of the United States lives in the White House _____ 1600 Pennsylvania Avenue, N.W., Washington, D.C.

9. Martin Luther King Jr., the famous civil rights leader, was assassinated _____ 1968.

10. Toni Morrison, a contemporary American writer who received the Nobel Prize for literature, was born _____ February 1931.

11. Hemingway arrived* _____ Spain _____ February 1937 to write about the Spanish Civil War for American newspapers.

12. Eleanor Roosevelt was First Lady _____ World War II.

Exercise 2: Expressions of Time—*since, for, ago*

Since and *for* refer to duration (length) of time, *ago* to one point in the past.		
Duration of past to present time		*One point in the past*
Use the present perfect tense		Use the past tense
Since (gives the beginning of the time)	*For* (gives the *length of the time* [a quantity])	*Ago* (gives a *quantity of time in relation to the present*)
Mr. Chang has lived in the United States _since_ 1997.	**Mr. Chang has lived in the United States *for* five years.**	**Mr. Chang came to the United States five years *ago*.**

For the following situations, give sentences with *since, for,* and *ago*. Use the present perfect tense with *since* and *for*, and use the past tense with *ago*.

1. Luis began to attend an American university in 1998. It is now 2000, and he is still attending the university.

    Since   *Luis has attended (or has been attending) an American university since 1998.*

---

* After *arrive, in* is used for a large geographic area (continent, country) and *at* for a smaller place (airport, station, library, etc.)

Since gives the date when the continuing event began. Note that the progressive form *(has been attending)* emphasizes the continuing action.

For   *Luis has attended (or has been attending) an American university for two years.*

For gives the length of time that the event lasts. (In this case, *for* is sometimes omitted.)

Ago   *Luis began to attend an American university two years ago.*
(Do not use *before* for *ago*.) Note that another verb must be used with this completed point in the past.

2. My friend is visiting me. It is now March, and he came to visit me in January.

Since _____

_____

For   _____

_____

Ago   _____

_____

3. It is now August 5. Dimitri got married on July 5.

Since _____

_____

For   _____

_____

Ago   _____

_____

4. It is now December. Anabel became a lawyer in February.

Since _____

_____

For   _____

_____

Ago   _____

_____

5. My older sister is in the United States. It is now 1996, and she arrived in the United States in 1976.

Since _____

_____

For _____

_____

Ago _____

_____

6. Georgia is studying medicine. It is now 1998, and she began to study medicine in 1995.

Since _____

_____

For _____

_____

Ago _____

_____

Exercise 3: Adjective Clauses (restrictive)

A *clause* contains a subject and a predicate. An *adjective clause* follows a noun and gives more information about the noun. The word beginning the clause depends on the noun the clause refers to.

A. Introductory word as *subject* in the adjective clause.

Noun Referred to	Introductory Word for the Clause	Sentence with an Adjective Clause
a person	*who* or *that*	I really appreciate the teacher *who* (or *that*) *taught me English.*
a thing	*which* or *that*	I attended the high school *which* (or *that*) *was near my home.*
a place	*where*	The high school *where I learned English* was a very good one.

57

Underline the word in parentheses that refers to the noun being described. Replace this word by *who* (or *that*), *which* (or *that*), or *where* used at the beginning of the adjective clause. Then write the complete sentence. (Use the *past tense* for the verbs within the parentheses.)

No commas are required in any part of exercise 3.

1. The *teacher* (<u>she</u>, teach, me, English) was very strict.

    The teacher who (or that) taught me English was very strict.

2. I'll never forget the *neighborhood* (I, live, <u>there</u>, my childhood).

    I'll never forget the neighborhood where I lived during my childhood.

3. The *subject* (it, give, me, most trouble) was English.

    _____

4. I attended the same *school* (my brother, go, there).

    _____

5. I didn't learn much English from the *teacher* (she, be teaching, subject).

    _____

6. There were many *friends* (they, come, say, good-bye, me).

    _____

7. The *city* (I, born, there) is very beautiful.

    _____

8. The *relative* (he, encourage, me, go, university) was my uncle.

    _____

9. I had a private *tutor* (he, help, me, learn, English language).

    _____

10. The *foreign languages* (they, be taught, my school) were English and French.

    _____

11. The *school* (I, study, there, four years) no longer exists.

    _____

B. Introductory word as *object of verb* in the adjective clause

> In section A you made clauses with *who* or *whom* or *which* or *that* as subjects of the clauses. *Who* or *which* may also be *objects* of the verbs in their clauses. As an object, *whom* is the formal equivalent of *who*.
>
> The girl *whom* (informal, *who*) I married lived next door to me.
> > *Whom* (= *the girl*) is the object of *married*.
>
> I went to the same school *which* my brother attended.
> > *Which* (= *the school*) is the object of *attended*.
>
> In these clauses the *whom* or *which* objects may be replaced by *that*.
>
> The girl *that* I married lived next door to me.
> I went to the same school *that* my brother attended.
>
> The omission of *whom, that,* or *which* as objects is very common in spoken English.
>
> The girl I married lived next door to me.
> I went to the same school my brother attended.

Underline the word in the parentheses that refers to the noun being described. Replace this word by *who(m)*, *that*, or *which* used at the beginning of the adjective clause. Then write the complete sentence. (Use the past tense for the verbs in the parentheses.)

1. The *teacher* (I, respect, <u>her</u>, the most) was my English teacher.

   The teacher whom (or that) I respected the most was my English teacher.

2. The *ambition* (I, have, it, a long time) was to be a doctor.

3. The *education* (I, receive, it, high school) was excellent.

4. I still see the *friends* (I, meet, them, elementary school).

5. I finally received the *application form* (I, have, to fill out, it).

6. The *elementary school* (I, attend, it) no longer exists.

7. My English *teacher* was the best teacher (I, ever, have, him).

8. The *subject* (I, like, it, the best) was English.

C. Go over the sentences you made in B and omit *whom, that,* or *which.*

> *The teacher I respected the most was my English teacher.*

D. Introductory word as *object of a preposition* in an adjective clause

> **In clauses that describe nouns, *who* or *whom* and *which* are not only subjects or objects of verbs, but also objects of prepositions. The preposition may begin or end the clause.**
>
> > **Preposition at the beginning of the adjective clause—formal usage**
> > **The children with *whom* I played lived on my block. (*who* is never used after a preposition)**
> > **I never liked the neighborhood in *which* I lived.**
> >
> > **Preposition at the end of the adjective clause—less formal usage**
> > **The children *who(m)* (or *that*) I played with lived on my block.**
> > **I never liked the neighborhood *which* (or *that*) I lived in.**
>
> **When this separation of the prepositions is made, the *whom* or *which* object may be omitted *(the children I played with).***

Underline the word in parentheses that refers to the noun being described. Replace this word by *whom, which,* or *that.* Move the preposition plus *whom* or *which* to the beginning of the parentheses. Then write the complete sentence. (Use the past tense for the verbs in the parentheses.)

1. The *person* (I, have to write, to this person) was the director of admissions.
   The person (I, have to write, to this <u>person</u>) was the director of admissions.

   The person to whom I had to write was the director of admissions.

2. The *teacher* (I, be, most fond, of this teacher) was my English teacher.

   _____

3. I would like to visit again the *street* (I, use, live, on this street).*

   _____

---

* In sentences 3, 7, and 8, it is also possible to use *where* without the preposition. If the preposition is *from,* however, it is kept with *where.*

4. The *teacher* (I, have, most respect, for this teacher) was my history teacher.

   _____

5. When I was a child the only *person* (I, use, have confidence, in this person) was my uncle.

   _____

6. For a long time, the only *thing* (I, can, think, about this thing) was becoming a doctor.

   _____

7. The *school* (I, go, to this school) was a small but a good one.

   _____

8. Everyone would enjoy visiting the *town* (I, come, from this town).

   _____

E. Go over the sentences you made in D and move the prepositions to the end of the clauses. Omit *whom, which,* or *that.*

   The person I had to write to was the director of admissions.

Exercise 4: Punctuation of Adjective Clauses (Restrictive and Nonrestrictive)

> If the adjective clause *identifies* or *restricts* a noun, no commas are used with the clause.
>
>   A mother *who is very strict* can also be very fair.
>
> In the above sentence, *who is very strict* is restrictive: it narrows down the whole class of mothers.
>
>   If the adjective clause comes after a noun that is already fully identified, the clause requires commas.
>
>   My mother, *who was very strict with me,* was also very fair.
>
> Here, the speaker has only one mother. *Who was very strict with me* is nonrestrictive: it does not identify the mother further.
>
>   Commas for nonrestrictive clauses are especially necessary after proper nouns (nouns beginning with capital letters).
>
>   Caracas, *where I was born,* has grown very fast.

Make adjective clauses from the words in parentheses. Be careful with the punctuation of restrictive and nonrestrictive clauses. (Use the past tense of the verbs in the parentheses.)

1. My favorite uncle (he, encourage, me, study, English) gave me the money to come to this country.

   My favorite uncle, who encouraged me to study English, gave me the money to come to this country. (The speaker is referring to only one particular uncle.)

2. The person (he, encourage, me, study, English) was my uncle.

   The person who encouraged me to study English was my uncle. (The class word *person* is narrowed down by *who encouraged me* to study English.)

3. The subject (it, give, me, most trouble, high school) was English.

   _____

4. English (it, give, me, most trouble, high school) is now very useful to me.

   _____

5. Everyone on the block is helping the family (their house, burn down, yesterday). (Use the possessive *whose* for the possessive *their.*)

   _____

6. The Johnsons (their house, burn down, yesterday) are being helped by everyone on the block.

   _____

7. I would like to visit again the street (I, use, live, this street).

   _____

8. Everyone would enjoy visiting Tokyo (I, grow up, there).

   _____

9. My parents (they, love, me, very much) gave me everything I needed.

   _____

10. A boy (his parents, have money) could afford to go abroad to study.

   _____

11. My best friend (her parents, have money) could afford to go abroad to study.

_____

12. The children (I, use, play, with, them) all lived on the same block (I, live, there).

_____

Exercise 5: Adjectival Phrases

Part of a sentence, with the subject and a form of *be* omitted, may be used as a phrase after a noun.

Thomas Edison, (he was) famous as the inventor of the phonograph, made many other important inventions.

Commas are required for the adjective phrase in this sentence because the phrase comes after a proper noun.

Change the sentences in parentheses to phrases by omitting the subject and *is* or *was*. Use commas for these phrases.

1. Albert Einstein (he was the most renowned scientist in the world) discovered the formula for atomic energy.

    Albert Einstein, the most renowned scientist in the world, discovered the formula for atomic energy.

2. Sigmund Freud (he is considered the founder of modern psychoanalysis) had a great influence on modern thought.

    _____

    _____

3. Maria Sklodowska-Curie (she was the first woman in Europe to earn her doctorate) won the Nobel Prize in physics for her discovery of radioactivity.

    _____

    _____

4. Charles Darwin (he was the originator of the theory of evolution) gathered his information on a five-year boat trip around the world.

_____

_____

5. Martin Luther (he was shocked by the corruption of the Catholic Church) finally broke with the established church and started the Reformation.

_____

_____

6. Niccolo Machiavelli (he was a patriot who wanted to see Italy made strong) outlined the political policy that the end justified the means.

_____

_____

Exercise 6: Word Forms

Use the correct form of the word in parentheses. You will need auxiliaries with some verbs.

1. Helen Keller became deaf and blind in early (child) _childhood_ .

2. The writer Edgar Allan Poe continued to have (infant) _____ fantasies even as an adult.

3. Catherine de Médicis (birth) _____ in Florence, Italy. She (death) _____ in Blois, France.

4. Edgar Allan Poe (marry) _____ a young cousin of his in 1836. The (marry) _____ lasted until her (die) _____ in 1847.

5. Johnny Appleseed (engage) _____ to a young woman. The (engage) _____ ended when she (dead) _____ .

6. Carl Sandburg is the famous (biography) _____ of Abraham Lincoln.

7. Mahatma Gandhi became (engage) _____ at the age of seven. He was (marry) _____ when he was fourteen.

8. When the rate of (born) _____ of people is much higher than the rate of (dead) _____, a country may become overpopulated. (Use plural for these words.)

9. Most children find friends in their (neighbor) _____.

10. A person's work is his or her (occupy) _____.

11. William Shakespeare was (marry) _____ to Anne Hathaway.

12. The vital statistics for someone include the dates of his or her (born) _____, (marry)_____, and (die) _____.

Exercise 7: Sentence Review

Make full sentences from the word groups below. Make whatever changes or additions are needed, but do not change the word order. Use commas, semicolons, or periods where necessary.

1. Karl Marx / born / Germany / 1818 / he / die / London / March 14, 1883.

   Karl Marx was born in Germany in 1818. He died (or and he died) in London on March 14, 1883.

2. Albert Camus / go / public schools / Algiers / then / enter / University / Algiers.

   _____

3. William Shakespeare / famous playwright / be / married / Anne Hathaway / have / three children.

   _____

4. Prime Minister / England / usually / reside / 10 Downing Street / London.

   _____

5. Abraham Lincoln / born / 1809 / Kentucky / he / assassinate / Washington / April 15, 1865.

   _____

6. Mahatma Gandhi / become / engage / age / seven / he / marry / when / fourteen years.

   _____

7. Sigmund Freud / founder / modern psychoanalysis / have / great influence / modern thought.

   _____

8. Edgar Allan Poe / marry / young cousin / his / 1836 / marriage / lasted / her death / 1847.

   _____

9. teacher / teach / me / English / be / very strict.

   _____

10. Everyone / would enjoy / visit / town / I / come / from this town.

    _____

11. The Johnsons / their house / burn down / yesterday / being helped everyone on the block.

    _____

▷ Extra Speaking and Writing Practice

Exercise 8: Questions and Answers

A. Working with a partner, take turns asking and answering *wh-* questions based on the following information about three famous people. The answers should be in full sentences.

The two kinds of *wh-* questions that you will be using are:

> **(1) Questions beginning with the adverbs *when, where, why,* or *how.***
> **These question words are always followed by the same auxiliary as the**
> **one used in a yes-no question.**
>
> | *Statement* | *Shakespeare was born in 1564.* |
> |---|---|
> | yes-no question | *Was* Shakespeare born in 1564? |
> | *wh-* question | When *was* Shakespeare born? |

If the verb does not have an auxiliary (simple present and simple past tenses), an auxiliary from *do* is added for most questions.*

Statement	*Shakespeare married Anne Hathaway.*
yes-no question	*Did* Shakespeare marry Anne Hathaway?
wh- question	When *did* Shakespeare marry Anne Hathaway?

(2) Questions beginning with the pronoun *who* (for a person), *what* (for a thing), and *which* (for a choice of a person or a thing). With one exception, these question words must also be followed by the same auxiliary that starts a yes-no question.

Statement	*Shakespeare married Anne Hathaway.*
yes-no question	*Did* Shakespeare marry Anne Hathaway?
wh- question	Who(m) *did* Shakespeare marry?

However, if the question word is the *subject*, it merely replaces the subject, with no change in word order and no addition of an auxiliary.

Statement	*Shakespeare married Anne Hathaway.*
wh- question	Who married Anne Hathaway?

1. *William Shakespeare*

Birth:	April 1564; Stratford, England
Marriage:	to Anne Hathaway, 1582
Family:	three children
Work:	wrote many famous plays and poems
Death:	April 23, 1616, Stratford
	52 years old

Example:	*When was Shakespeare born?*
	He was born in April 1564.
	Where was Shakespeare born?
	He was born in Stratford, England.
	How many children did Shakespeare have?†
	He had three children.

---

*An exception is the independent verb *be*. If this verb has no auxiliary, the verb itself is pulled forward to auxiliary position.

Statement	Shakespeare *was* famous for his plays.
yes-no question	*Was* Shakespeare famous for his plays?
wh- question	Why *was* Shakespeare famous?

† Note that the question word *how* may be followed by other words—*how many* (quantity), *how long* (time or measurement), *how old* (age), etc.

2. *Jacqueline Cochran*

    Birth: 1906

    Work: First woman to break the sound barrier; once held more flying records than any other pilot, male or female.

    Publications: *The Stars at Noon,* 1953

    Death: 1980

                   74 years old

3. *Leo Tolstoy*

    Birth: August 28, 1828; Yasnaya Polyana, Russia

    Education: first at home, then at the university

    Marriage: to Sofia Andreyevna Behrs, 1862

    Family: many children

    Publications: *War and Peace,* 1869

                   Anna Karenina, 1877

    Death: November 7, 1910; Astapovo, Russia

                   82 years old

B. Write a short dialogue in which someone asks you questions about a famous person, and you give the answers in full sentences. The questions might be about the famous person's birth, education, marriage and family, accomplishments, and death. (You may need to check an encyclopedia for some of this information.)

Exercise 9: Questions and Answers—Names

Working with a partner, ask and answer the following questions about the use of names in your home culture. (American customs are given in the right-hand column.) After you have finished your discussions, write a paragraph or two about customs regarding names. Use the order of the questions as your outline.

Questions	*American Customs*
1. How do people in your culture sign their names?	Americans first write the first (or given) name, then the last name (or surname, family name). The last name usually comes from the father.
2. What are some common first names in your culture?	John, Mary, Susan, James, Lily, William, Jane

3. What are some common last names?   Smith, Jones, Williams, Johnson

4. Do you use nicknames (sometimes   Jim or Jimmy for James; Bob or Bobby
   called pet names, especially for   for Robert; Meg or Peggy for Margaret;
   children)?   Bill or Billy for William[*]

5. What first names do you like?

6. Do you use hyphenated surnames
   in your culture? Explain.

Exercise 10: Questions and Answers—Interview

A. Below is a form that requires some information usually requested when a person applies for a job or for admission to a school. Working with a partner, take turns interviewing each other to get the required information. Begin each question of the interview with the question word to the left of the form. For the purposes of this exercise, you may answer only the questions you are comfortable answering.

The interviewer should take down notes in the blank spaces as the person being interviewed answers *in full sentences.*

What	Name	_____
Where	Address	_____
When	Date of birth	_____
Where	Place of birth	_____
What country	Citizenship	_____
What schools	Education:	
	high school	_____
	higher education	_____
What	Occupation	_____
What	Hobbies	_____
How many	Foreign languages	_____

Example: Student 1:   *What is your name?*
            Student 2:   *My name is _____.*

----

[*] These names ending in *y* are used especially for children, but they often continue into adult life.

B. Write up the interview you had with your partner. Begin with: "*(name of your partner)* told me she lived _____." For this practice, use the past tense *(lived)* because the main verb *(told)* is past (sequence of tenses). However, keep in mind that since most of the information after *told* consists of general statements, the present tense of the verbs in these statements is also appropriate. You may combine some of the information into one sentence (for example, date of birth and place of birth).

Exercise 11: Business Letter

Write a letter to a college or university requesting their catalog and an application for admission to their school. Tell them what you want to study and give them your previous education (graduation from high school or the university) so that they may know what your area of specialization is and whether you are applying for undergraduate studies (to get a bachelor's degree) or graduate studies (to get a master's degree or a doctorate).

If you are a foreign student, tell them so.

Use the form that follows as a model for a business letter.

Your street address
City, state, and zip code
Date

(3–4 single line spaces down)

Admissions Officer
Name of the university
Address of the university

Dear Admissions Officer:
Please send me _____

_____

_____

_____

_____

_____

_____

Thank you.

Sincerely, (or Sincerely yours,)
(sign your name)

(print or keyboard your name 3–4 single line spaces from *Sincerely,*)

Note: in this letter style, every part of the letter begins at the left margin. In a business letter it is better not to use abbreviations, except for the state in the address.

It is preferable to prepare a business letter on a computer, but a handwritten letter is acceptable if it is neat and follows the same form as the letter given here.

Exercise 12: Journal Writing

Write an entry on the following subject. Write freely since you are the only one who will see this entry.

Discuss someone that you consider a role model. Consider his or her life and accomplishments. Also, tell why you chose this person as your role model.

You may consult an encyclopedia before you write, but do not look at it while you are writing.

Using the information in this journal entry, prepare an outline for an oral report you will give to the class. Organize the points on your outline in some kind of logical order.

Exercise 13: Proverbs (short, wise sayings)

Discuss the following proverbs in groups or as a class. Do you have similar proverbs in your culture?

1. Heroes are made, not born.

2. Some are born great, some achieve greatness, and some have greatness thrust upon them.

3. The hand that rocks the cradle rules the world.

4. History teaches by example.

5. The apple doesn't fall far from the tree.

◎ Listening-Writing Practice

Exercise 14: Dictation

Your teacher will dictate the paragraph three times. The first time is for listening only, the second time is for writing, and the third time is for checking what you have written.

Immediately after you give your teacher the dictation you have written, check the dictation in the book for any problems you had in writing it.

> One of the most famous African-Americans who overcame prejudice was Marian Anderson. She was the first African-American opera singer to perform at the Metropolitan Opera and around the world. She became the subject of a nationwide controversy in 1939 when the Daughters of the American Revolution denied her the use of Constitution Hall for a concert in Washington, D.C., because of her race. Many Americans were indignant. Eleanor Roosevelt, the wife of the President, resigned her membership in this organization and helped sponsor another concert at the foot of the Lincoln Memorial, with a much larger audience. At this same memorial, several decades later, an African-American minister, Martin Luther King, Jr., gave his impassioned speech, "I Have a Dream." He asked that African-Americans be given the same civil rights as all other Americans.

Exercise 15: Dicto-comp

Take notes as your teacher reads the dicto-comp to you several times. Then reconstruct the dicto-comp from your notes. The dicto-comp does not need to be written exactly as you heard it, but it should be grammatically correct.

Before you write the dicto-comp, your teacher may ask the class to get together in groups to check with each other on what you heard.

Immediately after you give your teacher the dicto-comp you have written, check the dicto-comp in the book for any problems you had in writing it.

> Thomas Edison is well known all over the world for his many inventions, yet he had very little education. When his teachers criticized him for being stubborn and unwilling to learn, his mother decided to teach him herself. She encouraged his natural desire to read and to experiment. By the time he was ten years old, he had developed a strong taste for chemistry and made himself a laboratory.
>
> His first inventions were begun during his adolescence. With a little money made from one of his inventions, he started his own manufacturing business in New Jersey. This later developed into a research laboratory. Here he perfected the incandescent lamp, which enabled electricity to replace gas. Here too he first reproduced the sound of the human voice on an instrument he called the phonograph.

Constant experimentation played an important part in Edison's success. He slept very little and worked very hard. When people told him he was a genius, he answered, "Genius is 1% inspiration and 99% perspiration."

Reading-Writing Practice (summary: encyclopedia article on "Walt Whitman")

You are going to write a one to three paragraph summary of a reading selection. A summary is a restatement, in shortened form, of the main ideas of a selection.

In preparation for the summary, skim through the selection quickly to determine the way the ideas are developed (through comparison, contrast, listing, time, space, or example). Then reread the selection carefully, underlining the important points that should be included in the summary. (Do not underline too much.)

In writing the summary, use your own words as much as possible. You may include the important words from the reading selection, but use quotation marks around whole phrases taken directly from the selection.

Devote more attention to the main points than to their supporting details. Omit examples unless they are important to the development of the ideas. Do *not* give your own ideas in a summary.

The selection to be summarized has been adapted from an encyclopedia article. The article begins and ends with general statements about Walt Whitman. As in all biographies in encyclopedia articles, most of the information is presented chronologically (by time), beginning with the birth of Walt Whitman and ending with his death.

Walt Whitman is considered by many to be the greatest of all American poets. He celebrated the freedom and dignity of the individual and sang the praises of democracy and the brotherhood of man. His *Leaves of Grass,* unconventional in both content and technique, is probably the most influential volume of poems in the history of American literature.

Born in 1819 on Long Island, New York, Whitman had little public education. He first worked in the printing trade and then taught school for a short time. By 1841 he had become a full-time journalist, editing successively several papers and writing prose and verse for New York and Brooklyn journals. His active interest in politics during this period led to the editorship of the *Brooklyn Daily Eagle,* a Democratic party paper; he lost this job because of his **vehement advocacy** of **abolition** and the **"free-soil"** movement.

After a brief trip to New Orleans in 1848, Whitman returned to Brooklyn, continued as a journalist, and later worked as a carpenter. In 1855 he published at his own expense a volume of 12 poems, *Leaves of Grass.* Prefaced by a statement of his theories of poetry, the volume included the famous poem later known as "Song of Myself," in which the author proclaims himself the symbolic representation of the common people. Although some reviewers recognized the appearance of a bold new voice in poetry, the book was a commercial failure. At first it was criticized because of his **exaltation** of the body and also because of its **innovative** form; that is, the use of **free verse** in long rhythmic lines. Whitman continued to enlarge and revise further editions of *Leaves of Grass*; the last edition appeared in 1892.

From 1862 to 1865 Whitman worked as a volunteer hospital nurse in Washington. His poetry of the Civil War, *Drum-Taps,* included his two famous poems about Abraham Lincoln, "When Lilacs Last in the Dooryard Bloom'd," considered one of the finest **elegies** in the English language, and the much recited "O Captain! My Captain!" He continued to write and to revise his earlier work until his death in 1892.

Cultivating a bearded, shaggy appearance, Whitman saw himself as the **full-blooded rough and ready** spokesman for a young democracy. He had an **incalculable** effect on later poets, inspiring them to experiment in **prosody** as well as in subject matter.

Adapted from "Walt Whitman,"
Columbia Encyclopedia, 1993, pages 2966–67.

Vocabulary

1. **vehement**—full of strong feeling; passionate

2. **advocacy**—support for a cause, especially public support

3. **abolition**—putting a complete end to something; often referred to the legal end of African-American slavery in the United States

4. **free soil**—a region where slavery is illegal, especially a U.S. territory before the Civil War

5. **exaltation**—glorifying something

6. **innovative**—introducing something new

7. **free verse**—poetry without rhyme and without a measured rhythm of accented and unaccented syllables (called meters)

8. **elegy**—a song, poem, or speech expressing sorrow about someone's death

9. **full-blooded**—vigorous, virile, energetic

10. **rough and ready**—showing strong but unrefined vigor

11. **incalculable**—very great

12. **prosody**—a system of meters and rhyme in poetry

For Your Information
(poem: "O Captain! My Captain!"
by Walt Whitman)

The following is the strongly felt poem written by Walt Whitman to mourn the death of President Abraham Lincoln. Lincoln saw the country through the terrible period of the Civil War, 1861–65, when the North defeated the South and so kept the Union together. He was assassinated soon after the end of the war, in 1865.

"O Captain! My Captain!" differs from the free verse of most of Whitman's poetry. It uses rhyme, a measured rhythm, and a stanza form. Whitman symbolizes Lincoln's tragic death through the use of a captain of a ship that he has safely brought to port after much danger. As the people on the shore celebrate his success, the captain lies dead on the deck of the ship.

O Captain! My Captain!

O Captain! my Captain! our fearful trip is done,
The ship has weather'd every rack, the prize we sought is won,
The port is near, the bells I hear, the people all exulting,
While follow eyes the steady keel, the vessel grim and daring;
    But O heart! heart! heart!
       O the bleeding drops of red,
          Where on the deck my Captain lies,
            Fallen cold and dead.

O Captain! my Captain! rise up and hear the bells;
Rise up—for you the flag is flung—for you the bugle trills,
for you bouquets and ribbon'd wreaths—for you the shores a-crowding,
for you they call, the swaying mass, their eager faces turning;
    Here Captain! dear father!
       The arm beneath your head!
          It is some dream that on the deck,
            You've fallen cold and dead.

My Captain does not answer, his lips are pale and still,
My father does not feel my arm, he has no pulse nor will.
The ship is anchor'd safe and sound, its voyage closed and done,
From fearful trip the victor ship comes in with object won;
    Exult O shores, and ring O bells!
       But I with mournful tread,
          Walk the deck my Captain lies,
            Fallen cold and dead.

From *Leaves of Grass,* Random House, 1855.

Instructions (how to make or do something)

Grammar and Usage

Passive voice (for a process)

Conditions—possible and unreal

Conditions with *otherwise*

Auxiliaries—*mustn't* vs. *don't have to*

Have + VERB (for instructions)

Dangling participles

Subjunctive verbs in *that* clauses

Rhetoric

Using an outline to guide the composition

Using an introduction and a conclusion

Discussion and Composition

1. Discussion: Preliminary Outline for the Composition (prewriting stage)

Subject: (Tell what is being made or done.)

Outline *(To be placed on the board.* *Books are closed.)*	Discussion *(Ideas, Grammar and Usage, Vocabulary,* *Elements of Composition Building)*
	Give instructions for something you yourself can make or do well.
	Subjects for instruction:
	make: the end result is a *thing*
	make: a bookcase, a table
	a dress
	a particular food
	do: only an *activity* is involved
	play: football, tennis, cards (a game)
	the piano, the guitar (an instrument)
	collect: stamps, coins
	plant: flowers, vegetables
	use: a CD player, a computer
	bowl, swim, skate, dance,
	drive a car
Introduction: general statements, incentives	Mention what is being made or done.
	Try to catch the interest of the reader in the product or activity you are giving instructions for.
	easy to make or do
	quick
	useful
	beautiful
	inexpensive
	delicious, nourishing (for food)
	get lots of pleasure from it
	relaxing
	healthy
	satisfying
	Avoid negative remarks such as "It's hard to do," or "It will take a long time."

I. Tools, materials, equipment (if necessary)

For a recipe, give the ingredients (in exact quantities) and utensils (pot, pan, frying pan, casserole dish, mixing bowl).

For something to be constructed, specify needed tools: hammer, nails, saw, pliers, screws, screwdriver.

II. Steps in chronological order (include precautions)
(If the instructions are for a game, give the rules here.)

Form for giving the steps:
imperative: do this, do that
with *should:* you should do this, you should do that
first person: I do this, I do that
Note: Avoid changing from one form to another.

III.
IV.
V.
VI.
etc.

Transitions for the steps:
then, next, after this; afterward(s); after you do this; after *doing* this, you . . . (to avoid a dangling construction)

Form for precautions:
be sure to; be careful not to; you must . . . ; otherwise, . . .

Conclusion: general statements

Refer again to incentives mentioned in the introduction and repeat in other words.

Synonyms for adjectives in the introduction:
simple: for easy to make or do
not time-consuming: for quick
practical: for useful
attractive: for beautiful
economical, money-saving: for inexpensive
enjoyment: for pleasure
tasty: for delicious
nutritious: for nourishing
more general comments:
You can be proud of your accomplishment.
You can enjoy the compliments of your family and friends.
You can be satisfied with a job well done.

2. Composition (to be done before or after the grammar practice)

A. Organizing the Composition

Before writing your composition, fill in the required information on this organizational work sheet. The work sheet follows the preliminary outline used for the discussion. Suggestions for writing each paragraph are given at the right side of this work sheet. The pages of the discussion outline provide additional help for the composition.

You may use phrases on this work sheet except where it calls for full sentences.

Organizational Work Sheet
(Preliminary notes for the composition)

Title of the composition _____
(Do not use quotation marks or a period for a title at the top of the page. Use initial capital letters for the first word of the title and for all other words except articles, prepositions, and coordinate conjunctions *[and, or, but]*.)

Introduction: general statements
Opening sentence of paragraph _____

> Put the introduction in a separate paragraph.
>
> Use the present tense for general statements.
>
> Avoid negative remarks like "It's hard to do."

_____

_____

_____

Incentives

_____

_____

_____

I. Tools, materials, equipment (if necessary) (For a recipe, give the ingredients here.)
   Note: The recipe should be for something you know how to make yourself, not a recipe from a book.

> New paragraph
>
> Recipe ingredients may be listed in one or two columns.

_____

_____

_____

_____

_____

II. Steps in chronological order
    Include precautions
    (For a game, give the rules here.)

_____

_____

_____

III. _____

_____

_____

IV. _____

_____

_____

V. _____

_____

etc. _____

_____

Conclusion: general statements
Incentives restated

_____

_____

_____

_____

_____

_____

_____

_____

_____

New paragraph

Use short paragraphs for the steps (but avoid one-sentence paragraphs). Make the instructions clear and short, but do not leave out any necessary details.

Verbs:
    the imperative: *do this*, *do that*
Or: *you should do this, you must do that*
Or: *I do this, I do that*
Connectives between the steps: *then, next, after this, after doing that*

New paragraph

May be only one or two sentences

Repeat some of the incentives in the introduction, using other words.

Use the present tense for general statements.

B. Writing a 400/500-Word Composition

Write the composition based on your notes on the organizational work sheet. Be careful of your paragraphing. Use separate paragraphs for your introduction and your conclusion. (Long paragraphs may be broken in two at appropriate places, but avoid single-sentence paragraphs.)

C. Correcting/Rewriting the Composition (peer review)

When you bring your composition to class, you will be asked to exchange it with that of another student.

First check the other student's development of the composition, and then check the items listed under Editing.

1. Development of the Composition
Introduction and Conclusion
Transitional lead-in
Paragraphs—opening sentences and supporting details
Are these well done, or can you suggest ways to improve them? Write your
comments on the student's composition.

2. Editing
Grammar
Usage (spelling and punctuation)
Vocabulary
For grammar and usage, the information in the Symbol Chart for Correction of
Compositions in the Appendix can be helpful.

When the peer review is over, hand in your composition to your teacher, who will return it to you later with additional comments and correction symbols used for the mistakes. Then you will be asked to rewrite the composition, taking into account the suggestions of your fellow student and your teacher for the improvement of the composition.

After you have revised your composition, hand it in to your teacher together with your first draft.

☑ Grammar Practice

Exercise 1: Passive Voice (for a process)

Instructions can be given in the passive voice if we want to talk about a *process*—that is, *how something is made or done*—rather than how to make or do something.

Active:	*Hold* the fingers lightly over the keyboard keys.
Passive Process:	The fingers *are held* lightly over the keyboard keys.
Active:	You *should hold* the fingers lightly over the keyboard keys.
Passive Process:	The fingers *should be held* lightly over the keyboard keys.

Note that in the passive sentence the original object (the fingers) becomes the subject.

A. Change the following sentences to the passive voice in order to indicate a process. Begin each passive sentence with the object of the verb in the active sentence. The verbs to be made passive are in italics. Some of the sentences need two passive verbs.

1. *Simmer* the stew for two hours.
   The stew is simmered for two hours.

2. You *should simmer* the stew for two hours.
   The stew should be simmered for two hours.

3. *Plant* the seeds in even rows.

   _____

4. You *should sandpaper* the table before you *paint* it.

   _____

5. *Throw* the tennis ball high in the air and *serve* it into the proper box of your opponent.

_____

6. You *should preheat* the oven before you *put* the cake in it.

_____

7. You *should drink* plenty of fluids if you have a cold.

_____

8. *Use* a screwdriver to loosen the screws.

_____

9. You *should check* the air in the tires before you start on a long automobile trip.

_____

10. *Mix* all the dry ingredients and *add* them to the others.

_____

11. You *should do* these exercises regularly every morning.

_____

B. You are giving instructions on how to play a particular game (for example, tennis, soccer, Ping-Pong), how to drive a car, how to prepare a certain recipe, or do something else. Write five to ten sentences telling what *should* or *must be done* by the learner who is following your instructions.

Examples:

Preparing a recipe: *The batter should be well mixed before it is poured into the baking pan.*

Playing Ping-Pong: *The paddle must be held in a special way.*

Driving a car: *The oil and the water in the car should be checked at regular intervals.*

Exercise 2: Conditions—Possible and Unreal

An *if* clause in a sentence may express a possible condition or an unreal one. In instructions, a conditional sentence usually gives advice or suggestions.

Possible Condition	Your cold *will get* better if you *stay* in bed.
(Future Time)	(This kind of condition implies its opposite: *Your cold won't get better if you don't stay in bed.*)
Unreal Condition	
Present Time	Your cold *would get* better if you *stayed** in bed. (*Real situation:* You're not staying in bed.)
Past Time	Your cold *would have gotten* better if you *had stayed* in bed. (*Real situation:* You didn't stay in bed.)

Note: An *if* clause can be used at the beginning or the end of the sentence.

---

* The past form of the verb is used in the *if* clause. This is called the subjunctive use. In such sentences, *would* may also occur informally in the *if* clause: Your cold would get better if you would (were willing to) stay in bed.

A. The following sentences with possible conditions have been taken from instructions about how to do something. Change these sentences to sentences with *present unreal conditions*.

1. The cookies will taste better if you add some nuts.

   The cookies would taste better if you added some nuts.

2. Your health will improve if you do these exercises.

   _____

3. You will learn faster if you practice every day.

   _____

4. The piano will sound better if you have it tuned.

   _____

5. The garden will look better if you water the plants every day.

_____

6. The car can* last a long time if you take good care of it.

_____

7. You can save money if you buy food in season.

_____

8. If you take some driving lessons, you will learn to park the car.

_____

9. If you follow these instructions carefully, you will have no trouble.

_____

B. Change the sentences in A to sentences with *past unreal conditions.*

1. *The cookies would have tasted better if you had added some nuts.*

C. Combine these sentences to make *present unreal conditions.* Watch for negative-positive or positive-negative changes.

Real Situation	*The Speaker's Opinion or Advice about This Situation*
1. You aren't staying in bed.	Your cold will not get better.

If you stayed in bed, your cold would get better.
(This situation is *unreal now.* Note the negative-positive changes.)

| 2. You don't practice a lot. | You will not be an excellent pianist. |

_____

_____

* *Can* (or *may, might*) may be used instead of *will* in conditional sentences.

3. You don't study hard.   You won't become a good student.

_____

4. You don't shop wisely.   You won't save money.

_____

5. You don't watch the road carefully. You won't become a better driver.

_____

6. You look down at the keyboard keys. Your keyboarding speed won't improve.

_____

7. You go outside.   Your work won't get done.

_____

D. Combine these sentences to make *past unreal conditions.*

Real Situation	*The Speaker's Opinion or Advice about This Situation*

1. You didn't stay in bed.   Your illness didn't get better.

 If you had stayed in bed, your illness would have got(ten) better.
 (This situation was *unreal in the past.* Note the negative-positive changes.)

2. You didn't practice a lot.   You weren't an excellent pianist.

_____

3. You didn't study hard.   You didn't become a good student.

_____

4. You didn't shop wisely.   You didn't save money.

_____

5. You didn't watch the road carefully. You didn't become a good driver.

_____

6. You looked down at the keyboard
   keys.   Your keyboarding speed didn't improve.

   _____

7. You went outside.   Your work didn't get done.

   _____

Exercise 3: Conditions with *otherwise*

> **Precautions in instructions are often given in the imperative form of a verb, or with *you should* (advisability) or *you must* (necessity).**
>
> > *Learn* (or *you should learn*, or *you must learn*) **to drive defensively; *otherwise* you may get hit by another car.**
>
> **This precaution may also be stated as a condition.**
>
> > *If you don't* (or *Unless you*) **drive defensively, you may get hit by another car. (Note that this *if* clause is now negative.)**

Change the following conditional sentences to their equivalents with *otherwise.* You will need to watch for positive-negative changes. Be sure to use a semicolon before *otherwise.* (In sentences with *otherwise*, a period may replace the semicolon, especially if both parts of a sentence are long. Also, a comma is often used after *otherwise.*)

1. Unless you learn to swim with your face in the water, you will never become a good swimmer.

   Learn (or you should learn, or you must learn) to swim with your face in the water; otherwise you will never become a good swimmer.

2. If the roast isn't basted frequently, it will become dry and tough.

   The roast should (or must) be basted frequently; otherwise it will become dry and tough. (The imperative form is not used with a passive.)

3. If you don't pin the pieces of material together carefully, the dress won't come out right.

   _____

88

4. Unless the piano is tuned regularly, it won't sound right.

_____

5. If you don't hold your fingers in the right position over the keyboard keys, you will make mistakes.

_____

6. Unless you follow the instructions carefully, you won't get your new computer to work.

_____

7. If you don't turn on the ignition in the car with your key, the car won't start.

_____

8. Unless you serve the ball diagonally across into the box of your opponent, the serve doesn't count.

_____

9. If you don't learn to skim in reading, you will never become a fast, efficient reader.

_____

Note: You should is not an appropriate choice in sentences 7 and 8 since the conditions express *necessity*.

Exercise 4: Auxiliaries: *mustn't* vs. *don't have to*

Must and *have to* are synonyms when used in the positive. Their negatives, however, have different meanings.

If you want vegetables to taste right, you *mustn't* let them cook too long.

(*You mustn't* gives a warning; *mustn't* is a stronger form than *shouldn't*, which gives advice.)

You don't have to add the wine to this recipe if you prefer not to.

(*You don't have to* is the equivalent of *you aren't required to, you don't need to.*)

Use *mustn't* or *don't have to* with the verb in parentheses. Keep in mind that *mustn't* is a warning that is stronger than the advice of *shouldn't*; *don't have to* means *don't need to* or *aren't required to.*

1. You (add) _mustn't add_ much turpentine to the paint if you want the paint to cover the wood completely.

2. You (add) _don't have to add_ any turpentine to the paint; the paint is already mixed.

3. You (put) _____ on a second coat of paint if you don't want to.

4. However, if you are going to put on a second coat of paint, you (do) _____ it until the first coat is thoroughly dry.

5. You (leave) _____ on a camping trip until you have thoroughly checked all the equipment and the food supplies.

6. You (take) _____ a tent for a short camping trip; you can take sleeping bags instead.

7. You (drive) _____ in heavy traffic if you are just learning how to drive.

8. In the winter a baby (go) _____ out without a hat.

9. You (do) _____ these exercises every day; a few days a week will be enough to get you back in shape.

10. In stamp collecting, you (pick) _____ up the stamps with your fingers.

11. You (be) _____ an expert to enjoy the dance I am going to teach you.

Exercise 5: *have* + VERB (for instructions)

Instructions for a service to be performed are often given with the verb *have*. The service may be expressed in the active or the passive form.

Service Expressed as Active	I had the supermarket *deliver* some groceries.
	(*Deliver* is the infinitive, without *to*.) The service: The supermarket delivered some groceries.
Service Expressed as Passive	I had some groceries *delivered* (by the supermarket).
	(*Delivered* is the past participle from the passive verb.) The service: Some groceries were delivered by the supermarket.

In this passive use, the *by* phrase is often omitted.

A. Make sentences beginning with *I had* and ending with (a) a service expressed as active, and (b) a service expressed as passive. For the passive the *by* phrase may be omitted.

Instructions to: *Request for Service*

1. the maid   Please clean the house.

    (a) Active: *I had the maid clean the house.*

    (b) Passive: *I had the house cleaned (by the maid).*

2. the pharmacist   Please fill my prescription.

_____

_____

3. the bank teller   Could you please cash my check?

_____

_____

4. the lawyer   I'd like you to draw up my will.

_____

_____

5. the administrative assistant   Would you mind making the travel arrangements?

_____

_____

6. the shoemaker   My shoes need to be repaired.

_____

_____

7. the auto mechanic   Please change the rear tires.

_____

_____

8. the painter   The whole house needs to be painted.

_____

_____

9. the tailor   Would you please lengthen my skirt?

_____

_____

10. the carpenter   Could you please build some bookcases for me?

_____

_____

11. the gardener   You'll trim the hedges, won't you?

_____

_____

12. the handyman

Would you mind replacing the furnace filters?

_____

_____

B. Using one of the forms for requests from A, ask for a service from each of the following people. Then write sentences with *I had* to express the service as (a) active and (b) passive. The *by* phrase may be omitted in the passive.

1. the tailor

   Please shorten the sleeves of my coat.

   (a) *I had the tailor shorten the sleeves of my coat.*

   (b) *I had the sleeves of my coat shortened (by the tailor).*

2. the plumber

   _____

   _____

   _____

3. the dentist

   _____

   _____

   _____

4. the furnace repairman

   _____

   _____

   _____

5. the photographer

   _____

   _____

   _____

7. the barber/hairdresser

   _____

   _____

   _____

8. the car mechanic

   _____

   _____

   _____

9. the painter

   _____

   _____

   _____

10. the pharmacist

   _____

   _____

   _____

6. the doctor

_____

_____

_____

11. the salesclerk

_____

_____

_____

Exercise 6: Dangling Participles

When an introductory structure does not have its own subject, it often depends on the subject of the main verb for its agent. This is typically true for introductory structures containing the *-ing* participle or the *-ed* participle.

While *waiting* for the rice to cook, *you* should prepare the gravy.

If the subject of the main verb is not the agent of the *-ing* or *-ed* verb in the introductory structure, this structure is considered as unacceptably "dangling."

Dangling: While *waiting* for the rice to cook, *the gravy* should be prepared.

(*The gravy* is not the agent of *waiting*.)

Underline (1) the *-ing* or *-ed* participle in the introductory structure, and (2) the subject of the main verb that follows. Then correct any dangling constructions in the sentences in one or both of the ways suggested below. Mark "CORRECT" for those sentences that do not have dangling participles.

1. By practicing every day, your speed will improve rapidly.

　　By *practicing* every day, *your keyboarding speed* will improve rapidly.

Corrections:

　　By practicing every day, you will improve your keyboarding speed rapidly.

(The subject *you* is the agent of *practicing*.)

or

　　If you practice every day, your keyboarding speed will improve rapidly.

(*Practice* now has its own subject in the *if* clause and does not depend on the subject of the main verb for its agent.)

94

2. Once cooked, add the sautéed mushrooms to the chicken.

_____

_____

3. Leaving the pan on a low flame, the whole procedure will take 30 to 40 minutes.

_____

_____

4. After hemming the dress, the last step is ironing it.

_____

_____

5. Once having learned to drive, you will be able to have many enjoyable trips in the country.

_____

_____

6. When doing this dance step, your arms should be placed on your partner's hips.

_____

_____

7. If carefully constructed and finished, no one will know that you made the table yourself.

_____

_____

8. Before hanging a picture, carefully check the place where the nail is to be hammered in.

_____

_____

9. Prepared in advance, this stew will permit you to enjoy your guests without your having to run into the kitchen all the time.

_____

_____

Exercise 7: Subjunctive Verbs in *that* Clauses

Instructions given in the form of advice are often expressed indirectly in *that* clauses after certain verbs. The verbs in such *that* clauses are usually in simple, unchanged form (called the present subjunctive) *regardless of person or tense.*

In his book *How to Win Friends and Influence People,* Dale Carnegie suggested that a person *be* a good listener. He also recommended that we *become* genuinely interested in other people.

Note that the present subjunctive verbs *(be, become)* are those infinitives without *to.* (Sometimes the auxiliary *should* occurs in such *that* clauses: Carnegie suggests that a person *should* be a good listener.)

Below are some other suggestions given by Dale Carnegie in *How to Win Friends and Influence People.* Using verbs from the nouns at the beginning of each sentence, write sentences expressing Dale Carnegie's advice in *that* clauses. Use *we* as the subject in the *that* clause.

1. Advice: Make the other person feel important and do it sincerely.

   Dale Carnegie advised that we make the other person feel important and that we do it sincerely.

2. Suggestion: Show respect for the other person's opinions.

   _____

3. Urging: Never tell anyone he or she is wrong.

   _____

4. Advice: Let the other person do a great deal of the talking.

   _____

5. Insistence: Try honestly to see things from the other person's point of view.

   _____

6. Recommendation: Be sympathetic to the other person's ideas and desires.

   _____

7. Proposal: Call attention to other people's mistakes indirectly.

   _____

Exercise 8: Word Forms

Add the correct endings.

1. Something that is *cheap* is <u>econom-*ical*</u> or <u>inexpen-*sive*</u>.

2. Something that is *useful* is <u>practi-</u>_____.

3. Something that is *easy* is <u>sim-</u>_____.

4. Something that is *beautiful* is <u>attrac-</u>_____.

5. Something that is *tasty* is <u>delic-</u>_____.

6. Something that is *pleasant* is <u>enjoy-</u>_____.

7. Something that is *nourishing* is <u>nutri-</u>_____.

8. Something that is *lightly fried* is <u>saut-</u>_____.

9. Something that is *slowly cooked on low heat* is <u>sim-</u>_____.

10. A *safety measure* is a <u>precau-</u>_____.

11. *Something that encourages us to action* is an <u>incent-</u>_____.

12. *Any of the things that are mixed together* is an <u>ingred-</u>_____.

13. *Something that we do* is an <u>activ-</u>_____.

14. *Something that we do well and take pride in* is an <u>accomplish-</u>_____.

15. *Something that is done by a tailor to make our clothes fit better* is called an <u>altera-</u>_____.

Exercise 9: Sentence Review

Make full sentences from the word groups below and complete the unfinished words. Use the correct form of the verb, together with any auxiliaries that might be required (especially *must, should, would, had*). Do not change the word order. Use commas, semicolons, and periods wherever necessary.

1. Air / in tires / check / before / you / start / on / long / trip. (passive)

   The air in the tires should be checked before you start on a long trip.

2. screwdriver / use / loosen / screws (passive)

   _____

3. piano / sound / better / if / you / have / it / tune-_____.
   (*Note:* The piano isn't tuned now.) (unreal conditional)

   _____

4. car / last / long / time / if / you / take / care / it.
   (*Note:* You aren't taking care of it now.) (unreal conditional)

   _____

5. If / you / practice / every day / you / learn / faster.
   (*Note:* You didn't practice every day last year.) (unreal conditional)

   _____

6. your illness / get / better / if / you / stay / bed.
   (*Note:* You didn't stay in bed last week.) (unreal conditional)

   _____

7. you / learn / skim / in read-_____ / otherwise / you / never / become /
   fast / effici-_____ / reader.

   _____

8. you / turn on / ignition / in car / otherwise / car / not start.

   _____

9. you / not add / much turpentine / if / you / want / the paint / cover / wood /
   complete-_____.

   _____

10. Dale Carnegie / advise / we / make / other person / feel / important.
    (Use a *that* clause after *advise*.)

    _____

11. I / had / gardener / trim / hedge.

    _____

12. I / will have / some bookcases / build / by / carpenter.

    _____

▷ **Extra Speaking and Writing Practice**

Exercise 10: Composition—Adding an Introduction: Recipe

The following recipe for Potato and Vegetable Casserole comes from *The Complete Book of Vegetable Cookery*. Look it over to see why you would want to recommend it to a friend.

1½ pounds potatoes, peeled and sliced thin	1½ teaspoons salt
2 cups chopped tomatoes	½ teaspoon freshly ground black pepper
1½ cups thinly sliced carrots	1½ cups water
1 cup chopped onion	¼ cup olive oil
2 cloves garlic, minced	
¼ cup chopped parsley	

In a buttered baking dish, spread the potatoes. Mix together the tomatoes, carrots, onion, garlic, parsley, salt, and pepper; spread over the potatoes. Add the water; bake in a 375-degree oven for 45 minutes. Pour the oil over the top; bake 15 minutes longer. Serve hot or cold. Serves 4 to 6.

From *The Complete Book of Vegetable Cookery*

Note that in this kind of recipe, only the essential information is given. The simple imperative form of the verb is used, and there are no transitions to connect steps. In short instructions, articles and pronouns are often omitted.

Write a short introduction for this recipe. Give your reasons why someone would want to make this vegetable dish. You might use some of the reasons already suggested for making something: it is easy to make, economical, tasty, and nutritious. You might also refer to the idea of variety: this is an unusual way to serve vegetables, especially for those who are vegetarians or for those who don't usually like vegetables.

To catch the attention of the reader more easily in the introduction, you might put one or more of these reasons in the form of questions.

Exercise 11: Composition—Adding the Body and a Conclusion

The following is an introduction to a composition giving instructions on how to take care of a cold.

How to Take Care of a Cold

You've all had colds at some time and know how miserable a cold can make you feel. Your nose runs, your throat hurts, you're sneezing, you have a headache, and you may have a fever. Here is some advice about how to take care of your cold.

First, discuss as a class, or in groups, the remedies for taking care of a cold. Then copy the introduction given above and continue the composition. In full sentences arranged in paragraphs, tell the readers what they must do to take care of a cold. Some of the things to consider are rest, food, drink, medications, clothes to wear outdoors.

Also tell the readers what they mustn't do—for example, go outdoors when it is very cold, overeat, take too much medication, get too close to other people who can catch your cold.

Add a brief conclusion.

Exercise 12: Proverbs (giving advice)

Discuss the following proverbs in groups or as a class. Do you have similar proverbs in your culture?

1. An apple a day keeps the doctor away.

2. Too many cooks spoil the soup.

3. Hear no evil, see no evil, speak no evil.

4. Don't put all your eggs in one basket.

5. Look before you leap.

6. You can't make an omelette without breaking some eggs.

7. When in Rome, do as the Romans do.

8. Half a loaf is better than none.

9. A bird in the hand is worth two in the bush.

10. Better late than never.

11. Don't count your chickens before they hatch.

Exercise 13: Journal Writing

Write a journal entry on the following subject. Write freely since you are the only one who will see this entry.

Tell how you get back to your home from school. Begin from the time you leave the school and end with your arrival at home. Write about the directions you follow, the streets you walk on, where you cross, the transportation you use.

Now use your journal entry as the basis for a more careful letter to one of your classmates telling him or her how to get to your home from school. This letter is to be handed in to your teacher.

 # Listening-Writing Practice

Exercise 14: Dictation

Your teacher will dictate each paragraph three times. The first time is for listening only, the second time is for writing, and the third time is for checking what you have written.

Immediately after you give your teacher the dictation you have written, check the dictation in the book for any problems you had in writing it.

> If you want to find the pronunciation of a word in an American dictionary, check the information in parentheses right after the word. Within these parentheses, the word is rewritten phonetically with symbols for the sounds and with stress marks for the accented syllables. In an American dictionary, the symbols are mainly letters of the alphabet. Because there are many more vowel sounds than the five vowel letters, special marks above these letters differentiate the sounds. Look at the bottom of the dictionary page to find illustrations of the sounds of each symbol. If two pronunciations are given for a word, for example, the word *direction,* this means that either pronunciation is acceptable.

Exercise 15: Dicto-comp

Take notes as your teacher reads the dicto-comp to you several times. Then reconstruct the dicto-comp from your notes. The dicto-comp does not need to be written exactly as you heard it, but it should be grammatically correct.

Before you write the dicto-comp, your teacher may ask the class to get together in groups to check with each other on what you heard.

Immediately after you give your teacher the dicto-comp you have written, check the dicto-comp in the book for any problems you had in writing it.

Here are a few important rules of reading hygiene.

First, get expert help in relieving eyestrain. Get eyeglasses if you are nearsighted or farsighted or have other defects of vision.

Second, hold your book up when you read. Don't let your head bend over a book that is lying flat on your desk or table. Hold the book vertically in your hand or propped up on the desk at the best distance for you. For most persons the best distance is about fourteen inches from the eyes.

Third, read in a good light. Avoid reading in the bright sunlight and be careful to turn on the light before twilight falls. Sit with your back to the light. The light should fall over the left shoulder (or the right, if you are left-handed). In this way, you keep out of your own light and avoid having a bright light shining into your eyes.

Study Types of Reading Exercises by Ruth Strang,
Teachers College Press, 1951, page 74.

Reading-Writing Practice (summary: "Taking an Examination")

You are going to write a one to three paragraph summary of a reading selection. A summary is a restatement, in shortened form, of the main ideas of a selection.

In preparation for the summary, skim through the selection quickly to determine the way the ideas are developed (through comparison, contrast, listing, time, space, or example). Then reread the selection carefully, underlining the important points that should be included in the summary. (Do not underline too much.)

In writing the summary, use your own words as much as possible. You may include the important words from the reading selection, but use quotation marks around whole phrases taken directly from the selection.

Devote more attention to the main points than to their supporting details. Omit examples unless they are important to the development of the ideas. Do *not* give your own ideas in a summary.

The selection to be summarized was written by a well-known educator whose specialty was teaching reading skills. The selection comes from a chapter called "Reading Aids to Passing Examinations."

You will note that the ideas are developed through listing, first of general rules and then of specific rules for taking an essay examination or an objective examination.

Taking an Examination

Techniques for the actual taking of an examination vary according to the kind of examination. The most common forms are the essay and the **objective.** However, in any examination there are two **cardinal** rules:

1. Carefully study all directions whether they are included on the question sheet, written on the board, or given orally. Directions usually cover methods of indicating answers, credit value of various answers, methods of scoring the examination, number of questions that need to be answered, and other vital considerations.
2. Plan to use all the time allowed for writing the examination. Since most examinations represent the **culmination** of an activity that has taken considerable time and energy, failure to take advantage of the entire time **allotted** to them is a **short-sighted** policy.

Before beginning to write an essay examination it is profitable to take time to: (1) read the entire examination, (2) outline all your answers, (3) then budget your time in proportion to the credit value of the various answers. By outlining all your answers before writing any of them, you will often find it possible to transfer from one answer to another some of the items on which you are well informed. In this way you will improve the organization of all your answers, and include in each one some ideas about which you feel very sure.

In taking an objective examination, it is desirable to follow these rules: (1) on your first reading of the examination, answer only those questions about which you feel absolutely certain; (2) on your second reading answer only those you can confidently do with a minimum of **computation** or thought; (3) having completed these two steps, determine how many more times you can go through the questions in the time remaining and budget your time accordingly; (4) answer all questions before the end of the examination period—leave no blanks; (5) change your answers only if you are certain that your first response was incorrect.

Study Types of Reading Exercises by Ruth Strang,
Teachers College Press, 1951, pages 145–46.

Vocabulary

1. **objective** (test)—In this type of test, the test taker must choose the right answer to a question from among a choice of answers that are given (multiple choice). The test does not depend on anyone's opinion about the right answer.

2. **cardinal**—very important

3. **culmination**—end point

4. **allot**—divide or distribute, set apart as a portion

5. **short-sighted**—unable to see far, without sufficient thought

6. **computation**—calculation

 **For Your Information**
(recipe for curried chicken and rice)

You might be interested in trying out the following recipe for a tasty dish that doesn't cost much and is easy to prepare.

How to Make Curried Chicken and Rice
(simplified American style)

Curried chicken and rice is one of the easiest dishes to prepare. It requires very few ingredients and makes a tasty meal with your favorite salad. Here is all you need.

    4 good-sized chicken parts
    ½ cup brown rice
    1 heaping tablespoon mild curry (The next time you may want
    more or less curry depending on your taste.)
    1 tablespoon salt
    This recipe will serve four people.

Wash the chicken parts and place them in a pot with enough water to cover them. Add the curry and the salt; then cover the pot. When the water boils, add the rice, and then lower the heat. Stir occasionally to prevent the rice from sticking to the bottom of the pan. Continue cooking on low heat for 45 minutes or until both the rice and the chicken are done. If the water is absorbed before the rice is done, add a little more water. If there is too much water, raise the heat and cook uncovered until most of the water has evaporated.

You are now ready to serve your curried chicken and rice dish with the salad you have prepared. If you have followed the simple instructions given in this recipe, you will get many compliments from your family or guests for a delicious meal that was very easy to prepare and didn't cost a great deal.

———————————————————————

Holidays

Grammar and Usage

Prepositions of time— *in, on, at*

Definite article—*the*

Noun phrases—*the* + verbal noun + *of*

Subject-verb agreement

Passive voice

much-many, (a) *little,* (a) *few*

Questions and answers

Spelling—noun plurals in *-es*

Rhetoric

Using an outline to guide the composition

Using an introduction and a conclusion

Using a transitional lead-in to the body of the
composition

Discussion and Composition

1. Discussion: Preliminary Outline for the Composition (prewriting stage)

Subject: *The Celebration of* (name of holiday) *in* (name of country)

Outline	*Discussion*
(To be placed on the board. Books are closed.)	*(Ideas, Grammar and Usage, Vocabulary, Elements of Composition Building)*

Introduction: general comments about kinds of holidays in any country	Possible comments: My country, like all other countries, has holidays. Some are national, some religious, some social. (An example of each may be given.) Some are days when people get off from work or school; some are not.
Transitional lead-in: connection with your subject of *one* holiday	Possible transitions: One of the holidays I enjoy the most is a national (or religious, social) one. *or* My favorite holiday is a national (or religious, social) one. *or* The national (or religious, social) holiday I always look forward to is _____.
I. Date of the holiday and background (if possible)	Points of usage: 1. prepositions of time: *in*—season, year, month, part of the day *at*—noon, midnight, time of the day *on*—days of the week, dates, holidays 2. Initial capitals: holidays, days of the week, months 3. No *the* with the name of a holiday (except with the Fouth of July)
II. What people do to celebrate this holiday III. IV. V. VI.	Possible activities: have a vacation from work or school clean the house wear special clothes or costumes go to a place of worship: a church, temple, synagogue, mosque

VII.   watch parades
   etc.   listen to speeches
                                                shoot off firecrackers
                                                watch fireworks
                                                put out flags
                                                place flowers on graves
                                                have parties, dances
                                                eat special foods
                                                go to the beach or to the country
                                                decorate homes, stores, streets

Conclusion: general statements   Possible comments:
                                                enjoyment of the holiday
                                                looking forward to next year's
                                                    celebration
                                or end with an interesting final detail, a
                                              personal anecdote, or a special feeling
                                              about the holiday

---

2. Composition (to be done before or after the grammar practice)

A. Organizing the Composition

Before writing your composition, fill in the required information on this organizational work sheet. The work sheet follows the preliminary outline used for the discussion. Suggestions for writing each paragraph are given at the right side of this work sheet. The pages of the discussion outline provide additional help for the composition.

    You may use phrases on this work sheet except where it calls for full sentences.

Organizational Work Sheet
(Preliminary notes for the composition)

Title of the composition _____
(Do not use quotation marks or a period for a title at the top of the page. Use initial capital letters for the first word of the title and for all other words except articles, prepositions, and coordinate conjunctions *[and, or, but].*)

Introduction: general statements

Opening sentence of paragraph _____

_____

_____

_____

Put in a separate paragraph.

Use the present tense for general statements.

Keep this paragraph short.

Kinds of holidays

_____

_____

_____

Transitional lead-in connecting the general statements of the introduction to the specific subject of *one* holiday

Full sentence _____

_____

_____

_____

Do not use *the* with the name of a holiday (except with the Fourth of July).

I. Date and background of the holiday

_____

_____

_____

_____

_____

Keep this short—may be included in the paragraph with the transition.

Be careful of your use of prepositions and initial capitals.

II. What people do on this holiday

_____

_____

_____

III. _____

_____

_____

IV. _____

_____

_____

V. _____

_____

_____

etc. _____

_____

Conclusion: general statements

_____

_____

_____

_____

_____

_____

_____

_____

_____

_____

_____

Use chronological order.

This is the main part of the composition.

Use several paragraphs, but avoid one-sentence paragraphs.

New paragraph

The conclusion may simply be an interesting final detail, anecdote, or feeling regarding the celebration of the holiday.

B. Writing a 400/500-Word Composition

Write the composition based on your notes on the organizational work sheet. Be careful of your paragraphing. Use separate paragraphs for your introduction and your conclusion. (Long paragraphs may be broken in two at appropriate places, but avoid single-sentence paragraphs.)

C. Correcting/Rewriting the Composition (peer review)

When you bring your composition to class, you will be asked to exchange it with that of another student.

First check the other student's development of the composition and then check the items listed under Editing.

1. Development of the Composition
Introduction and Conclusion
Transitional lead-in
Paragraphs—opening sentences and supporting details
Are these well done, or can you suggest ways to improve them? Write your comments on the student's composition.

2. Editing
Grammar
Usage (spelling and punctuation)
Vocabulary
For grammar and usage, the information in the Symbol Chart for Correction of Compositions in the Appendix can be helpful.

When the peer review is over, hand in your composition to your teacher, who will return it to you later with additional comments and correction symbols used for the mistakes. Then you will be asked to rewrite the composition, taking into account what your fellow student and what your teacher suggested for the improvement of the composition.

After you have revised your composition, hand it in to your teacher together with your first draft.

☑ Grammar Practice

Exercise 1: Prepositions of Time—*in, at, on*

The following are the most common prepositions for specific time.

in	with seasons	in (the) spring, in (the) summer
		in (the) fall, in (the) winter
	with years	in 1976
	with months	in February
	with certain parts of the day	in the morning, in the afternoon, in the evening
at	with certain parts of the day	at night, at noon, at midnight
	with the time of the day	at five o'clock
on	with days	on Sunday (day of the week) *on* may be
		on February 22 (date) omitted except
		on Labor Day at the beginning
		on New Year's Eve (holiday) of the sentence

Note that names of days of the week and names of months begin with capital letters. Initial capital letters are also required for every word in the name of a holiday (*Independence Day, Christmas Eve*). Note also that *the* is not used with names of holidays, except for *the Fourth of July,* an alternative name for Independence Day.

A. Use the time expression *in, at,* or *on.*

1. The Declaration of Independence was signed __*on*__ July 4, 1776.

2. Boxing Day is observed in Canada __on__ December 26.

3. Many people go to church __on__ Christmas Eve.

4. Santa Claus is supposed to arrive __at__ night to put presents under the Christmas tree.

5. Columbus Day celebrates the discovery of America __in__ 1492.

6. __On__ Independence Day, it is customary to have fireworks displays __at__ the evening.

7. Mother's Day is observed __in__ May, Father's Day __in__ June.

113

8. _on_ New Year's Eve, parties often begin late, _at_ ten or eleven _at_ night.

9. Cinco de Mayo is observed _on_ May 5.

10. Many holidays that occur _on_ Sundays are celebrated _at_ the following Monday.

B. In full sentences, give the dates of five holidays. Use capital letters for the word *Day* if it is part of the name of the holiday. Use capital letters for the name of the day or the month. Do not use *the* with the name of the holiday.

> *Independence Day is observed (or is celebrated) on July 4.*

Exercise 2: Definite Article—*the*

> *The* is usually required with ordinal numbers: the first, the second, the third. (Ordinals are ranking numbers. Their primary forms, which express amount, are called cardinals: one, two, three.)
>
> Labor Day is observed on *the first* Monday in September.
>
> *The* also occurs with other words that establish a sequence: the next, the following, the last.
>
> New Year's Eve is celebrated on *the last* day of the year.
>
> *The next* day begins the New Year.
>
> *The* is not used when *next* or *last* simply marks a time that is future or past from the present.
>
> Present: The store is having a sale *this* week.
>
> Future: The store will have a sale *next* week.
>
> Past: The store had a sale *last* week.
>
> *Note:* No preposition of time appears with these points of time.
>
> Dates are usually written as cardinal numbers but are spoken as ordinals. Thus the written date *May 1* is spoken as May *first* or May *the first*. If the date is written *1 May*, it is spoken as *the first* of May.

Use *the* where required. If cardinal numbers are given, change them to ordinals.

1. Thanksgiving Day in the U.S. is celebrated on (four) _the fourth_ Thursday of November.

2. Valentine's Day falls on February 14 (spoken form) _(the) fourteenth_ .

3. Mexican Independence Day is celebrated on September 16 (spoken form) _____

   _____.

4. Memorial Day is observed on _____ last Monday in May.

5. In _____ next few years we may have more holidays than we had _____ last year.

6. April Fool's Day, which occurs on April 1 (spoken form) ____, is the day we play tricks on each other.

7. Many people stay up late on New Year's Eve. On _____ next day they are very tired.

8. The birthday of Martin Luther King, Jr., is observed on (three) _____ Monday in January.

9. Christmas Day falls on December 25 (spoken form) _____.

10. Election Day occurs on _____ first Tuesday after _____ first Monday in November.

Exercise 3: Noun Phrases—*the* + Verbal Noun + *of*

By changing the verb in a sentence to its noun form, we can often use this sentence as a noun phrase within another sentence.

Sentence: Both Americans and Canadians celebrate Thanksgiving.

New Sentence: The celebration of Thanksgiving is a tradition in both the U.S. and Canada.

(The verb *celebrate* has been changed to the verbal noun *celebration.*)

Note that the noun phrase begins with the word *the.* The word *of* comes before the original object.

> The original subject, both *Americans and Canadians,* can be
> included in the noun phrase by
>
> using the possessive form (without *the* before it): Both
> Americans' and Canadians' celebration of Thanksgiving is a tra-
> dition or in a *by* phrase at the end: The celebration of Thanks-
> giving by both Americans and Canadians is a tradition.

A. In the following sentences, change the words in parentheses to noun phrases following the pattern: *the* + verbal noun + *of.* If the verbal noun has a subject, place the subject in possessive form or in a *by* phrase.

1. (decorate their homes for Halloween) takes some people a long time.

   The decoration of their homes for Halloween takes some people a long time.

2. (Columbus discovered America) is commemorated on the second Monday in October.

   Columbus's discovery of America (or the discovery of America by Columbus) is commemorated on the second Monday in October.

3. (children enjoy holidays) is greatest at Christmas time.

   _____

4. Thanksgiving Day (in the U.S.) honors (the Pilgrims celebrated the good harvest of 1621).

   _____

5. On Election Day, certain public places, especially schools, are used for (elect government officials).

   _____

6. In the United States, (declare Independence) was signed in 1776.

   _____

7. At Christmas time, (exchange gifts) around the Christmas tree is a popular custom.

   _____

8. (Americans observe Memorial Day) takes place on the last Monday in May.

   _____

B. Sometimes a verbal noun is interchangeable with an *-ing* gerund—*the decoration of their homes* or *decorating their homes.*

Go over the sentences in A and see how many *-ing* gerunds may also be used.

Exercise 4: Subject-Verb Agreement

The verb in a sentence must agree with the subject in number. This kind of agreement is especially required with verbs in the simple present tense.

The girl remembers. (A singular noun requires a verb ending in *-s.*)
The girls remember. (A plural noun requires a verb that has no *-s.*)

Agreement is also needed with those auxiliaries that have different forms for the singular and plural.

Singular	*Plural*
is	are
was	were
has	have
does	do

If the subject is long, the verb agrees with the main word used in the subject.

The *atmosphere* during the Christmas holidays *is* very festive.

A subject used with *each* or *every* is singular and requires a singular verb.

Everyone *enjoys* getting the day off from work on a holiday.
Each holiday *is* celebrated in a different way.

Where *there* is used in subject position, the verb (usually *be*) agrees with the noun that follows it.

There *is* one *holiday* that I especially love.
There *are* some *holidays* that I especially love.

117

Underline the word in parentheses that agrees with the subject.

1. Everybody (like, <u>likes</u>) to have a holiday from work.

2. Memorial Day (honor, honors) the service personnel who (was, were) killed in past wars.

3. At a New Year's party, each guest (wear, wears) a funny hat and (have, has) a noisemaker.

4. The cooking many people (have, has) to do to prepare for some holidays often (take, takes) a long time.

5. There (is, are) a lot of noise on New Year's Eve.

6. The children in every town (enjoy, enjoys) Halloween.

7. Everyone (is, are) sad on Labor Day because it (mark, marks) the end of the summer.

8. There (is, are) few people who (do, does) not enjoy getting off from work.

9. Every person who (get, gets) a valentine on Valentine's Day (is, are) pleased.

10. The police (is, are) needed to preserve order during a parade. (*Police* is always plural.)

11. The size of the box of Valentine chocolates (depend, depends) on how much money the giver (have, has) or on how much he or she (care, cares) for someone.

12. Traditional food prepared with special ingredients (is, are) served.

13. Each of their children (get, gets) a handmade gift for this holiday.

Exercise 5: Passive Voice

Change the following sentences to the passive. Start the passive sentence with the original object, and omit the subject *people*.

1. People send greeting cards at Christmastime.

   Greeting cards are sent at Christmastime.

2. People buy flowers on Memorial Day for those who died in service to their country.

   _____

3. People sometimes wear new clothes on Easter Sunday.

   _____

4. People eat turkey on Thanksgiving Day.

_____

5. People observe many holidays on Mondays.

_____

6. People decorate store windows for the Christmas holidays.

_____

7. People sometimes spend a lot of money to prepare for a holiday.

_____

8. People blow horns on New Year's Eve.

_____

9. People put a wreath on the Tomb of the Unknowns in Arlington, Virginia, on Memorial Day.

_____

10. People sing Christmas carols during the Christmas holidays.

_____

11. People display the flag on the Fourth of July.

_____

12. People make New Year's resolutions on December 31 or January 1.

_____

Exercise 6: *much-many,* (a) *little,* (a) *few*

> Adjectives generally do not change their form when they are used with plural nouns. Exceptions are *much* and *little.* These two adjectives occur only with noncountable nouns. With plural countable nouns, *much* becomes *many,* and *little* becomes *few.*
>
> | *Noncountable Noun* | *Plural Countable Noun* |
> |---|---|
> | Too *much* music was played. | *Many* songs were sung. |
> | *(A) Little* music was played. | *(A) Few* songs were sung. |
>
> *A little* and *a few* stress the presence of something in a small quantity *(I have a little money; I have a few friends). Little* and *few* (without the word *a*) stress the absence of almost all quantity *(I have little money, I have few friends);* their use has a negative effect.

Underline the correct form.

1. Christmas dinner is served in (much, <u>many</u>) restaurants.

2. Even though their hosts had made elaborate preparations for the Halloween party, (few, a few) children came because of the bad weather.

3. (Much, many) people go to the beach on Independence Day.

4. Too (much, many) noise is heard on July 4.

5. Everyone was happy that only* (few, a few) speeches were made.

6. Not (much, many) work gets done on a holiday.

7. (Few, a few) people came to the parade because of the heat.

8. Even after shopping all day, she still had (little, a little) more shopping to do to prepare for the holiday.

9. Only (little, a little) turkey was left from their Thanksgiving dinner.

10. Very (little, a little) turkey was left from their Thanksgiving dinner.

11. Very (few, little) people work on New Year's Day.

12. They spent so (much, many) money on Christmas presents that now they have (little, few) money in the bank.

---

* *Only* requires the form with *a*: Only a few days are left before Christmas.

Exercise 7: Word Forms

Use the correct form of the word in parentheses and complete the unfinished words.

1. The (observe) _observation_ of Labor Day takes place on the first Monday in September.

2. It is (custom) _____ for families to eat Thanksgiving dinner together.

3. On St. Patrick's Day the Irish honor the day of St. Patrick's (die) _____.

4. Many (religion) _____ services are held at Eastertime.

5. During Christmas the brightly (decorate) _____ stores make the shopping areas look very (festival) _____.

6. On Easter morning children look forward to the (appear) _____ of a basket filled with candy.

7. The exchange of gifts adds to the (enjoy) _____ of the Christmas holidays.

8. On the Fourth of July, Americans express their (proud) _____ in their great (inherit) _____.

9. Christmas is a time for (merry) _____.

10. Memorial Day (commemor- _____ those who died in the service of their country in all wars.

11. During the celebration of Mardi Gras in New Orleans, there are many joyous (festiv- _____ that take place.

12. The valentine sent on Valentine's Day (symbol) _____ the love we feel for the one who receives it.

13. Christmas (origin- _____ celebrated the (born) _____ of Christ. Now the Christmas (celebrate) _____ has (wide) _____ to include many (enjoy) _____ (activ- _____.

14. Some holidays are (basic) _____ religious. Others are (general) _____ observed by everyone in the country, (especial) _____ the (nation) _____ holidays.

Exercise 8: Sentence Review

Make full sentences from the word groups below, and complete the unfinished words. Make whatever changes or additions are needed, but do not change the word order. Use commas, semicolons, or periods wherever necessary.

1. Santa Claus / suppose / arrive / night.

   Santa Claus is supposed to arrive at night.

2. Mother's Day / observe / May, / Father's Day / June.

   _____

3. Many holidays / occur / Sunday / celebrate / following / Monday.

   _____

4. It is / custom- / families / eat / Thanksgiving dinner / together.

   _____

5. Exchange / gifts / add / enjoy- / Christmas holidays.

   _____

6. Memorial Day / observe / last Monday / May.

   _____

7. Decorate / their homes / take / some people / long time.

   _____

8. Everybody / like / have / holiday / work.

   _____

9. There / be / few people / who / not enjoy / holidays.

   _____

10. Few / people / came / parade / because / heat.

    _____

11. In / United States / Election Day / occur / first Tuesday / after / first Monday / November.

_____

12. There / be / lot / noise / New Year's Eve.

_____

13. Each / their children / get / a handmade gift / for / holiday.

_____

14. Lot / money / spend / prepare / for / holiday.

_____

15. Some / holiday / be / basic / religious / others / be / general / observe / everyone in the country.

_____

▷ Extra Speaking and Writing Practice

Exercise 9: Questions and Answers—Holidays

A. Below is some information about holidays. Halloween and Thanksgiving are American and Canadian holidays. New Year's is celebrated in many countries.

    Working with a partner, take turns asking and answering questions about the information given for each holiday. The answers should be in full sentences.

Halloween

Date:	October 31
Time began:	in pre-Christian Great Britain and Ireland
Activities (what people do):	(1) no vacation from school or work
	(2) children in costume go from door to door saying "Trick or treat" (treats: candy or coins)
Decorations:	(1) harvest fruit and vegetables
	(2) paper images of witches on broomsticks, black cats, skeletons
	(3) lighted pumpkins (called jack-o'-lanterns)
	(4) colors of decorations are black and orange

Example:

Question:	*When is Halloween?* or *When does Halloween take place?* or *When is Halloween celebrated?* or *What is the date of Halloween?*
Answer:	Halloween is October 31. Or, *Halloween takes place on October 31.* Or, *Halloween is celebrated on October 31.* Or, *The date of Halloween is October 31.*

Thanksgiving (in the U.S.)

Date:	fourth Thursday of November
Commemorates:	the Pilgrims' good harvest of 1621
Activities (what people do):	(1) vacation from school or work
	(2) family reunions
	(3) festive dinners: turkey, sweet potatoes, cranberry sauce, pumpkin pie
Decorations:	harvest fruit and vegetables (especially yellow or orange ones), autumn leaves

New Year's

Date:	December 31 and January 1
Purpose:	(1) say goodbye to the old year
	(2) greet the new year
Activities (what people do):	(1) vacation from school or work
	(2) watch football games on TV
	(3) have big parties on New Year's Eve
	lots of drinking
	stay up to midnight to greet the new year
Decorations:	elaborate decorations for New Year's Eve parties at home and in restaurants, with confetti, streamers, noisemakers, funny hats

B. Using the information given in A, write one paragraph for each of the three holidays.

C. Write a short dialogue in which an English-speaking person asks you questions about another holiday with which you are familiar and you give the answers. (Do not use the holiday you wrote about in your composition.)

The questions can be about: the date of the holiday

what the holiday celebrates

what people do:

     parties, dancing

     religious activities

     special clothes worn

     special foods eaten

     decorations

public activities

     speeches, parades, demonstrations,

     fireworks, pageants

Exercise 10: Spelling—Noun Plurals Ending in *-es*

The regular plural ending for a noun is *-s*.

     games, symbols, tricks

However, after certain letters, *-es* is added:

  (1) after sibilants, spelled *ch, sh, s, x*

     churches, dishes, classes, boxes

  (2) after nouns ending in *-y* preceded by a consonant. The *y* is

     changed to *i* before the *es*.

     countries, activities

If a vowel comes before *y*, only *-s* is added.

     holidays

Many *one-syllable nouns* ending in *-f* or *-fe* in the singular end in *-ves* in the plural.

     leaves, knives

Use *-s* or *-es* for the plural of the nouns in parentheses. Make whatever change is necessary before adding the plural ending.

1. Many (festivity) _festivities_ take place during the Christmas (holiday) _holidays_ .

2. (Box) _____ of candy are given to (sweetheart) _____ _____ on Valentine's Day.

3. During the summer vacation, many (bus)* _____ take people to the different (beach) _____.

---

* The final *-s* in this word may also be doubled before the plural ending.

4. Several holidays take place when the (leaf) _____ are falling from the (tree) _____.

5. On festival (day) _____ many (people) _____ use their best (dish) _____.

6. Halloween is based on some old pre-Christian (belief) _____.

7. On religious holidays, the (church) _____ are full of people giving (prayer) _____ of thanks for their (blessing) _____.

8. At Halloween (party) _____ people wear (costume) _____ and play (game) _____.

9. On New Year's Day, no (class) _____ are held and almost all (business) _____ are closed.

10. On Halloween (witch) _____ are (symbol) _____ of evil.

11. Good (wish) _____ are exchanged on New Year's Day.

12. On Memorial Day, people visit the (cemetery) _____ to place (wreath) _____ on the (grave) _____ of the dead.

13. On Independence Day, we may hear many (speech) _____ and see many (parade) _____.

Exercise 11: Journal Writing

Write a journal entry on the following subject. Write freely since you are the only one who will see this entry.

Tell about an American holiday that you found interesting. Talk about what people do, the decorations they use, and the meaning of the holiday. Tell how you felt about the celebration of the holiday.

Now use your journal entry as the basis for a more careful letter to your teacher that is to be handed in.

◎ Listening-Writing Practice

Exercise 12: Dictation

Your teacher will dictate the paragraph three times. The first time is for listening only, the second time is for writing, and the third time is for checking what you have written.

Immediately after you give your teacher the dictation you have written, check the dictation in the book for any problems you had in writing it.

> One of the most festive ways of celebrating our multicultural heritage is having parades. The most famous of these parades is the St. Patrick's Day parade. St. Patrick's Day, celebrated on March 17th, was first observed in the United States in Boston in 1737. Named after the patron saint of Ireland, it is a day to celebrate Irish culture. Today, whether or not we are descended from the Irish, we may join in the St. Patrick's Day celebration. It is customary to wear something green in honor of the occasion. The symbol of the holiday is the Irish shamrock or three-leafed clover. It is supposed to bring good luck. If you can find one, the rare four-leafed clover is even luckier.
>
> Adapted from *Here/There*, English in Action, a program
> of the English-Speaking Union of the U.S., March, 1998.

Exercise 13: Dicto-comp

Take notes as your teacher reads this dicto-comp to you several times. Then reconstruct the dicto-comp from your notes. The dicto-comp does not need to be written exactly as you heard it, but it should be grammatically correct.

Before you write the dicto-comp, your teacher may ask the class to get together in groups to check with each other on what you heard.

Immediately after you give your teacher the dicto-comp you have written, check the dicto-comp in the book for any problems you had in writing it.

> The United States, like other countries, has many kinds of holidays. Some are national, like Independence Day and Thanksgiving, which celebrate historical events. Others are of religious origin but are observed nationally because of the enjoyable nonreligious activities connected with them. Still others are social, for example, Mother's Day and Valentine's Day. Most of these are celebrated without people getting off from work or school.
>
> One of the social holidays I greatly enjoy is Halloween. It is observed on October 31, and it is a day just for fun. It originated in pre-Christian times in Great Britain and Ireland as a festival of the dead. Evil spirits like witches, ghosts, and goblins were supposed to roam the earth and cause a lot of mischief.

On Halloween we see many decorations associated with death, for example, skeletons, skulls, and ghosts. There are also witches on broomsticks with black cats as traveling companions. We also see lots of jack-o'-lanterns. These are hollowed-out pumpkins with cut-out eyes, nose, and mouth, and a light inside. Favorite colors for decorations on Halloween are orange and black.

On this day children dress in costumes, many of them scary, and visit neighboring homes saying "trick or treat." The treats they expect are candy, cookies, fruit, or coins. The "trick" is now just a meaningless threat going back to old days when it was common to play all kinds of mischievous pranks on Halloween.

The day often ends with costume parties, with fanciful outfits and masks worn by all. People play a lot of games, and they tell ghost stories. The children's parties are in the late afternoon or early evening; the adult parties are later in the evening.

Everybody has fun on Halloween.

Reading-Writing Practice (summary: encyclopedia article on "Carnival")

You are going to write a one to three paragraph summary of a reading selection. A summary is a restatement, in shortened form, of the main ideas of a selection.

In preparation for the summary, skim through the selection quickly to determine the way the ideas are developed (through comparison, contrast, listing, time, space, example). Then reread the selection carefully, underlining the important points that should be included in the summary. (Do not underline too much.)

In writing the summary, use your own words as much as possible. You may include the important words from the reading selection, but use quotation marks around whole phrases taken directly from the selection.

Devote more attention to the main points than to their supporting details. Omit examples unless they are important to the development of the ideas. Do *not* give your own ideas in a summary.

The following selection comes from an encyclopedia article. It begins with a definition of carnival and then traces the historical development of carnivals. The article concludes with a reference to the looser use of the word today.

Carnival is a communal celebration, especially the religious celebration in Catholic countries that takes place just before **Lent**. Since early times, carnivals have been accompanied by parades, **masquerades, pageants,** and other forms of **revelry** that had their origins in pre-Christian **rites,** particularly **fertility** rites that were connected with the coming of spring and the re-birth of vegetation.

One of the first recorded instances of an annual spring festival is the festival of Osiris in Egypt; it commemorated the renewal of life brought about by the yearly flooding of the Nile. In Athens, during the 6th century B.C., a yearly celebration in honor of the god **Dionysus** was the first recorded instance of the use of a **float**. It was during the Roman Empire that carnivals reached an unparalleled peak of civil disorder and wild behavior. In Europe the tradition of spring fertility celebrations persisted well into Christian times, where carnivals reached their peak during the 14th and 15th centuries.

Because carnivals are deeply rooted in **pagan** superstitions and the folklore of Europe, the Roman Catholic Church was unable to stamp them out and finally accepted many of them as part of church activity. Eventually, however, the church succeeded in dominating the activities of the carnivals, and they became directly related to the coming of Lent. The major celebrations are generally in February; however, in Germany the carnival begins on January 6 in Bavaria and on November 11 in the Rhineland.

The term **carnival** is now also used to mean local festivals, traveling circuses, **bazaars**, and other celebrations of a joyous nature, regardless of their purpose or their season.

Adapted from "Carnival," *Columbia Encyclopedia*, 1993, pages 460–61.

Vocabulary

1. **Lent**—in the Christian religion, a period of fasting (especially going without meat) for forty days before Easter

2. **masquerade**—a costume party at which masks are worn

3. **pageant**—a spectacular procession or celebration

4. **revelry**—wild, unrestrained festivity

5. **rite**—a ceremonial act

6. **fertility**—power to produce vegetation, crops, etc.; power of producing offspring

7. **Dionysus**—in Greek mythology, the god of wine

8. **float**—a platform on wheels carrying a display in a parade

9. **pagan**—not believing in the one God of the Christian, Jewish, or Muslim religions; believing in many gods

10. Two of the famous carnivals called Mardi Gras take place in New Orleans and in Rio de Janeiro, Brazil in late winter. In Rio de Janeiro, special music clubs prepare almost all year long for their parades, competing with each other for the best songs, costumes, dances, and floats.

11. **bazaar**—a marketplace; a fair or sale, especially for charity

For Your Information
(summary: "The Loy-Krathong Festival in Thailand")

The following is a collaborative composition about the Loy-Krathong Festival in Thailand. The composition was written by three Thai students working together[*] in the author's writing class at the American Language Institute of New York University in the fall semester of 1997.

The Loy-Krathong Festival in Thailand

In Thailand, there are many holidays and festivals, but one of the most beautiful is the Loy-Krathong. It takes place in early November, when the moon is full. It is the night for Thai people to pay respect to the goddess of the river. Thai people believe that this goddess plays an important role in their lives.

Loy means "to float," and a *Krathong* is a lotus-shaped vessel made of fresh banana leaves. It is decorated beautifully with flowers, candles, incense sticks, and coins and floated down the river. People who are too busy to prepare the Krathongs by themselves can buy them ready-made.

By the light of the full moon that night, Thai people gather at the nearest river. They light the candles and the incense and then clip just a little of their nails and hair to be put in the Krathongs together with some money. This cutting of hair and nails is meant to ward off all misfortune while the Krathong is floating away. The money is intended for merit-making.[†]

Before floating the Krathongs, people will apologize to the goddess of the river for offending her by using her water to take a bath or to wash their clothes. Then people will make a wish that she will bring them all prosperity and happiness.

Then Thai people float their Krathongs down the river. It is believed that the Krathongs carry away the past year's sins as well as bring hopes for the future.

At the full of the moon that night, the whole river gleams with the reflection of the moon and glitters with light specks from the millions of Krathongs floating downstream. All the river looks as though a stardust carpet were laid on it.

At midnight people make their wishes and wash their faces or splash water on their bodies for expiation of their sins. They all look at the same full moon and sing a song, "Loy, Loy Krathong, Loy, Loy Krathong, then happiness will be with us forever."

It is a fantastic night which nobody can ever forget. Thai people always look forward to the next year's festival, when they can again show their appreciation for the gifts of the river in this beautiful ceremony of flickering lights floating down the moonlit river.

---

[*] The students are Phornratna Jongwilaikasem, Chantra Sukhaviriya, and Wasin Suwansukroj.
[†] *Merit-making*—rebirth into a better state.

Illustration by Xavier Urquieta

Telling Stories

Grammar and Usage

Direct and indirect statements
Direct and indirect questions
Exclamations
Adjective structures after nouns

Rhetoric

Using an outline to guide the composition
Using an introduction and a conclusion
Using a transitional lead-in to the body of the
   composition

Discussion and Composition

1. Discussion: Preliminary Outline for the Composition (prewriting stage)

Subject: (*Name of Story*—a fairy tale, folktale, myth, or legend)

Outline *(To be placed on the board. Books are closed.)*	Discussion *(Ideas, Grammar and Usage, Vocabulary, Elements of Composition Building)*
	Note: The kind of story being discussed is a fairy tale. Students who want to write about a folktale, myth, or legend can get information for a definition in exercise 4 or can consult a dictionary.

Introduction: general statements, including a definition of fairy tale	Definition of a fairy tale: a simple narrative that deals with supernatural beings and is told for the amusement of children
	A fairy tale often reflects the values, beliefs, and customs of a society.
	Kinds of persons, other creatures, and magical things in fairy tales:
	    fairy godmother, wicked stepmother and stepsisters, kings and queens, princes and princesses, magicians
	    fairies, witches, giants, dwarfs, mermaids, monsters, dragons
	    enchanted animals, fish
	    enchanted castles, forests
	    magic lamps, rings, carpets, mirrors
	Themes in fairy tales:
	    Moral—often good wins out over evil
	    takes place far away and long ago
	    impossible tasks to perform
	    magical spells—transformation of a person into an animal
	    breaking an enchantment through kindness and love
	    help is given the good person by a creature with magical powers
	    three wishes, chances, or challenges
	    third and youngest son succeeds when the first two fail

third and youngest daughter is the most
    beautiful and the most virtuous

jealousy of older brothers and sisters

wickedness of the stepmother (not the
    natural mother)

Transitional lead-in: connecting the
    general statements of the
    introduction to the *one* story
    you are going to talk about

One of my favorite fairy tales is . . .

Let me tell you about about the fairy tale I
    like best.

A fairy tale I remember from my childhood
    is . . .

A fairy tale that my mother (or
    grandmother) often told me is . . .

A fairy tale that is very famous in my
    country is. . . .

I. What happened in the story (use
   chronological order)

Opening sentence of first paragraph begins:
    Once upon a time . . .
    A long time ago . . .
    Long ago and far away . . .

Direct speech:

II.
III.
IV.
V.
etc.

    (1) use of quotation marks for the actual
        words spoken

    (2) use of a comma to separate *said,*
        told, asked, etc., from the spoken
        words

Indirect speech:

    (1) sequence of tenses (past verbs after a
        past main verb): The wicked fairy *told*
        the queen that her daughter *would* die
        when the girl *was* fifteen.

    (2) normal word order in indirect
        questions:
            direct: "How can I go to the ball?"
            indirect: Cinderella asked her
              fairy godmother how *she*
              could go to the ball.

    (3) use of *if* or *whether* to introduce indi-
        rect yes-no questions
            direct: "Can I go to the ball?"
            indirect: Cinderella asked her
              fairy godmother *whether* (or
              if) she could go to the ball.

    (4) change in pronouns

    (5) *said to* becomes *told* in indirect speech.

Conclusion: general statements

Can end with the end of the story, a natural conclusion (often, They lived happily ever after) or a general comment about good conquering evil (or any other moral)

2. Composition (to be done before or after the grammar practice)

A. Organizing the Composition

Before writing your composition, fill in the required information on this organizational work sheet (pp. 135–36). The work sheet follows the preliminary outline used for the discussion. Guidance for writing each paragraph is given at the right side of this work sheet. The pages of the discussion outline provide additional help for the composition.

You may use phrases on this work sheet except where it calls for full sentences.

B. Writing a 400/500-Word Composition

Write the composition based on your notes on the organizational work sheet. Be careful of your paragraphing. Use separate paragraphs for your introduction and your conclusion. (Long paragraphs may be broken in two at appropriate places, but single-sentence paragraphs should be avoided.)

C. Correcting/Rewriting the Composition (peer review)

When you bring your composition to class, you will be asked to exchange it with that of another student.

First check the other student's development of the composition and then check the items listed under Editing.

1. Development of the Composition

Introduction and Conclusion
Transitional lead-in
Paragraphs—opening sentences and supporting details
Are these well done, or can you suggest ways to improve them? Write your
    comments on the student's composition.

2. Editing

Grammar
Usage (spelling and punctuation)
Vocabulary
For grammar and usage, the information in the Symbol Chart for Correction
    of Compositions in the Appendix can be helpful.

When the peer review is over, hand in your composition to your teacher, who will return it to you later with additional comments and correction symbols used for the mistakes. Then you will be asked to rewrite the composition, taking into account what your fellow student and what your teacher suggested for the improvement of the composition.

After you have revised your composition, hand it in to your teacher together with your first draft.

Organizational Work Sheet
(Preliminary notes for the composition)

Title of the composition _____
(Do not use quotation marks or a period for a title at the top of the page. Use initial capital letters for the first word of the title and for all other words except articles, prepositions, and coordinate conjunctions *[and, or, but]*.)

Introduction: general statements
Opening sentence of paragraph _____

_____

_____

_____

_____

_____

Put in a separate paragraph.

Use the present tense for general statements. (For a definition of a folktale, myth or legend, see exercise 4 or consult a dictionary.)

Include a definition of fairy tale (or other type of story).

_____

_____

_____

_____

_____

Transitional lead-in connecting the general statements of the introduction to the *one* story you are going to write about _____

_____

_____

_____

_____

_____

New paragraph

The story can begin in this same paragraph.

I. What happened in the story

_____

_____

_____

_____

_____

II. _____

_____

_____

III. _____

_____

_____

IV. _____

_____

_____

V. _____

_____

_____

(Additional events may be listed on another sheet of paper.)

Conclusion: general statements

_____

_____

_____

_____

_____

_____

Use chronological order.

Use the past tense for these past events.

Separate these events into paragraphs at natural points; avoid long paragraphs.

Use the correct forms of direct and indirect speech.

(may be omitted if the end of the story provides a natural conclusion)

New paragraph

Use the present tense for general statements.

✓ Grammar Practice

Exercise 1: Direct and Indirect Statements

> Statements in direct speech become noun clause objects in indirect speech.
>
> | | |
> |---|---|
> | Direct Statement | The Beast said to (or told) Beauty, "I love you." |
> | Indirect Statement | The Beast told Beauty that he loved her. |
> | | (The word *that* may be omitted in indirect speech.) |
> | | (*Say* may be used without an object. *Tell* requires an object.) |
>
> Note these changes from direct speech:
>
> The past main verb *(told)* requires a past verb *(loved)* in the indirect statement. (sequence of tenses)
>
> *Told* replaces *said to* in indirect speech.
>
> The pronouns change in indirect speech: *I* becomes *he, you* becomes *her.*
>
> There is no comma before the indirect statement.

A. Rewrite the sentences, changing the quoted statements to indirect speech. Be sure to change the pronouns and the tense of the verb. Do not use a comma before *that.*

  1. The fairy godmother said to Cinderella, "You're also going to go to the ball."

    The fairy godmother told Cinderella that she was also going to go to the ball.

  2. Chicken Little said to Ducky-Lucky, "The sky is falling and we have to tell the king."

    _____

  3. Rumpelstiltskin said to the maiden, "I'll spin the gold if you'll give me your firstborn child."

    _____

4. The Beast said to Beauty, "You forgot* your promise, and so I decided to die, for I could not live without you."

_____

5. The giant said to his wife, "I smell the blood of an Englishman."

_____

6. The wolf said to the little pig, "I'll huff and I'll puff and I'll blow your house in."

_____

7. Bluebeard said to his wife, "You will die at once because you have disobeyed me."

_____

8. Father Bear said to Mother Bear, "Someone's been sleeping in my bed."

_____

B. Change the indirect statements to direct speech. Use a comma after _said_ and use the correct form of the pronouns and the verbs.

1. The weavers said that they could weave the finest cloth in the world.

    The weavers said, "We can weave the finest cloth in the world."

2. They said that clothes made of this cloth were invisible to a stupid person.

    _____

3. The emperor said that if he wore such clothes he could distinguish the clever people from the stupid.

    _____

4. The emperor said that he had to have this cloth woven for him immediately.

    _____

---

* Formal usage requires the use of the past perfect (with _had_) with this verb.

5. The people who saw the emperor in the procession said that he looked marvelous in his new clothes.

_____

6. A little child said that the emperor had nothing on at all.

_____

7. All the people finally said that the emperor was not wearing any clothes at all.

_____

Exercise 2: Direct and Indirect Questions

Questions in direct speech become noun clause objects in indirect speech.

Yes-No **Question**

Direct: **Cinderella asked, "Can I go to the ball?"**

Indirect: **Cinderella asked _whether (if)_ she could go to the ball.**

Wh- **Question**

Direct: **Cinderella asked, "How can I go to the ball?"**

Indirect: **Cinderella asked _how_ she could go to the ball.**

Note these changes from direct to indirect questions:

The sentence ends with a period, not a question mark (unless the whole sentence is a question).

The past main verb _(asked)_ requires a past verb _(could)_ in the indirect question. (sequence of tenses)

Whether or _if_ introduces a noun clause object made from the yes-no question.

The pronouns in the indirect questions are changed—_I_ becomes _she_.

Normal subject-verb order is used in the indirect questions.

A comma is not used to set off the indirect question from the word of asking.

Rewrite the sentences, changing the quoted questions to indirect speech. Be careful of the punctuation and the subject-verb order. Use the correct form of the pronouns and the verbs.

1. Her stepsisters asked Cinderella mockingly, "Do you want to go to the ball?"

   Her stepsisters asked Cinderella mockingly whether (or if) she wanted to go to the ball.

2. Cinderella asked her stepsisters, "Did you enjoy yourselves at the ball?"

   _____ whether they had enjoyed themselves at _____

3. The genie of the lamp asked Aladdin, "What is your wish?"*

   _____ what his wish was _____

4. Bluebeard asked his wife, "Why is there blood on the key?"

   _____ why there was blood _____

5. The two thieves asked the emperor, "Isn't it a beautiful piece of cloth?"

   _____ it was n't a _____

6. The emperor asked, "Doesn't my suit fit me marvelously?"

   _____ his suit doesn't fit him _____

7. A little child who was watching the procession asked, "Why isn't the emperor wearing any clothes?"

   _____ why the emperor wasn't _____

8. At the ball, all the people asked, "Who is that beautiful girl?"*

   _____

---

* If the verb is a form of the independent verb *be* (not an auxiliary), the verb is placed at the *end* of the indirect question.

Exercise 3: Exclamations

Exclamations begin with *what* or *how*.

		Exclamatory Phrase		Balance of Sentence
what	*with* **nouns**			
	singular (countable)	What a	magnificent castle	this is.
	singular (noncountable)	What	exquisite food	this is.
	plural	What	luxurious things	this castle has.
how	*with* **adjectives** *and* **adverbs**			
	adjective	How	kind	the owner of the castle is.
	adverb	How	mysteriously	all the food has appeared.

All exclamations may end with a period or an exclamation mark.

Use the information given below to make exclamations with *what* or *how*. Underline the noun that requires *what* or *what a* or the adjective/adverb that requires *how*. Use normal word order in the exclamatory phrase.

1. When Little Red Riding Hood saw her "grandmother," she exclaimed:

    a.   You have big <u>teeth</u>
         What big teeth you have!

    b.   Your ears are <u>long</u>
         How long your ears are!

    c.   You have big legs

    d.   You are behaving strangely

Illustration by Xavier Urquieta

2. When Snow White came to the
   dwarfs' cottage, she exclaimed:

   a.   This is a nice cottage

   b.   The beds look small

   c.   This food tastes good

   d.   I am tired and sleepy

   e.   I have gone very far

3. When the prince saw Snow White, he exclaimed:

   a.   I am lucky to see such a beautiful girl

   b.   She is beautiful

   c.   She is a beautiful girl

4. The thieves exclaimed to the emperor:

   a.   The cloth is a beautiful color

   b.   The clothes fit well

   c.   Your new clothes are magnificent

Exercise 4: Adjective Structures after Nouns

A noun may be modified by several grammatical structures that follow it. This kind of modification is especially common in *definitions*.

Definition: A fairy tale is a simple narrative of folk origin dealing with supernatural beings, which is told for the amusement of children.

The adjective structures that modify the noun *a simple narrative* are:

of folk origin	*prepositional phrase* begins with a preposition
dealing with supernatural beings	*participial phrase* begins with an *-ing* or *-ed* participle
which is told for the amusement of children	*adjective clause* begins with the pronoun *which, that,* or *who*

The adjective structures usually follow the order given in the sentence above: prepositional phrase, then participial phrase, then adjective clause.

Working with a partner, combine each group of sentences into one sentence that gives a definition of a particular kind of story. Use the structures given at the right of each group. (Some definitions will have only two of these structures, and others will have two of the same structures that will need to be joined by *and*.)

1. A **folktale** is:

   Noun: *a story*

It is about ordinary people.	*prepositional phrase*
It forms part of an oral tradition.	*participial phrase* (use a comma at the beginning of the phrase)
It reveals the customs and beliefs of a particular group of people.	*participial phrase* (connect with *and*)

   •   *Sentence:* A folktale is a story about ordinary people, forming part of an oral tradition and revealing the customs and beliefs of a particular group of people.

2. A **fable** is:

   Noun: *a fictitious narrative*

It is intended to teach some moral truth.	*participial phrase*
In a fable animals act like human beings.	*adjective clause* (begin the clause with *in which*)

3. A **legend** is:

   Noun: *an oral narrative*

It is about some wonderful event.	*prepositional phrase*
It has been handed down for generations among a people.[*]	*participial phrase* (use a comma at the beginning of the phrase)
It is popularly believed to have a historical basis.	*participial phrase* (connect with *and*)

---

[*] *A people* is used here in the singular to refer to a particular group of persons—racial, national, or religious. Only in this sense does the word have the plural, *peoples*.

4. A **myth** is:

Noun: *a traditional story*

It is about gods and heroes.	*prepositional phrase*
It serves to explain some natural phenomenon, the origin of man, or the customs and institutions of a people.	*participial phrase* (use a comma at the beginning of the phrase)

5. An **epic** is:

Noun: *a long narrative poem*

It is in very dignified style.	*prepositional phrase*
It celebrates episodes of a people's heroic tradition.	*participial phrase*

Exercise 5: Word Forms

Use the correct form of the word in parentheses, and complete the unfinished words.

1. Fairy tales are (imagine) _imaginary (also imaginative)_ stories dealing with magic and the supernatur-__al__.

2. The words "Once upon a time" are often (find) _____ at the (begin) _____ of fairy tales.

3. Fairies are (diminu-_____ creatures with magic powers. They are (rare-_____ (harm) _____ but some of them are (mischief) _____.

4. In some fairy tales, the hero (final) _____ wins the (hero-_____ either through his great (strong) _____ or his (clever) _____ or through the (assist) _____ of magical powers.

5. We expect the hero in a fairy tale to be (attract) _____ in (appear) _____. He often marries a (love) _____ and (virtue) _____ (prince-_____.

6. In some fairy tales, troubles are (cause-_____ by the (jealous) _____ of (wick-_____ sisters or brothers.

7. *Snow White and the Seven Dwarfs* is a (favor) _____ movie of many people both old and young.

8. Snow White had great (pure) _____ and (innocent)_____.

9. Cinderella was so (beauty) _____ that the prince fell in love with her (immediate) _____.

10. Hansel and Gretel were (abandon-_____ in the woods by their father and their stepmother.

11. Bluebeard killed many of his wives because of their (disobey) _____. They all opened a door which was (forbid-_____ to them.

12. Aladdin, the lazy son of a (China) _____ tailor, was enticed by a (magic-_____ from Morocco to enter a cave and obtain a lamp for him.

Exercise 6: Sentence Review

Make full sentences from the word groups below. Make all the verbs *past* except those in direct speech. Make whatever changes or additions are needed, but do not change the word order. Watch the punctuation.

1. Beast / tell / Beauty / he / love / her.
   The Beast told Beauty (that) he loved her.

2. Cinderella / say / her stepsisters / "I / help / you / get ready / ball."

   _____

3. Little Red Riding Hood / say / wolf / "Grandmother / what / big / teeth / have."

   _____

4. Weavers / say / they / can / weave / finest / cloth / world.

   _____

5. All / people / finally / say / emperor / not wear / clothes / at all.

   _____

6. Bluebeard / ask / his wife / "Why / blood / on / key?"

   _____

7. Genie / ask / Aladdin / "What / your / wish?"

_____

8. Sultan / ask / his minister / he / ever / see / such / precious / jewels.

_____

9. Aladdin / ask / magician / why / they / come / to cave.

_____

10. When / Hansel / touch / house / he / cry / "Gretel / it / good enough / to eat!"

_____

11. Queen / ask / magic mirror / "Who / most / beautiful / woman?"

_____

12. Cinderella / ask / how / she / can get / to ball.

_____

▷ Extra Speaking and Writing Practice

Exercise 7: Vocabulary Derived from Greek Mythology

There are many words in the English language that are based on Greek mythology. In this exercise, the source from Greek mythology is given for each word, along with the meaning of the word.

English word	Source from Greek Mythology	Meaning
odyssey	From Odysseus, a Greek leader who traveled home after the Greek armies defeated Troy. His journey took ten years, with many adventures along the way.	a long, adventurous journey
titanic	From Titans. In ancient times they were giants who were overthrown by Zeus, who became ruler of the heavens.	having enormous size, strength, power; immense; huge; gigantic

chaotic	From Chaos, the beginning of the ancient world when there was confusion, disorder, darkness	completely disordered; confused; unorganized
herculean	From Hercules, a hero who accomplished many difficult tasks because of his superhuman strength	requiring great strength; very hard to perform
Spartan	From Sparta, an ancient Greek city famous for strict discipline and training of soldiers	rigorously self-disciplined; simple; frugal; austere
tantalizing	From Tantalus, a king condemned to the underworld for his crimes. He was tortured by thirst, standing in water that always receded when he tried to drink it, and by hunger, standing under branches of fruit that always remained out of reach.	teasing by arousing expectations that cannot be fulfilled; desirable but out of reach; tempting but unobtainable
morphine	From Morpheus, god of dreams	a medication used to reduce pain or to induce sleep
hypnosis	From Hypnos, the god of sleep	a state of sleep induced by suggestion
lethargic	From River Lethe, the river of forgetfulness in the Greek underworld	drowsy; dull; sluggish; lacking energy

In the space provided, write the meaning of the underlined words.

1. The civil war left the country in a <u>chaotic</u> condition, with a complete breakdown of law and order.

   _____

2. They are building a sports arena of <u>titanic</u> proportions, seating more than 150,000 spectators.

   _____

3. The American writer Thoreau went to live in the woods to escape civilization and to live a <u>Spartan</u> life.

    _____

4. To finish so much work in one week will require a <u>herculean</u> effort.

    _____

5. The doctor went on a long <u>odyssey</u> all over the world for her research on the medicinal benefits of different herbs.

    _____

6. When the patient's pain became too intense, the doctor prescribed <u>morphine</u>.

    _____

7. The graduating student was offered some <u>tantalizing</u> prospects of good jobs overseas, but he could accept a job only in his home town because he had to care for his sick mother.

    _____

8. This pill often makes people <u>lethargic</u>, so they are advised not to drive after they take it.

    _____

9. <u>Hypnosis</u> is sometimes used in surgery as a substitute for anesthesia.

    _____

Exercise 8: Spelling—Final Silent *e*

> **A.** *Drop* final silent *e before a vowel* (or before *y*).
>
>   admire + -ation   = admiration
>
>   arrange + -ing   = arranging
>
> *Keep* final silent *e before a consonant.*
>
>   arrange + -ment   = arrangement
>
>   care + -ful   = careful

Rewrite each word with the endings that are given. Remember to *drop* the final silent *e* before a vowel (or *y*) and *keep* the final silent *e* before a consonant.

please + ure _____ *pleasure* _____   fortunate + ly _____

confuse + ion _____   continue + ing _____

engage + ment _____   practice + ing _____

advertise + ment _____   safe + ty _____

nine + ty _____   nature + al _____

arrive + al _____   complete + ly _____

excite + ment _____   nerve + ous _____

observe + ance _____   noise + y _____

immediate + ly _____   entire + ly _____

shine + ing _____   announce + ment _____

use + ful _____   judge + ment* _____

dine + ing _____   argue + ment* _____

accurate + ly _____   love + ly _____

shine + y _____   finance + ial _____

invite + ation _____   write + ing _____

_____

* This word is an exception in American usage. British usage follows the rule.

> **B.** There are some exceptions to the rule about final silent *e*.
>
> (1) To prevent *c* and *g* from becoming "hard" before *a, o,* and *u,* keep the *e*:
>
> *serviceable, outrageous*
>
> (2) Drop *e* before *–th*: *width, ninth*

Rewrite each word with the endings that are given.

wide + th _____*width*_____   change + able _____

notice + able _____   nine + th _____

advantage + ous _____   courage + ous _____

twelve + th (change the *v* to *f*) _____   five + th (change the *v* to *f*) _____

Exercise 9: Journal Writing

Write a journal entry on the following subject. Write freely since you are the only one who will see this entry.

Have you found a story in the United States that is similar to one from another country? Tell the story and discuss the similarities and the differences.

Now use your journal entry as the basis for a more careful letter to a friend. This letter is to be handed in to your teacher.

◎ Listening-Writing Practice

Exercise 10: Dictation

Your teacher will dictate each paragraph three times. The first time is for listening only. The second time is for writing, and the third time is for checking what you have written.

Immediately after you give your teacher the dictation you have written, check the dictation in the book for any problems you had in writing it.

> Although a fairy tale is told for the amusement of children, it usually reflects the customs, beliefs, and values of a society. It may deal with supernatural beings such as fairies, witches, and dragons. There may be en-

chanted forests, castles, and animals in the story. Human beings may have magical powers, superhuman strength, or great wisdom. The good characters are beautiful or handsome, and their goodness defeats the wickedness of the evil characters. The language in a fairy tale is usually old-fashioned. Often the story begins with "Once upon a time" and ends with "They lived happily ever after."

Exercise 11: Dicto-comp

Take notes as your teacher reads this dicto-comp to you several times. Then reconstruct the dicto-comp from your notes. The dicto-comp does not need to be written exactly as you heard it, but it should be grammatically correct.

Before you write the dicto-comp, your teacher may ask the class to get together in groups to check with each other on what you heard.

Immediately after you give your teacher the dicto-comp you have written, check the dicto-comp in the book for any problems you had in writing it.

When we were children, we were often delighted by fairy tales. Such strange and wonderful things happened in them. There were enchanted castles and forests where supernatural beings like dragons, fairies, and witches lived. There were carpets that could fly and animals that could talk. There were good characters and bad characters. But whatever happened, the good characters won in the end.

One story from my childhood that I loved was "Little Red Riding Hood." This is the way the story goes. Once upon a time a pretty little girl called Red Riding Hood was going through the woods to take some cake to her grandmother. On the way she met a wolf, who asked her where she was going. "To my grandmother's house," she replied. "It is the first in the village over there."

The wolf ran ahead by a shorter way and reached the grandmother's house first. He knocked on the door.

"Who's there?" asked the grandmother.

"It's your granddaughter, Red Riding Hood," said the wolf, disguising his voice.

She told him to come in. As soon as he was inside, he quickly ate her up.

Soon Red Riding Hood came to her grandmother's house and entered. The wolf was lying in her grandmother's bed. Red Riding Hood was surprised at the way her grandmother looked.

"Grandmother, dear," she exclaimed, "what big arms you have!"

"The better to embrace you, my child," said the wolf.

"Grandmother, dear, what big ears you have!"

"The better to hear you with, my child."

"Grandmother, dear, what big teeth you have!"

"The better to eat you with!"

With this, the wicked wolf leaped upon Little Red Riding Hood and was ready to eat her up. Just then a hunter came into the house and killed the wolf. He cut open the wolf's stomach and rescued the grandmother.

Reading-Writing Practice (summary: "The Judgment of Paris")

You are going to write a one to three paragraph summary of a reading selection. A summary is a restatement, in shortened form, of the main ideas of a selection.

In preparation for the summary, skim through the selection quickly to determine the way the ideas are developed (through comparison, contrast, listing, time, space, example). Then reread the selection carefully, underlining the important points that should be included in the summary. (Do not underline too much.)

In writing the summary, use your own words as much as possible. You may include the important words from the reading selection, but use quotation marks around whole phrases taken directly from the selection.

Devote more attention to the main points than to their supporting details. Omit examples unless they are important to the development of the ideas. Do *not* give your own ideas in a summary.

The selection to be summarized comes from a well-known book on mythology. It tells the story of how the Trojan War began. Like most stories, this story is told in chronological order. It has a short introduction and conclusion.

The Judgment of Paris

Thousands of years ago, near the eastern end of the Mediterranean, there was a very rich and powerful city called Troy. Troy is famous today because of a long war that was the subject of one of the world's greatest poems, **The Iliad**. The poem tells us that the cause of the war went back to a dispute among three jealous goddesses.

It was the evil goddess of Discord who brought about the **discord**. Because she was the only one of the **divinities** that was not invited to an important marriage, that of King Peleus and the sea **nymph** Thetis, out of deep resentment she threw into the banqueting hall a golden apple marked "For the fairest." Of course all the goddesses wanted it, but in the end the choice was narrowed down to three: **Aphrodite, Hera,** and **Pallas Athena**. They asked **Zeus** to judge between them, but very wisely he refused to have anything to do with the matter. He told them to go to Mt. Ida, near Troy, where the young prince Paris was keeping his father's sheep. He was an excellent judge of beauty, Zeus told them. Paris, though a royal prince, was sent away to do a shepherd's work because his father Priam, the king of Troy, had been warned that this prince would some day be the ruin of his country.

Paris's amazement can be imagined when there appeared before him the wondrous forms of three great goddesses. He was not asked, however, to gaze at the radiant divinities to choose which of them seemed fairest, but only to choose the bribe each offered that seemed best worth taking. The choice was not easy. Hera promised to make him Lord of Europe and Asia; Athena, that he would lead the Trojans to victory against the Greeks and lay Greece in ruins; Aphrodite, that the fairest woman in the world should be his. Paris, a weakling and somewhat of a coward, too, as later events showed, chose the last. He gave the apple to Aphrodite.

That was the Judgment of Paris, famed everywhere as the real reason why the Trojan War was fought.

Adapted from *Mythology* by Edith Hamilton,
New American Library of World Literature, 1942, pages 178–79.

Vocabulary

1. **The Iliad**—This poem about the Trojan War is by the Greek poet Homer. The poem tells us that after Paris gives the golden apple to Aphrodite, the goddess leads him to the most beautiful woman in the world, Helen, the wife of a Greek king. When Paris steals her away, the Greek kings band together to get her back, and thus the Trojan War begins.

2. **discord**—conflict, lack of harmony

3. **divinity**—a divine being, a god

4. **nymph**—a lesser goddess who inhabited the sea, rivers, woods, or mountains

5. **Aphrodite**—goddess of love (Roman name: Venus)

   Hera—wife of the king of gods, Zeus—goddess of marriage and domestic life (Roman Name: Juno)

   (Pallas) Athena—goddess of wisdom, technical skill, and invention (Roman name: Minerva)

6. **Zeus**—king of the gods (Roman name: Jupiter)

▐▛▜▌ **For Your Information**
(story: "The Old Lady in the Cave")

In the introduction to the book *Favorite Folktales from around the World,* the editor makes the point that a story can be a "permissible lie." Her example of such a "permissible lie," together with the paragraphs that lead into the story, is given here.

> The accumulated stories from the world's many societies are a catalog of people, places, events—and wonder. Often such tales are described as "cultural history," as if they constituted a fixed body of lore. However, this is a fluid tradition that is as migratory as a winter bird, feeding as it goes from place to place and leaving something of itself behind.
>
> In the very center of these stories, of course, is human truth. But as in the old story of the man who searched for truth, it is served up to us in different guises. As folklorist Roger Abrams puts it, "Tales are, in the ears of their hearers, permissible lies."

The Old Lady in the Cave

There was once a man who was successful in all things. He had a fine wife, a loving family, and a craft for which he was justly famous. But still he was not happy.

"I want to know Truth," he said to his wife.

"Then you should seek her," she replied.

So the man put his house and all his worldly goods in his wife's name (she being adamant on that point) and went out on the road as a beggar after Truth.

He searched up the hills and down the valleys for her. He went into small villages and large towns; into the forests and along the coasts of the great wide sea; into dark, grim wastes and lush meadows covered with flowers. He looked for days and for weeks and for months.

And then one day, on top of a high mountain, in a small cave, he found her.

Truth was a wizened old woman with but a single tooth left in her head. Her hair hung down onto her shoulders in thin, greasy strands. The skin on her face was as brown and dry as old parchment and stretched over prominent bones. But when she signaled to him with a hand shriveled with age, her voice was low and lyrical and pure, and it was then that he knew that he had found Truth.

He stayed a year and a day with her and he learned all that she had to teach. And when the year and a day was up, he stood at the mouth of the cave ready to leave for home.

"My Lady Truth," he said, "you have taught me so much and I would like to do something for you before I leave. Is there anything you wish?"

Truth put her head to one side and considered. Then she raised an ancient finger. "When you speak of me," she said, "tell them I am young and beautiful!"

Adapted from *Favorite Folktales from around the World,* edited by Jane Yolen, Pantheon Books, a division of Random House, Inc., 1986, pages 3–4.

_____

Superstitious Beliefs

Grammar and Usage

Cause-result with *if* clauses
Cause-result with *if* clauses or gerund phrases
Unreal conditions
Conjunctive adverbs—*therefore, however, otherwise*
Articles—definite: *(the)* and indefinite *(a, an)*
most, most of the, the most

Rhetoric

Using an outline to guide the composition
Using an introduction and a conclusion
Using a transitional lead-in to the body of the
    composition
Using transitions between paragraphs

Discussion and Composition

1. Discussion: Preliminary Outline for the Composition (prewriting stage)

Subject: *Superstitious Beliefs in* (name of country)

Outline *(To be placed on the board.* *Books are closed.)*	*Discussion* *(Ideas, Grammar and Usage, Vocabulary,* *Elements of Composition Building)*
Introduction: general statements, including a definition of superstition	Definition of superstition: an unreasonable belief that supernatural forces can cause good or bad things to happen Results from ignorance and fear of the unknown Often involves magic and witchcraft May have a religious origin
Transitional lead-in to the kinds of superstitions that will be discussed	Final sentence of introductory paragraph may mark a transition to the main points of the superstition: Superstitions are often attached to numbers, animals and birds, and things.
I. Superstitions about numbers	Possible opening sentences and connectives within the paragraph: There are several superstitions about numbers in my country. For example, we have one about number 13. . . . Another one is about . . . Or for the second sentence: The most common one concerns (or, is about) number 13. luck, lucky: Number 13 will bring bad *luck*. Number 13 is *unlucky*. Number 13 is an *unlucky* number.
II. Superstitions about animals and birds may include insects	Possible opening sentence of paragraph and connectives within the paragraph: We also have a few (some, many) superstitions about animals and birds. One is about the owl. . . . Another (or, a second) concerns . . .

Vocabulary

    omen, sign, symbol(ize)

    a good luck (or, a lucky) charm

    the cry of an owl

    the cry of a crow, raven (black birds)

    a rabbit's foot

    a black cat crossing your path

In sentences with *if:* present tense in the *if*

    clause, future with the main clause

    If you *hear* the cry of an owl,

    a death *will* occur in the family.

III. Superstitions about things   Possible opening sentence of paragraph:

    We have still other superstitions

    concerning things. Or, other

    superstitions are *about* things.

Coherence may be established through

    parallel *if* clauses beginning sentences.

If you: break a mirror

    walk under a ladder

    find a four-leaf clover

    spill salt on the table

    find a penny

    open an umbrella in the house

    put a horseshoe over your door

Conclusion: general statements   Your own belief

---

2. Composition (to be done before or after the grammar practice)

A. Organizing the Composition

Before writing your composition, fill in the required information on this organizational work sheet. The work sheet follows the preliminary outline used for the discussion. Guidance for writing each paragraph is given at the right side of this work sheet. The pages of the discussion outline provide additional help for the composition.

    You may use phrases on this work sheet except where it calls for full sentences.

Organizational Work Sheet
(Preliminary notes for the composition)

Title of the composition _____
(Do not use quotation marks or a period for a title at the top of the page. Use initial capital letters for the first word of the title and for all other words except articles, prepositions, and coordinate conjunctions *[and, or, but]*.)

Introduction: general statements, including a definition of superstition

Opening sentence of paragraph _____

_____

_____

_____

Put in a separate paragraph.

Use the present tense for general statements in this paragraph and in the rest of the composition.

Definition of a superstition

_____

_____

_____

_____

_____

Transitional lead-in connecting the general statements of the introduction to the kinds of superstitions that will be discussed

Full sentence _____

_____

_____

_____

May be included at the end of the introductory paragraph

I. Superstitions about numbers

Opening sentence of paragraph _____

_____

_____

_____

New paragraph
Mention the subject, *numbers.*

Examples: _____

_____

_____

_____

Expressions for examples:
for example, for instance,
or, one example is,
another example is . . .

II. Superstitions about animals and birds
Opening sentence of paragraph _____

_____

_____

Examples: _____

_____

_____

_____

New paragraph

Mention the subject,
animals and *birds* (or only
one of these).

III. Superstitions about things
Opening sentence of paragraph _____

_____

_____

Examples: _____

_____

_____

_____

New paragraph

Mention the subject,
things.

Conclusion: general statements

_____

_____

_____

New paragraph

B.   Writing a 400/500-Word Composition

Write the composition based on your notes on the organizational work sheet. Be careful of your paragraphing. Use separate paragraphs for your introduction and your conclusion. (Long paragraphs may be broken in two at appropriate places, but single-sentence paragraphs should be avoided.)

C. Correcting/Rewriting the Composition (peer review)

When you bring your composition to class, you will be asked to exchange it with that of another student.

First check the other student's development of the composition, then check the items listed under Editing.

1. Development of the Composition
Introduction and Conclusion
Transitional lead-in
Paragraphs—opening sentences and supporting details
Are these well done, or can you suggest ways to improve them? Write your
    comments on the student's composition.

2. Editing
Grammar
Usage (spelling and punctuation)
Vocabulary
For grammar and usage, the information in the Symbol Chart for Correction of
    Compositions in the Appendix can be helpful.

When the peer review is over, hand in your composition to your teacher, who will return it to you later with additional comments and correction symbols used for the mistakes. Then you will be asked to rewrite the composition, taking into account what your fellow student and what your teacher suggested for the improvement of the composition.

After you have revised your composition, hand it in to your teacher together with your first draft.

☑ Grammar Practice

Exercise 1: Cause-Result with *if* Clauses

> A conditional *if* clause often represents a cause. The rest of the sentence (the main clause) is the result.
>
> Cause: If you *hear* the cry of an owl or a raven,
> Result: there *will be* a death in the family. (main clause)
>
> The verb in the *if* clause is in the *present* tense, the verb in the main clause is in the *future tense* with *will.*[*]

Combine each group of words about superstitions so that the cause is placed in an *if* clause. Use the present tense in the *if* clause and the future tense with *will* in the main clause.

1. Cause: a bridesmaid (catch) the bridal bouquet
   Result: she (be) married herself soon

   If a bridesmaid catches the bridal bouquet, she will be married herself soon.

2. Result: you (have) seven years of bad luck
   Cause: you (break) a mirror

   You will have seven years of bad luck if you break a mirror.

3. Cause: a woman (want) to have a baby boy
   Result: she (wear) blue colors during her pregnancy

   If a woman wants to have a baby boy, she will wear blue colors during her pregnancy.

4. Result: the groom (carry) his bride over the doorstep of their new home
   Cause: he (want) to avoid the evil spirits that are gathered outside every threshold

   _____

5. Cause: your left hand (itch)
   Result: you (receive) money

   If your left hand itch you will receive money

6. Result: you (give away) money
   Cause: your right hand (itch)

   You will give away money if your right hand itch.

---

[*] *Be going to* can also be used in the main clause: If you hear the cry of the raven, there is *going to be* a death in the family.

Exercise 2: Cause-Result with *if* Clauses or Gerund Phrases

A cause may be expressed not only in a conditional *if* clause, but in a gerund phrase.

		Cause	Result
1.	A conditional *if* clause	*If you break a mirror,*	you will have seven years' bad luck.
2.	A gerund phrase	*Breaking a mirror*	will bring you seven years' bad luck.

Combine the word groups so that the *cause* is expressed once in an *if* clause and once in a gerund phrase.

1. Cause: carry a rabbit's foot
   Result: good luck

   If clause: *If you carry a rabbit's foot, you will have good luck.*
   Gerund phrase: *Carrying a rabbit's foot will bring you good luck.*

2. Cause: walk under a ladder
   Result: bad luck

   if you walk under a ladder, you will have a bad luck
   walking under a ladder will bring you a bad luck.

3. Cause: a black cat crosses your path
   Result: bad luck

   if a black cat crosses your path you will have
   a black cat crossing your path will bring you bad luck

4. Cause: spill salt on the table
   Result: bad luck

   if you spill salt on the table you will have bad luck
   spilling salt on the table will bring you bad luck

5. Cause: find a four-leaf clover
   Result: good luck

   if you find a four-leaf clover you will have a good luck
   finding a four-leaf clover will bring you good luck

6. Cause: find a penny
   Result: good luck all day

if you find a penny you will have good luck all day.
finding a penny will bring you good luck all day

7. Cause: open an umbrella in the house
   Result: bad luck

if you open an umbrella in the house you will have a bad luck
opening an umbrella in the house will bring you bad luck

8. Cause: break off the bigger end of the wishbone
   Result: good luck because your wish will be granted

if break off the bigger end of the wishbone.

Exercise 3: Unreal Conditions

> The form of verbs in a conditional sentence can indicate that the fact
> stated in the sentence is not real. Such verbs may refer to present or
> past time.
>
> | *Present Time* | *Verb Form* |
> |---|---|
> | (Real fact: No one is sneezing now.) | |
> | Unreal fact: If someone *sneezed,* | past tense |
> | I *would* say, "God bless you." | auxiliary *would* |
>
> | *Past Time* | |
> |---|---|
> | (Real fact: No one sneezed.) | |
> | Unreal fact: If someone *had sneezed,* | past perfect tense |
> | I *would have* said, "God | auxiliary *would have* |
> | bless you." | |

A. Use the correct forms of the verbs to make conditions about facts that are unreal at the
present time.

1. If I (spill) _spilled_ salt on the table, I (throw) _would throw_ some
   over my left shoulder to avoid bad luck.

2. If I (give) _gave_ a woman a present of a purse, I (put) _would put_ a good-luck penny in the purse.

3. If a black cat (try) _tried_ to cross my path, I (get) _would get_ out of the way fast.

4. If I (decide) _decided_ to get married, I (not have) _would not have_ the wedding on Friday the thirteenth.

5. If my sister (get) _got_ married, at the wedding she (wear) _would wear_ "something old, something new, something borrowed, and something blue."

6. If a friend (give) _gave_ me a present of a knife, I (give) _would give_ him a coin to avoid cutting our friendship.

7. If someone (step) _____ between me and another person as we were walking together, I (say) _____ "bread and butter."

B. Use the correct forms of the verbs in A to make conditions about facts that were unreal in the past tense.

1. *If I had spilled salt on the table, I would have thrown some over my left shoulder to avoid bad luck.*

Exercise 4: Conjunctive Adverbs—*therefore, however, otherwise*

A sentence with *therefore, however,* or *otherwise* can be joined to the preceding sentence by a semicolon.

A friend gave me a present of a knife; therefore(,) I gave him a coin to avoid cutting our friendship.

A comma after a word like *therefore* depends on whether the writer would pause at that point in speaking.

Words like *therefore* may also appear in other positions in the second part of the combined sentence.

A friend gave me a present of a knife; I therefore gave him a coin to avoid cutting our friendship.

Note that the semicolon remains at the beginning of the second sentence. (In fact, a period can also be used here.)

Replace the words in italics with *therefore, however,* or *otherwise,* and join the sentences with a semicolon. See if these words can go in positions other than the beginning of the second part of each sentence. However, make sure that the semicolon remains where the period was.

1. He spilled some salt on the table. *For this reason* he will have bad luck.

   He spilled some salt on the table; therefore(,) he will have bad luck.
   and . . .; he will therefore have bad luck.

2. He spilled some salt on the table. *But if he throws salt over his left shoulder, he can avoid bad luck.*

   He spilled some salt on the table; however, if he throws salt over his left shoulder, he can avoid bad luck.
   and . . .; if he throws salt over his left shoulder, however, he can avoid bad luck.

3. He must throw salt over his left shoulder. *If he doesn't,* he'll have bad luck.
   He must throw salt over his left shoulder; otherwise(,) he'll have bad luck.
   and . . .; he'll have bad luck otherwise.

4. I put a horseshoe over my door. *As a result of this,* I expect to have good luck.

   _____

   _____

   _____

5. You mustn't walk under a ladder. *If you do,* some misfortune will befall you.

   _____

   _____

   _____

6. They live on the thirteenth floor. *In spite of this,* they don't expect any bad luck.

   _____

   _____

   _____

7. I broke off the bigger end of the wishbone. *For this reason,* my wish will be granted.

_____

_____

_____

8. People believe that a crow is a sign of death. *But* I think this belief is only a superstition.

_____

_____

_____

9. She always carries a rabbit's foot with her. *For this reason,* she thinks she can avoid bad luck.

_____

_____

_____

10. You mustn't open an umbrella in the house. *If you do,* something bad will happen.

_____

_____

_____

Exercise 5: Articles—Definite *(the)* and Indefinite *(a, an)*

A. The most basic rule about articles is that *a* or *the* is required with a *singular countable* noun.

> She spilled salt on *the* table. (*the* means a *known* person or object)

> She broke *a* mirror. (*a* means *any one* person or object) (The only exception to this rule occurs when another determiner [such as *this, her, any, some*] is used: She broke *her* mirror.

Because of its basic meaning of *one*, the word *a* occurs mostly with a singular countable noun.

A plural noun does not usually require an article.

> She doesn't believe in ghosts.

The is not used with a noncountable noun when this noun stands alone.

> Many people believe in magic.

However, *the* precedes many nouns, countable or noncountable, *that are followed by modifiers.*

Noncountable Noun:	Many people believe in *the* magic *performed by their witch doctors.*
Countable Noun:	*The* number *we consider unlucky* is thirteen. (With countable nouns, *a* meaning *one* may also be used in such a sentence.)

Use *a, an, the,* or nothing. (In some cases there are two possibilities.)

1. _The_ house where he used to live is haunted by _____ ghosts.

2. Breaking _a_ mirror will cause you _____ trouble.

3. _____ crow is _____ symbol of _____ death.

4. She knocked on _____ wood so that nothing bad would spoil _____ plan she had made.

5. There was once _____ belief that _____ gold could be made by _____ people.

6. _____ superstitions that I remember were told to me by _____ my grandmother.

7. _____ superstitions are _____ result of _____ fear and _____ ignorance.

8. Walking under _____ ladder will bring _____ bad luck.

9. _____ house which is supposed to be haunted by _____ ghost is hard to sell.

B. The definite article *the* is generally used for someone or something *known.*

Known because it is already mentioned	A black cat was walking toward him. He crossed the street so that *the* black cat would not come near him.
Known because it is a familiar person or object in the environment	
immediate environment	She was worried because *the* mirror had fallen off *the* wall in *the* bedroom.
more distant environment	Some people feel that *the* sun, *the* moon, and *the* stars affect our daily lives.

Use *a, an, the,* or nothing.

1. If you spill _____ salt on _the_ table, you can avoid _____ bad luck by throwing _____ salt over your left shoulder.

2. Yesterday my friend gave me _____ horseshoe for _____ good luck. I'm putting _____ horseshoe over _____ door of _____ my house.

3. When _____ moon is full, _____ evil spirits wander over _____ earth.

4. Opening _____ umbrella in _____ house will bring you _____ bad luck.

5. She always wears _____ good luck charm. _____ charm was given to her by _____ friend of hers.

6. On Halloween you may see decorations of _____ witch flying on _____ broomstick. _____ witch may be accompanied by _____ black cat.

C. Use *a, an, the,* or nothing. Keep in mind that *a* or *an* refers to *one* and is used only with singular countable nouns. Remember also that *an article must be used with a singular countable noun.*

1. _A_ rabbit's foot is carried by _a (or the)_ person who wants to have _____ good luck.

2. _____ young bride hopes it doesn't rain on _____ day of her wedding.

3. _____ man will carry his bride over _____ threshold of their new house to avoid _____ evil spirits that are gathered there.

4. _____ number thirteen is _____ unlucky number.*

5. _____ superstition is _____ unreasonable belief in _____ supernatural.†

6. It is often _____ ignorant and _____ uneducated who believe that _____ lives of _____ people are affected by _____ supernatural forces.

7. _____ uneducated person often believes in _____ magic and _____ witchcraft.

8. In some countries, _____ number four is avoided in buildings because _____ number is unlucky.

Exercise 6: *most, most of the, the most*

> ***The*** has different uses with *most,* depending on whether *most* has the meaning of quantity or whether it is the *superlative* of an adjective or an adverb.
>
> | | |
> |---|---|
> | | ***Most as Quantity (part of a whole)*** |
> | *most* | ***Most educated people** still believe in some superstitions.* |
> | | (***Most*** without *of* is used mainly with plural nouns.) |
> | *most of the* | ***Most of the educated people in my country** still believe in some superstitions.* |
> | | (If *of* follows ***most,*** *the* [or another determiner] is usually required after *of.*) |
> | | ***Most as a Superlative*** |
> | *the most* | Only ***the most superstitious people** believe in magic and witchcraft.* |
> | | (***The*** is used before ***most*** only with superlatives.) |

---

* Articles are often omitted with cardinal numbers (one, two, etc.): Number 13 is an unlucky number. But: No one likes to live on the thirteenth floor.

† Adjectives used as nouns are usually preceded by *the*: Superstition results from a fear of the *unknown.*

In the following sentences, supply *the* wherever it is required with *most*. Be sure to use *the:* (1) after *most of* and (2) before *most* as a superlative.

1. At _____ most _____ weddings, birdseed is thrown at the married couple as they leave the church.

2. _____ most of _the_ wedding guests threw birdseed at the married couple as they left the church.

3. _The_ most _____ interesting superstitions are about animals and birds.

4. _____ most of _____ people I know avoid staying on the 13th floor of a hotel.

5. _____ most _____ people avoid walking underneath a ladder.

6. _____ most _____ widespread superstition of all is the one about number thirteen.

7. Some people believe that _____ most _____ accidents happen in threes.

8. _____ most of _____ accidents that happened here occurred in threes.

9. _____ most of _____ superstitions that children believe in involve magic.

10. _____ most _____ superstitions that children believe involve magic.

11. _____ most of _____ actors in the play are superstitious.

12. _____ most _____ actors are superstitious about the opening night of their play.

Exercise 7: Word Forms

Complete the words in the following sentences. Some words are already complete.

1. Anyone who belie- __ves__ in supersti- __tion__ is supersti- __tious__.

2. Supersti-_____ is an unreason-_____ belie-_____ in the supernatur-_____.

3. It often origin-_____ because of ignor-_____ of natur-_____ cause-_____.

4. It may come from a fear- _____ of the unknown-_____ and the myster-_____.

5. Many sign-_____ and omen-_____ symbol-_____ good luck-_____ or bad luck-_____.

6. Number thirteen is an unluck-_____ number.

7. See-_____ a crow may sign-_____ a dea-_____ in the family.

8. Misfort-_____ can result from break-_____ a mirror.

Exercise 8: Sentence Review

Make full sentences from the word groups below. Make whatever changes or additions are needed, but do not change the word order. Use commas, semicolons, or periods wherever necessary.

1. If / you / walk / under / ladder / you / have / bad luck.

   If you walk under a ladder, you will have bad luck.

2. If / black cat / cross / your path / you / be / unlucky.

   _____

3. Break / mirror / bring / you / bad luck.

   _____

4. If / bridesmaid / had caught / bridal bouquet / she / become / bride / herself / within / following / year.

   _____

5. If / someone / sneeze / I would say / "God / bless / you."

   _____

6. If / I / decide / get / marry / I would not have had / wedding / Friday / 13.

   _____

7. He / was / worry / because / mirror / fall / off / wall / in / bedroom.

   _____

8. Superstition / be / result / fear / unknown.

   _____

9. House / where / he / used to / live / haunt / ghosts.

_____

10. Tradition / has / preserve / many / superstition.

_____

11. There / be / once / belief / gold / can / be / make / man.

_____

12. See / crow / be / sign / death.

_____

▷ Extra Speaking and Writing Practice

Exercise 9: Writing about Personal Characteristics

Those who follow astrology believe that a person's character is determined by the date and time of birth. Astrologers divide the year into the twelve signs of the zodiac and describe the characteristics of persons born under each of these signs. (_Zodiac_ is the narrow path in which the sun, the moon, and the planets travel in the heavens. The zodiac is divided into twelve equal parts.) Some people feel that this kind of analysis of a person's character is pure superstition; others feel that many of the things the astrologers say are quite accurate. Astrologers try to predict what will happen each day; these predictions are called _horoscopes_. They are printed in most daily newspapers.

Following is a list of personal qualities that astrologers say are characteristic of people born under each of the zodiac signs. Remember that because they represent so many people, they are usually generalized. Discuss these characteristics as a class or in groups to see how true each one is for you. Look up the words that are unfamiliar to you.

Next write a short composition choosing one or two personal characteristics included under your sign and _give examples to show why you agree or disagree with this description._

Begin the composition with: "According to the astrologers, persons born under my sign, _____, are . . . (or, have . . .)." (Give only the characteristics you will agree or disagree with and write about only one characteristic at a time.) You may include statements such as: "I (dis)agree with that. . . ." or "This characteristic is certainly (not) true for me. For example, . . ."

Signs of the Zodiac—
Personal Characteristics*

Aries 3/21–4/19

(*Mars*†—rules energy, courage, aggressiveness,
action, ambition, and pioneering)

has initiative, courage, drive, enthusiasm
resourceful, self-confident, impulsive, imaginative
dynamic, a doer who wants to be first in everything
independent, restless, wants challenges and adventures
outgoing, enjoys competition in work but not monotony
a natural organizer with executive ability
faults: impatient, not persistent, thoughtless, selfish, quick-tempered

Taurus 4/20–5/20

(*Venus*—rules art, beauty, love,
peace and harmony, and perfection)

stubborn determination, slow starter, persistent, courageous
kind, but with a violent temper when pushed too far
sense of material values, talent for acquiring money
has great vitality and sensuality, love of beauty
conservative, very practical, methodical, shrewd
faults: hard to adapt to change, moody, carries grudges (doesn't forget
      or forgive), greedy, overly possessive, extremely conservative

Gemini 5/21–6/21

(*Mercury*—rules the mind and communication)

lighthearted, whimsical, talkative, witty conversationalist
alert, changeable, a quick and intelligent thinker with an excellent
      sense of humor
has need for novelty and variety, versatile and adaptable, skilled with
      hands
faults: superficial, lacks warmth, fickle, easily bored, restless, nervous,
      not persistent

---

* Not all sources show exactly the same beginning or ending date for each sign.
† The name in parentheses after each sign of the zodiac is the heavenly body (sun, moon, or planet) that rules the sign.

Cancer 6/22–7/22

(*Moon*—rules moods, emotions,
intuition, change, and domesticity)

tenacious, versatile, moody, sensitive, idealistic
possessive, very changeable, home-loving, protective of the family
romantic, affectionate, gentle
faults: overpossessive, jealous, tends to accumulate, emotionally
insecure, inconsistent

Leo 7/23–8/22

(*Sun*—rules the will, drive, and executive power)

a born leader, bold, energetic, ambitious, honest, enthusiastic
generous, loyal, optimistic, cheerful, sympathetic, self-confident
a strong personality, wants to be noticed and admired
emotionally intense, melodramatic, favors dramatic gestures
faults: arrogant, vain, self-centered, dictatorial, bossy, thoughtless,
vulnerable to flattery

Virgo 8/23–9/22

(*Mercury*—rules the mind and communication)

intellectual, logical and analytical mind, level-headed
methodical, meticulous, master of detail, hard-working, practical
dependable, enjoys routine work, perfectionist
modest, neat, loyal, reserved
faults: fanatic about neatness and order, emotionally cold, nervous,
critical and nagging, faultfinding, insecure, intolerant of ignorance

Libra 9/23–10/22

(*Venus*—rules art, beauty, love,
peace and harmony, and perfection)

poised, diplomatic, peace-loving, imaginative, fair-minded, intellectual
hates arguments, can see both sides, never totally committed
dislikes hard work, romantic but not sensual
loves beauty, especially beauty of human relationships
has artistic talent, good at working with people
faults: indecisive, gets discouraged easily, hesitant, not practical

Scorpio 10/23–11/21

(*Pluto*—rules power, intensity, everything
beneath the surface and behind the scenes)

strong drive, magnetic personality, great vitality
hard worker, has great patience and power of concentration, ambitious
realistic, practical, sensible, courageous, self-assured, loyal
unshakable determination of the kind that makes martyrs and fanatics
competes to win, not for the fun of it

subtle and secretive, manipulates people from the background
very sensual (the sexiest sign of the zodiac)
faults: lacks control over the emotions, ruthless and unfair, suspicious,
    jealous, overly possessive, selfish, arbitrary

Sagittarius 11/22–12/21

(*Jupiter*—rules sociability, kindness,
enthusiasm, generosity, and optimism)

warm, friendly, tolerant, good-natured, honest, curious
talkative, extrovert, fun to have around
restless and independent, needs action, travel, adventure
likes sports, but plays for enjoyment
not very domestic, doesn't like to be tied down
faults: fickle, not persistent, extravagant, impatient, forgetful, depends
    too much on luck

Capricorn 12/22–1/19

(*Saturn*—rules self-discipline, hard work,
responsibility, patience, and cautiousness)

works hard but wants it to count, wants to rise to the top
ambitious, authoritative, industrious, self-disciplined
conservative but forceful, practical, orderly, cautious
excellent organizer, plans large-scale ventures well
values honor and respectability
faults: single-minded in pursuing success, gloomy, pessimistic,
    impatient, distrustful

Aquarius 1/20–2/18

(*Uranus*—rules originality, invention, freedom, and individualism)

independent thinker but unpredictable, nonconformist
intellectual, rational, objective, fair-minded, tolerant
inventive, progressive, thinks in large-scale terms
friendly, good-humored, kind, spontaneous
faults: impersonal, resists intimate contact, impractical, eccentric,
    irresponsible

Pisces 2/19–3/20

(*Neptune*—rules vagueness, confusion,
creativity, illusion, and changeability)

imaginative, original, sympathetic, generous, honest
unrealistic, highly emotional, intuitive, impressionable
creative in all arts, also mathematics and science
faults: jealous, possessive, gloomy, lacks confidence, impractical,
    easily led

Exercise 10: Word Forms

Use the correct word form for the following characteristics typically associated with people born under each of the twelve signs of the zodiac. Remember these are generalizations. Do you fit with the characteristics of your sign?

1. The Capricorn person: is (ambition) _____ _ambitious_ _____
   (12/22–1/19)   (order) _____

                             (caution) _____

                          lacks (origin) _____ _originality_ _____

                             (self-confident) _____

                          is a (material) _____ _materialist_ _____

                             a (plan) _____

2. The Aquarius person: is (friend) _____
   (1/20–2/18)   (not predict) _____

                             has (good-humored) _____

                             (object) _____

                          resists (intimate) _____

                          is a (not conforming) _____

3. The Pisces person: is (imagination) _____
   (2/19–3/20)   (change) _____

                             (no organization) _____

                          has (subtle) _____

                          lacks a sense of (secure) _____

                             and (real) _____

4. The Aries person: is (courage) _____
   (3/21–4/19)   (impulse) _____

                          has (aggressive) _____

                             (initiate) _____

                          lacks (patient) _____

                             (persist) _____

5. The Taurus person: is (determine) _____

   (4/20–5/20)   (conserve) _____

                     has (vital) _____

6. The Gemini person: is (talk) _____

   (5/21–6/21)   (adapt) _____

                     has (versatile) _____

                     lacks (warm) _____

7. The Cancer person: is (possess) _____

   (6/22–7/22)   (change) _____

                     has (intuitive) _____

                     lacks emotional (secure) _____

8. The Leo person: is (cheer) _____

   (7/23–8/22)   (dictator) _____

                     has (arrogant) _____

                     (generous) _____

9. The Virgo person: is (modesty) _____

   (8/23–9/22)   (diligence) _____

                     is a (fanaticism) _____ about neatness

10. The Libra person: is (hesitate) _____

   (9/23–10/22)   (intellect) _____

                     is not (emotion) _____

                     lacks (commit) _____

11. The Scorpio person: is (suspect) _____

   (10/23–11/21)   has (determine) _____

                     (loyal) _____

12. The Sagittarius person: is (friend) _____

   (11/22–12/21)   (enthusiasm) _____

                     lacks (persist) _____

Exercise 11: Composition on Similarities and Differences— Western and Eastern Zodiacs

Page 181 gives the charts of the Western zodiac and the Asian animal cycle. As a class or in groups, discuss the similarities and the differences between the two zodiac charts. Then write three paragraphs about these similarities and differences. Use the following outline:

First paragraph   *Introduction:* general statements (Keep this short.)

Second paragraph   I.   *Similarities*
> (Use an opening sentence that tells the reader you are going to discuss the similarities.)
> expressions for similarity:
>> similar to . . . in that
>> like (or alike) . . . in that
>> both
>> one similarity between . . .
>> another (or a second) similarity
>> the same as, or the same . . . as

Third paragraph   II.   *Differences*
> (Use an opening sentence that tells the reader you are going to discuss the differences.)
> expressions for difference:
>> different from . . . in that
>> but; however; on the other hand
>> while, whereas
>> one difference between . . .
>> another (or a second) difference

Wherever possible, give *examples* for the similarities or differences you point out.

As you look for similarities and differences between the two zodiac charts, you might consider the following:

the shape of each zodiac	the symbols used in each zodiac
the divisions of each zodiac	the relation to people's lives of each zodiac
the period of time covered by each zodiac	the center of each zodiac

Duality (double character or nature) at the center of the Asian animal cycle:

Yang	*Yin*
heaven	earth
active	passive
positive	negative
male	female
firm	yielding
strong	weak
light	dark

The two together (yang and yin) represent the whole universe.

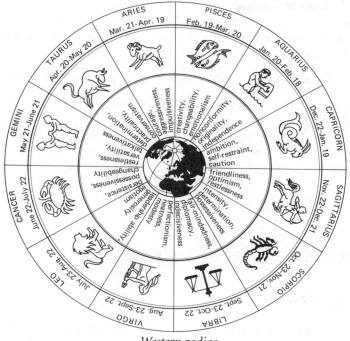

Western zodiac

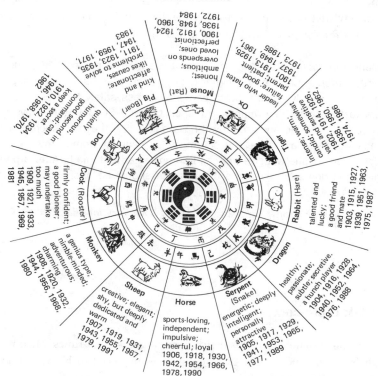

Asian animal cycle.

(Adapted from the Western and Oriental Animal (horoscope) Cycles
by Frank V. Rubens, New York Times Pictures, Copyright © 1976 New York Times.)

Exercise 12: Journal Writing

Write a journal entry on one of the following subjects. Write freely since you are the only one who will see this entry.

1. Write about some superstitions you found in the United States that surprised you.

2. Do you read the horoscopes in the daily newspapers? What do you think of them?

Now use your journal entry as the basis for a more careful letter to your teacher that is to be handed in.

◎ Listening-Writing Practice

Exercise 13: Dictation

Your teacher will dictate the paragraph three times. The first time is for listening only, the second time is for writing, and the third time is for checking what you have written.

Immediately after you give your teacher the dictation you have written, check the dictation in the book for any problems you had in writing it.

> Many superstitions deal with important events in a person's life, such as birth, entering adulthood, marriage, pregnancy, and death. Such superstitions supposedly ensure that a person will pass safely from one stage of life to the next. For example, a person born on Sunday will always have good luck. A bride and groom will have bad luck if they see each other on their wedding day before the ceremony. A pregnant woman must eat the right food, or she will give her child an unwanted birthmark. After a person dies, the doors and windows of the room should be opened so the spirit can leave.
>
> From "Superstition," *World Book Encyclopedia*, 2000, page 995.

Exercise 14: Dicto-comp

Take notes as your teacher reads this dicto-comp to you several times. Then reconstruct the dicto-comp from your notes. The dicto-comp does not need to be written exactly as you heard it, but it should be grammatically correct.

Before you write the dicto-comp, your teacher may ask the class to get together in groups to check with each other on what you heard.

Immediately after you give your teacher the dicto-comp you have written, check the dicto-comp in the book for any problems you had in writing it.

Superstitions have existed for a long time all over the world. They often originate because of ignorance of natural causes. They may come from a fear of the unknown and the mysterious.

In many countries superstitions concern numbers, animals or birds, and things. Here are some that are common in Western cultures.

With regard to numbers, the most common superstition is about number 13. This number is felt to be unlucky. In some buildings there are no floors with the number 13; the floors go from 12 to 14. Thirteen is also considered unlucky if it falls on Friday. People often avoid doing anything important on this day.

Western countries also have superstitions about animals and birds. Probably the most widespread superstition is that if a black cat crosses your path, you will have bad luck. Another unlucky omen is seeing a bat flying low. Seeing a crow is a sign of death.

The superstitions about things in Western cultures are particularly numerous. For example, if you break a mirror, you will have seven years' bad luck. Also, it is considered unlucky to open an umbrella in the house or to walk under a ladder. Good luck may come from finding a four-leaf clover or hanging a horseshoe above a doorway. Evil consequences may be avoided by knocking on wood.

Today people in most parts of the world are better educated, and so superstitions are gradually disappearing. Our education teaches us that superstitions are irrational beliefs that are not based on natural causes. Still, if we have a choice, we would rather not live on the thirteenth floor.

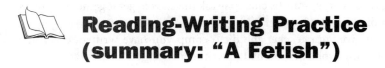

Reading-Writing Practice
(summary: "A Fetish")

You are going to write a one to three paragraph summary of a reading selection. A summary is a restatement, in shortened form, of the main ideas of a selection.

In preparation for the summary, skim through the selection quickly to determine the way the ideas are developed (through comparison, contrast, listing, time, space, example). Then reread the selection carefully, underlining the important points that should be included in the summary. (Do not underline too much.)

In writing the summary, use your own words as much as possible. You may include the important words from the reading selection, but use quotation marks around whole phrases taken directly from the selection.

Devote more attention to the main points than to their supporting details. Omit examples unless they are important to the development of the ideas. Do *not* use your own ideas in a summary.

The selection to be summarized comes from a book entitled *Amulets, Talismans and Fetishes*. It gives a definition of a fetish and two examples of their power.

A Fetish

Found in many cultures throughout the world, a fetish may have the form of an animal or human statuette, an Indian medicine bundle, a picture, a buffalo horn, or a sword. It is different from other magical objects because it is supposed to have human thoughts and feelings. It may also be the home of a spirit or other supernatural being.

In central Africa, the Bakongo tribe once had a fetish called *Nkosi* which consisted of two parts: an image of a man and a sack which held parts of birds and animals. When a theft was reported in the village, the Nkosi and his human caretaker were summoned to the scene of the crime. While the villagers beat their drums, the caretaker set off gunpowder under the nose of Nkosi, begging him to point out the **culprit**. Then they watched to see if anyone in the community developed a nosebleed soon after. If so, Nkosi was given the credit for identifying the person as the thief.

Nkosi was no ordinary **amulet** that functioned automatically to bring good luck or avert misfortune. It was treated as though it were a person who could be **implored** or frightened into revealing the truth.

Another example of a fetish comes from a Cambodian legend. There was once a king who possessed a sword containing a spirit. If the king were to draw the sword a few inches out of its **sheath,** the sun would hide its face, and all men and animals would fall into a deep sleep. If the king were to draw the sword out completely, the world would come to an end.

What is interesting about the sword is not its power, but the behavior of people toward it. The sword was clothed in the most costly silks and linens and annually presented with gifts of pigs, chickens, and buffalo. In return it was expected to bring rain to the country. The sword was the dwelling place of a powerful spirit on whose goodwill the prosperity of the people depended.

Adapted from *Amulets, Talismans and Fetishes* by Arthur S. Gregor, Atheneum Books for Young Readers, an imprint of Simon & Schuster Children's Publishing Division,1975, pages 77–78.

Vocabulary

1. **culprit**—a guilty person
2. **amulet**—a charm worn to avoid evil or to bring good luck
3. **implore**—beg
4. **sheath**—outer covering for the blade of a sword or knife

bread plate   glass

napkin   salad fork   fork   plate   knife   teaspoon   soup spoon

Rules of Etiquette (politeness)

Grammar and Usage

Verb-preposition combinations

Separable verb-preposition combinations

Pronouns in general statements

Negative prefixes

Rhetoric

Using an outline to guide the composition

Using an introduction and a conclusion

Using a transitional lead-in to the body of the composition

Using transitions between paragraphs

Discussion and Composition

1. Discussion: Preliminary Outline for the Composition (prewriting stage)

Subject: *Rules of Etiquette in* (name of country)

Outline *(To be placed on the board.* *Books are closed.)*	*Discussion* *(Ideas, Grammar and Usage, Vocabulary,* *Elements of Composition Building)*

Introduction: general statements
  Purpose of rules of etiquette
	Possible comments:
	Every country has its own rules of etiquette.
	Etiquette is polite social behavior that makes
	  life easier and more pleasant.
	It helps people to get along with each other.
	It often reflects a country's social values and
	  beliefs.

Kinds of rules:
1. conventional
2. social
	Example: serving and eating food
	  Example: respectful behavior toward older
	  people and toward women

Transitional lead-in to suggest that
both types of rules will be discussed
	This composition will deal with both types
	  of rules of etiquette in my country.
	Or, I want to discuss both types . . .
	Or, I would like to give examples of both
	  types . . .

I. Conventional rules—serving and
  eating food
	Opening sentence of paragraph: mention the
	  subject, conventional rules about serving
	  and eating food

A. serving the food	Time when meals are served Number and order of courses served Eating utensils used and their place on the table (place setting)
B. eating the food	Behavior of the people at the table (table manners)

II. Social rules—respectful behavior	Opening sentence of paragraph: mention the
	  subject, rules about respectful social
	  behavior

A. toward older people	Behavior of children toward grown-ups Behavior of students toward teachers

B. toward women	Examples: (U.S.)
	  dining in a restaurant
	  opening doors in buildings or cars
	  walking in the street

	Note: This point may be reversed (respect shown by women to men) in some cultures.
Conclusion: general statements	Possible comments:
	Rules of etiquette not so strictly observed now
	Changing customs—more informality now
	Influence of Western customs

2. Composition (to be done before or after the grammar practice)

A. Organizing the Composition

Before writing your composition, fill in the required information on this organizational work sheet. The work sheet follows the preliminary outline used for the discussion. Guidance for writing each paragraph is given at the right side of this work sheet. The pages of the discussion outline provide additional help for the composition.

You may use phrases on this work sheet except where it calls for full sentences.

Organizational Work Sheet
(Preliminary notes for the composition)

Title of the composition _____

(Do not use quotation marks or a period for a title at the top of the page. Use initial capital letters for the first word of the title and for all other words except articles, prepositions, and coordinate conjunctions *[and, or, but].*)

Introduction: general statements   Put in a separate paragraph.
Opening sentence of paragraph _____
                                                    Use the present tense for
_____   general statements in this
                                                    paragraph and in the rest
_____   of the composition.

_____

Purpose of rules of etiquette _____

_____

_____

_____

_____

Kinds of rules (conventional and social, with examples)

_____

_____

_____

_____

_____

Transitional lead-in connecting the general statements of
the introduction to the two kinds of rules of etiquette

Full sentence _____

_____

_____

_____

_____

May be the conclusion of
the introductory paragraph,
or may begin the paragraph
that follows it

I. Conventional rules—serving and eating food
   Opening (or second) sentence of paragraph _____

_____

_____

_____

New paragraph
Mention the subject,
conventional rules about
serving and eating food.

A. Serving the food

_____

_____

_____

_____

_____

B. Eating the food

_____

_____

_____

_____

_____

_____

II. Social rules—respectful behavior

    Opening sentence of paragraph _____

_____

_____

_____

_____

_____

New paragraph

Mention the subject, rules about respectful social behavior.

A. Respect shown to older people

_____

_____

_____

_____

_____

_____

B. Respect shown to women

_____

_____

_____

_____

_____

_____

(Or respect shown to men by women)

Conclusion: general statements

_____

_____

_____

_____

_____

_____

New paragraph

B. Writing a 400/500-Word Composition

Write the composition based on your notes on the organizational work sheet. Be careful of your paragraphing. Use separate paragraphs for your introduction and your conclusion. (Long paragraphs may be broken in two at appropriate places, but single-sentence paragraphs should be avoided.)

C. Correcting/Rewriting the Composition (peer review)

When you bring your composition to class, you will be asked to exchange it with that of another student.

First check the other student's development of the composition and then check the items listed under Editing.

1. Development of the Composition
Introduction and Conclusion
Transitional lead-in
Paragraphs—opening sentences and supporting details
Are these well done, or can you suggest ways to improve them? Write your comments on the student's composition.

2. Editing
Grammar
Usage (spelling and punctuation)
Vocabulary
For grammar and usage, the information under Symbol Chart for Correction of Compositions in the Appendix can be helpful.

When the peer review is over, hand in your composition to your teacher, who will return it to you later with additional comments and correction symbols used for the mistakes. Then you will be asked to rewrite the composition, taking into account what your fellow student and what your teacher suggested for the improvement of the composition.

After you have revised your composition, hand it in to your teacher together with your first draft.

☑ Grammar Practice

Exercise 1: Verb-Preposition Combinations

Many combinations of verbs and prepositions have meanings that are different from each of their two parts. For example, *get up* = awake, *keep on* = continue, *take after* = resemble.

Replace the verb in parentheses with a verb-preposition combination. Use the proper verb form. (If you have any difficulties with this vocabulary, consult the list of verb-preposition combinations at the end of this exercise.) Many of these rules of etiquette given in the following exercises are not observed today, although most were in earlier decades in the U.S.

1. Rules of etiquette are (transmit) _handed_ _down_ from generation to generation to help people (be in harmony) _get_ _along_ _with_ each other.

2. Parents should (raise) _____ _____ their children to have good manners so that when the children (mature) _____ _____ they will be well-bred.

3. It's polite to (telephone) _____ _____ friends before you visit them.

4. A man (remove) _____ _____ his hat in the elevator of a residence building or a hotel when a woman (enter) _____ _____ the elevator.

5. At a social gathering, it is best not to (raise) _____ _____ unpleasant or very controversial subjects.

6. Good table manners should be observed whether you (have food at home) _____ or (have food in a restaurant) _____.

7. In a restaurant the man may help the woman (remove) _____ _____ her coat.

8. It's in better taste for a woman not to (put on cosmetics) _____ _____ at the table while dining in a restaurant.

9. A man (rise from his seat) _____ _____ when a woman (enter) _____ _____ the room.

10. In the United States, the fork is (lift) _____ _____ with the right hand.

11. It is not polite to (appear) _____ _____ at a party without having called to say you were coming.

12. It took many hours for the firefighters to (extinguish) _____ _____ the fire.

Verb-Preposition Combinations for Exercise 1

bring up (a child), *raise*	grow up, *mature*
bring up (a subject), *raise*	hand down, *transmit*
call on, *ask a question in class*	make up, *put on cosmetics*
call up, *telephone*	pick up, *lift*
come into, *enter*	put out, *extinguish*
eat in, *have food at home*	
eat out, *eat in a restaurant*	
get along with, *be in harmony with*	take off (clothing), *remove*
get (stand) up, *rise from one's seat*	turn up, *appear*

Exercise 2: Separable Verb-Preposition Combinations

Many verb-preposition combinations are *separable:* their objects may appear either after the combination or between the two parts. However, a pronoun object appears *only between* the two parts.

Noun Object:	You should call up *your friends.*
	or
	You should call *your friends* up.
Pronoun Object:	You should call *them* up.

Other verb-preposition combinations are *nonseparable:* the noun or pronoun object comes *only after* the two parts.

Noun Object:	The teacher called on *all the students.*
Pronoun Object:	The teacher called on *them.*

Use pronouns for the italicized words along with the proper form of the verb-preposition combinations for the verbs in parentheses. (If you have any difficulties with this vocabulary, consult the list of verb-preposition combinations at the end of this exercise.)

1. I just received an invitation, but the *date* is illegible. I can't (understand)
   _____make_____ _____it_____ _____out_____.
   (separable combination)

2. She's wearing a beautiful *dress*, but nothing else that she has on (harmonize)
   _____goes_____ _____with_____ _____it_____.
   (nonseparable combination)

3. When her boyfriend made her an *offer of marriage*, she (reject) _____
   _____ _____ as kindly as possible.

4. You should write a *thank-you note* to your hostess. It's not polite to (postpone)
   _____ _____ _____.

5. They are worried about *their son*. They're afraid that they (not raise)_____
   _____ _____ _____ as well as possible.
   (several possibilities for the verb tense)

6. If a friend is in the hospital with an *illness*, we often send him a card wishing that he
   will (recover) _____ _____ _____ soon.

7. He never wears *clothes* that suit the occasion. He doesn't know how to (choose)
   _____ _____ _____. He is so impetuous that
   he (not test for fit or appearance) _____ _____
   _____ _____ _____.

8. She has some *friends* in Washington. If she plans to visit them, it would be polite to
   (telephone) _____ _____ _____ first.

9. If you are wearing a *hat* you should (remove) _____ _____
   _____ before you enter the classroom.

10. When a young man dates a *young woman,* he should (come to get) _____
    _____ _____ when he (escort somewhere)
    _____ _____ _____.

11. The *concert* never took place. They had to (cancel) _____
    _____ _____ because the singer became ill.

Verb-Preposition Combinations for Exercise 2

Separable combinations are marked *(S)*; nonseparable combinations are marked *(NS)*.

bring up (a child), *raise* (S)

call for (someone or something),
   come to get (NS)

call off (something), *cancel* (S)

call on (someone), *ask a question
   in class* (NS)

call up (on the telephone),
   telephone (S)

get over (an illness), *recover from* (NS)

go with (something, usually clothes),
   harmonize with (NS)

make out (some writing),
   understand (S)

pick out (something), *choose* (S)

put off (something), *postpone* (S)

take off (an item) of clothing,
   remove (S)

take out (someone), *escort
   somewhere* (S)

try on (an item of clothing),
   test for fit or appearance (S)

turn down (a person or an
   offer), *reject* (S)

Exercise 3: Pronouns in General Statements

Personal pronouns are often used in general statements to represent everybody that the statement is about.

We: In my country, *we* often eat dinner very late.

You: In my country, *you* must respect your elders.

One: *One* learns *one's* (or *his* or *her*) manners at home at an early
         age.

In using these pronouns for general statements, we must be consistent. If we start with *we,* then we must continue using this pronoun and not shift to one of the others.

Pronoun shift: *We* should not forget that the rules of etiquette
                  depend on the culture where *you* are.

Correction: *We* should not forget that the rules of etiquette de-
                  pend on the culture where *we* are. (Or, use *you* for
                  both pronouns.)

Correct the faulty pronoun shifts used in the following general statements about customs in different countries. (The verbs that follow the pronouns may also need to be corrected.)

1. Good manners should be observed whether one eats in a restaurant or whether you eat at home.

   Good manners should be observed whether one eats in a restaurant or whether one eats at home. (Or, use *you* in both places instead of *one.*)

2. We say a prayer to bless the food. Then one starts eating.

   _____

3. After we finish eating, we put the fork and the knife to the right on the plate. If you put your fork and knife back on the table, this means you are not finished eating.

   _____

4. First, we serve soup and vegetables, and then we usually eat sashimi and drink rice wine. Finally, you eat some dessert.

   _____

5. When one is invited to dinner, the host expects you to arrive on time. (In this sentence, change the first pronoun.)

   _____

6. When we sit at the table, we must wait for everyone to start eating. Sometimes you have to wait until the head of the family or host begins eating.

   _____

7. One should not talk about unpleasant subjects at a social gathering. Also, you should avoid any subject that might hurt the feelings of the people you are with.

   _____

Exercise 4: Negative Prefixes

Words may be made negative by adding the prefixes *in-* (*im-* before *p* or *m),* *un-,* *dis-,* or *mis-*.

Use the correct form of the negative.

1. It is (not pleasant) ____*unpleasant*____ to be with people who are (not courteous) ____*discourteous*____ and always do the (not correct) ____*incorrect*____ thing.

2. (Not obedient) _____ children who (not behave) _____ have not been brought up well by their parents.

3. It is (not polite) _____ to be (not respectful) _____ to one's elders.

4. People who are (not considerate) _____ or (not decent) _____ will gain the (no approval) _____ of others.

5. If we are (not accustomed) _____ to the ways of another culture, we may behave in an (not acceptable) _____ way and possibly commit an (no propriety) _____.

6. Long ago, it was considered (not modest) _____ for a woman to use the words *stomach* and *leg*.

7. It is bad taste to make (not appropriate) _____ or (not proper) _____ remarks to others.

8. A person who is (not able) _____ to like other people often has the (no ability) _____ to be polite to them.

9. A host will (not approve) _____ of a guest who (not regard) _____ the social amenities.

Exercise 5: Word Forms

Use the correct form of the word in parentheses. In sentences with choices, select the correct word.

1. Rules of etiquette have long been in (exist) ___*existence*___ in (social) ___*society*___ to make life more (please) ___*pleasant*___ and more (harmony) ___*harmonious*___.

2. Some of our rules of etiquette are remnants of (Middle Ages) _____ customs when knights were very (chivalry) _____ toward the women.

3. The person who follows the rules of etiquette has (good manners). He is ___-___-ed. If he does not follow these rules, he is ___-___-ed. (both words are hyphenated)

4. We also say that people who follow the rules of etiquette have (good breeding). They are _____. If they do not follow the rules, they are _____. (both words are hyphenated)

5. The rules of etiquette tell us what kind of (behave) _____ is (courtesy) _____ and what kind is (not polite) _____.

6. The person who observes the rules of etiquette shows (courteous) _____ and (consider) _____ toward others. He or she always (behavior)_____ with (proper) _____ and (decent) _____.

7. To be (social) _____ acceptable, a person must observe the (custom) _____ rules of etiquette.

8. Some parents today have been too (permit) _____ and have not trained their children in the rules of (polite) _____ and common (courteous) _____.

9. In the United States, an (obey) _____ and (respect) _____ child will ask for his or her parents' (permit) _____ to leave the dinner table.

10. In a restaurant, a woman should not leave her purse (lying, laying) _____ on the table.

11. RSVP (from the French *Répondez s'il vous plaît*) means "Please reply." You should reply (prompt) _____ to an (invite) _____.

12. Also, you should arrive (punctual) _____ when you are (invite)_____ to dinner.

Exercise 6: Sentence Review

Make full sentences from the word groups that follow. Make whatever changes or additions are needed, but do not change the word order. Be careful of the punctuation.

A. For the verbs in parentheses, use verb-preposition synonyms. If these combinations have objects, put the objects in the correct position.

1. If / you / plan / visit / friends / it's / polite / (telephone them) / first.
   If you plan to visit friends, it's polite to call them up first.

2. Parents / should / (raise) / their children / have / good manners / so that / when / children / (mature) / they / be / well-bred.

_____

3. Date / this invitation / be / illegible / I / can't / (understand it).

_____

4. They / be / worried / their son / they / be / afraid / they (not raise him) / well. (More than one tense is possible.)

_____

5. He / never / wear / clothes / that / suit / the occasion. / He / not know / how (choose them).

_____

6. She / wear / beautiful dress / but / nothing else / that / she / have on / (harmonize) / it. (More than one tense is possible.)

_____

B. As you make these sentences, add the correct negative prefixes or the correct word endings.

1. It / be / (not) -polite / be / (not) -respectful / one's / elders.

_____

2. Person / who / be / (not) -able / like / other / people / often / have / the / (no) -ability be / polite / them.

_____

3. It / be / (not) -pleasant / be / with / people / who / be / (not) -courteous.

_____

4. They / have / (not) -obedient / children / who / (not) -behave.

_____

5. Rules / etiquette / tell / us / what kind / behav-_____ / be /
   courte-_____ / and / consider-_____.

_____

6. You / should / arrive / punctual-_____ / when / you / be /
   invite-_____ / dinner.

_____

▷ Extra Speaking and Writing Practice

Exercise 7: Skit—Dinner in an American Restaurant

Work in groups of three to act out and then write a skit (a short play) about dining in a moderately priced American restaurant.

To make this skit more realistic, you might bring in two place settings (flatware, plates, glasses, napkins) for the table where Maria and John will sit. See the illustration at the beginning of this unit for the arrangement of the place settings.

Use the information in the left column for your skit. This column tells what the characters in the skit do or say. Use the present tense for the action.

The right column is for your information only. It explains some American customs about dining in a restaurant. You may incorporate some of this information within the skit.

There are two main characters in the skit: John, a young American man, and Mary, a young American woman. The third student plays all the other characters.

The skit must include both the directions for the actions and the dialogue that gives the actual words spoken. The skit is begun for you at the end of this introductory section.

Dinner in an American Restaurant

What Is Being Said and Done	*Explanation of American Customs*
It's 6:00 P.M. Mary and John enter the restaurant. The hostess greets them. She asks whether he has a reservation. He replies that he does and he gives his name.	A young man often calls for the young woman at her home to escort her to the restaurant. In a large city they may also meet at the restaurant.
They follow the hostess to the table, Mary going first.	At a popular restaurant, especially a small one, it's customary to make a reservation in order to be sure of getting a table at the desired time.
	A man (called a host or maître d') or a woman (the hostess) leads diners to their table. The woman diner precedes the man.
John helps Mary to her seat. He asks her whether he may help her with her coat. She answers yes.	The host or hostess or the woman's escort helps to seat her and helps her with her coat. In many large or expensive restaurants the man may check their coats.
The waiter or waitress approaches. He or she asks if they want to order a drink. John asks Mary to order first. The server brings the drinks and offers them the menus. He or she then tells them what the specials of the day are. John asks Mary what she would like to order.	The menu at the end of this exercise is a short but typical American menu. The price of the entrée (main course) includes the whole dinner. The courses in a full dinner are: appetizer, salad, entrée, dessert, and beverage. The same restaurant may also serve food *à la carte,* which means each course has a separate charge.
Mary looks over the menu. (Note: Use the menu at the end of this exercise.) She asks a few questions about any items she's interested in.	If steak or roast beef is ordered, you must tell the waiter whether you want the meat rare (not cooked much), medium, medium-rare, or well-done. Some American eating customs: A popular time to come to a restaurant is between 6 and 7 P.M., especially if the diners are going afterward to the theater (which usually starts at 8 P.M.). In big cities it is considered more fashionable to dine later. The salad is served before the main course.
The waiter or waitress approaches to take their order. The couple orders the appetizers, salads, and entrées from the full-course dinner.	

The appetizers, the salads, and the entrées are brought to their table at appropriate intervals.

Some U.S. table manners:
using the same hand to hold
the knife and then the
fork (different from Europe)
not cutting up all one's food at once
breaking off only a small piece of
bread at a time and buttering it
not putting elbows on the table

After the main course is finished, someone removes the plates and the flatware. The server shows the diners the menus again. He or she asks what they would like to order for an after-dinner beverage and dessert.

The diner indicates that he or she has finished eating the main course by placing the knife and fork together in the middle of the plate. (This custom is often disregarded.)

They order.

They finish the dessert and beverage. Soon John suggests that they'd better leave so that they can get to the theater on time.

He asks the waiter or waitress for the bill.

In a restaurant, the man and woman diners often go Dutch, that is, they each pay for their own meal.

The bill is checked, and they pay with either cash or a credit card.
John and Mary leave the restaurant.

A usual tip in a restaurant is 15 percent. In elegant restaurants, 20 percent may be given.

Beginning of the Skit

Dinner in an American Restaurant

It's 6:00 P.M. Mary and John enter the restaurant.
The hostess or host approaches.

Hostess: Good evening. Do you have a reservation?
John: Yes, I have a reservation for two for six o'clock in the name of John Smith.
Hostess: Yes, come with me, please.

(Continue the skit. Supply both action and the conversation.)

American Restaurant Dinner Menu

Appetizers

Fresh fruit in season   Fruit cocktail   Half grapefruit

Juice (tomato, orange, grapefruit)

Soup du jour*

Shrimp cocktail ($2.00 extra)

Salads

Green salad   Hearts of lettuce   Sliced cucumber

Dressing: French, Russian, Oil and vinegar, Roquefort

Entrées

Roast chicken	18.00
Pot roast	16.00
Baked ham	18.00
Lamb stew	16.00
Fried liver	15.00
Sirloin steak	21.00
Roast beef	20.00
Sautéed filet of sole	18.00
Broiled halibut	18.00
Baked flounder	18.00
Fried shrimp	19.00
Seafood platter	20.00

Vegetables (choose two)

Potatoes (baked, mashed, or French fried), Corn, Peas, Carrots,
Cabbage, Squash, Stewed tomatoes, String beans

Desserts

Assorted French pastries

Chocolate cake

Strawberry shortcake ($2.00 extra)

Apple pie, Blueberry pie, Cherry pie (à la mode, $1.50 extra)†

Banana cream pie

Ice cream or Sherbet

Fresh fruit salad

Cheese and Crackers

Beverages

Coffee (regular or decaf), Tea, Milk

Espresso, Cappuccino ($2.00 extra)

---

* Each day a different soup is served. The diner must ask the waiter what the soup is for that day.
† *A la mode* means with a scoop of ice cream (used for pie or cake).

Exercise 8: Proverbs

Discuss the following proverbs about etiquette in groups or in the whole class. Do you have similar proverbs in your culture?

1. If you can't say something nice about someone, don't say anything.

2. A little courtesy goes a long way.

3. Courtesy begins in the home.

4. Courtesy opens many doors.

5. People who live in glass houses shouldn't throw stones.

6. Courtesy costs nothing.

7. Children should be seen and not heard.

Exercise 9: Journal Writing

Write on one of the following subjects. Write freely since you are the only one who will see this entry.

1. Give your impressions of the behavior and social attitudes of someone from another culture with whom you have come in contact.

2. Give your impression of the way food is served and eaten in the United States or another country.

Now use your journal entry as the basis for a more careful letter to your English teacher that is to be handed in.

◎ Listening-Writing Practice

Exercise 10: Dictation

Your teacher will dictate the paragraph three times. The first time is for listening only, the second time is for writing, and the third time is for checking what you have written.

Immediately after you give your teacher the dictation you have written, check the dictation in the book for any problems you had in writing it.

> Good manners form the basis of modern etiquette. Its component parts are courtesy, promptness, a sense of decorum, good taste and—most important—consideration of and respect for others. The Golden Rule applies: "Do unto others as you would have them do unto you." These attitudes and their application are essential to the functioning of society at every level. Etiquette must be learned. The child, self-centered and demanding, must be taught the social behavior that will equip him or her for living in harmony with others.
>
> Adapted from "Etiquette," *Encyclopedia International,*
> Grolier Incorporated, 1967, page 544.

Exercise 11: Dicto-comp

Take notes as your teacher reads this dicto-comp to you several times. Then reconstruct the dicto-comp from your notes. The dicto-comp does not need to be written exactly as you heard it, but it should be grammatically correct.

Before you write the dicto-comp, your teacher may ask the class to get together in groups to check with each other on what you heard.

Immediately after you give your teacher the dicto-comp you have written, check the dicto-comp in the book for any problems you had in writing it.

> Every country has its own rules of etiquette. Etiquette is polite social behavior that makes life easier and more pleasant so that people can get along with each other. Some of the rules of etiquette are merely conventional and arbitrary. For example, they deal with the manner in which certain things are done, such as the serving and eating of food. Other rules reflect more deeply the values of a society; for example, the rules about respectful behavior toward older people or toward women.
>
> Let's look at some rules of etiquette in the United States. With regard to the way food is served, we have definite rules about where eating utensils are placed on the table. For example, the knife and the spoon are placed to the right of the serving plate; the forks and napkins are placed to the left. With regard to table manners, some rules are: (1) do not cut up all

your food at once; (2) break off and butter only a small piece of bread at a time; (3) do not use a toothpick at the table.

When we come to respectful behavior toward others, American rules are not as strict as in some other cultures. Many rules about polite behavior toward older people are breaking down. Respectful terms of address have all but disappeared, except perhaps in the South. Young children often are allowed to call adults by their first names. Teachers and others in authority often do not get the respect they once had from young people.

A few rules may still be observed about respectful behavior toward women. A man may still open the door for a woman in a building or a car. In a restaurant, or getting on and off an elevator, a man may allow the woman to go first. On a date, a man still usually pays, but today it's also common for the two to go Dutch, that is, share the bill.

On the whole, because of the freer lifestyle of the younger generation, more and more rules of etiquette are ignored. Even polite society does not insist on as many of the social rules as it once did.

 # Reading-Writing Practice (summary: encyclopedia article on "Etiquette")

You are going to write a one to three sentence paragraph summary of a reading selection. A summary is a restatement, in shortened form, of the main ideas of a selection.

In preparation for the summary, skim through the selection quickly to determine the way the ideas are developed (through comparison, contrast, listing, time, space, example). Then reread the selection carefully, underlining the important points that should be included in the summary. (Do not underline too much.)

In writing the summary, use your own words as much as possible. You may include the important words from the reading selection, but use quotation marks around whole phrases taken directly from the selection.

Devote more attention to the main points than to their supporting details. Omit examples unless they are important to the development of the ideas. Do *not* use your own ideas in a summary.

The selection to be summarized comes from an article on "Etiquette" in a recent encyclopedia. It begins with a definition of etiquette and continues with a chronological development to the present time.

As prehistoric people began to interact with one another, they learned to behave in ways that made life easier and more pleasant. Any manners that developed among these people probably had a practical purpose.

Early civilizations, such as those of ancient Greece and Rome, also developed rules for proper social conduct. Such rules became more formal during the Middle Ages in Europe, when boys training to become knights learned a code of conduct called *chivalry*. According to this code, a **knight** was devoted to the Christian church and his country and treated women with great respect. Some aspects of **chivalry,** particularly the special treatment of women, became a traditional part of manners.

Much of today's formal etiquette originated in the French royal courts during the 1600s and 1700s. King Louis XIV had drawn up a daily list of functions, giving time, place, and proper dress. It was posted at Versailles as an *etiquette*—a French word meaning *ticket*—to help the nobles know what to do. It brought order to a **chaotic** court society, and the code of behavior was quickly adopted by the courts of other nations' monarchs. In time, upper classes throughout the Western world adopted the code.

Etiquette today concerns itself less with **rigid** rules governing formal occasions, and more with everyday living. The goal is to help people of all lifestyles get along well with one another. Etiquette today is based on common sense and consideration of the other person.

Etiquette is as **dynamic** as the society it reflects. In the United States, prior to the mid-1960s, men were raised to treat women with special politeness. Most women were assumed to be in need of protection, and many appeared to be satisfied with ambitions confined to family and home. Since 1950, however, the roles of women have changed rapidly. For example, many women have become more **assertive,** and large numbers of women work outside the home.

As the roles of people in society have changed, so have the rules of etiquette that apply to these people and situations. What used to be considered the correct behavior of a young man who had been brought up properly—emphasizing male **gallantry** and chivalry—no longer has a place in the business world. When men and women work together, good manners decree that they help each other when help is needed, without any reference to a person's sex.

Adapted from "Etiquette," *World Book Encyclopedia*, 2000, page 374.

Vocabulary

1. **knight**—a man, usually of noble birth, who after an apprenticeship was raised to honorable military rank and bound to chivalrous service
2. **chivalry**—the combination of qualities expected of a knight, including courage, generosity, and courtesy (chivalrous—considerate and courteous to women)
3. **chaotic**—completely confused or disordered
4. **rigid**—strict, firmly fixed

5. **dynamic**—changing, moving (as opposed to static—not moving)

6. **assertive**—acting in a positive or confident way

7. **gallantry**—politeness and attentiveness to women

FYI For Your Information
(reading selection from *The Complete Idiot's Guide to Etiquette*)

The reading selection that follows comes from a recent book on etiquette. The rules of etiquette are presented in a lively, easy-to-read style. As with so many other informational books today, the title of the book, *The Complete Idiot's Guide to Etiquette,* gives the promise that even the most uninformed reader will be able to understand all the information in the book.

This selection is adapted from the beginning section of the book, "Etiquette in America—What Happened." It traces the development of guides to etiquette in America from early colonial days to the present. (Later sections in the book are on: "Dining Etiquette," "Business Etiquette," "Correspondence," "Home Etiquette," "Saying the Right Thing," "Sports," "Traveling," and "Weddings.")

Through all of the changes and crises that molded American society over the years, there has been a willingness and even an eagerness to accept information and advice about behavior.

It was only in the early days, when life was difficult and the pioneers had little time for the social graces, that no authoritative literature was consulted about rules of etiquette. It was only the law and the church that established minimum standards of civility and decent behavior.

But as leisure and wealth increased in the country, the Southern plantation owners and the prosperous merchants of the Northern port cities looked about for a standard of decorum and even elegance to serve as a reflection of their wealth and power. For this purpose, they looked back to England for the literature of civility. The English books that were imported were very often translations, adaptations, or outright plagiarism of French works. France, since the age of chivalry, had been Europe's chief instructor in matters of manners. The bookshelves of the wealthy soon contained volumes dealing with specifics as to dress, dining, and deportment.

As Americans marched into the 19th century, they discarded many of the social forms and practices of the Old World. Ordinary people believed that they could make themselves into whatever they wanted to be. The idea was that any man could become a gentleman. Until the time of the Civil

War, there was a flood of home-grown etiquette advice books. Americans wanted to learn the rules of behavior that would enable them to move comfortably in society.

After the Civil War came the era of the robber barons, the steel and railroad magnates, merchant princes, Napoleons of finance. A new nobility was created, the most prominent of which were called the "Four Hundred." The old simplicities of society were overturned by these new plutocrats, who turned to what has been called "conspicuous consumption." Ordinary people followed their activities avidly, mostly through "society" columns of the newspapers. Magazines, particularly women's magazines, devoted space to "deportment departments." Newspapers began running etiquette columns, and advice to the lovelorn columns also often included advice on proper, or at least acceptable, behavior.

The dining room became an arena for conspicuous consumption, with a bewildering display of goblets, plates, and silverware. The etiquette of the ballroom was complex and severe. Formal introductions were imperative, and the style and form of the dances themselves were strictly prescribed.

In the first half of the 20th century, the rules of etiquette again loosened. There seemed to be a national consensus that appropriate behavior could be simpler, more spontaneous, more genuine. But there was still some concern with correct behavior. Good manners, fitting in, dressing right, and being part of the crowd were still vitally important. Advice columns and magazine features on behavior remained popular, although the approach was perhaps more chatty than instructional.

But then came the 1960s, the hippies, the drug culture, long hair, longer dresses, denim, and disobedience. There was a pronounced decline in the popularity of books and magazine articles written on etiquette. In an era of rebellion, it was deemed unworthy even of protests. But even in those years, experts on etiquette emerged and were, if not honored, at least consulted.

And now, as America approaches the 21st century, this desire for knowledge and advice on behavior continues, but the wish to acquire information about etiquette is more sharply focused than ever before. Career-oriented people have come to realize that social skills often equal or surpass technical skills in importance. The "social scene" is often merged with the world of work. The arenas in which we are judged by our behavior are no longer primarily the ballroom and the dining room but the boardroom and the marketplace and, as our world shrinks, the international stage.

Adapted from *The Complete Idiot's Guide to Etiquette* by Mary Mitchell with John Corr, Alpha Books, 1996, pages 4–9.

Photo courtesy of Don Ward

Vacations

Discussion and Composition

1. Discussion: Preliminary Outline for the Composition (prewriting stage)

Subject: *An Invitation to Visit* (name of country)
(This is a letter (or email) recommending that a friend or classmate visit a country of your choice.)

Outline *(To be placed on the board.* *Books are closed.)*	*Discussion* *(Ideas, Grammar and Usage, Vocabulary,* *Elements of Composition Building)*
	Note: The address and the date are at the top left side of the paper.
Opening of the letter: Dear _____,	This opening begins at the left-hand margin. A comma is used with the opening of a friendly letter.
Introduction: greeting	Suggestions: give some friendly greeting such as: Hi, How are you? Or, refer to a letter received from your friend.
Transitional lead-in from the greeting to the visit you are suggesting Invitation to the country	I would like to invite you to visit _____. Or, I would enjoy having you come to_____.
Suggestion that your friend visit	Explain that you will be there at the time of the suggested visit. Please come to see me. You can be my guest. I will accompany you for all or part of your trip.

I. Tell why your friend would enjoy visiting the country
    A. The people
    B. The attractions and where they are found
	Opening sentence of paragraph: mention the subject, *enjoyment of the country*
	friendly, hospitable, helpful, unhurried
	Natural attractions:
	    good climate
	    mountains, beaches, lakes, waterfalls, canyons, volcanoes
	Recreational attractions:
	    sports: swimming, boating, fishing, camping, hunting

Historical and religious attractions:
    castles, palaces, monuments,
      archaeological ruins, old towns,
      churches, cathedrals, shrines,
      temples, statues

Cultural attractions:
    concerts, plays, dance, museum
      exhibitions

Handicrafts (handmade products) which your
    friend can buy at a good price:
    pottery, ceramics, leather goods, jewelry,
    copperware, brassware, silverware,
    clothes, fabrics

Grammar:

that clause after *recommend, suggest:*
    I recommend that you visit this market.
    vs. I recommend this market to you.
    I suggest that you visit these interesting
      places.
    vs. I want to suggest some interesting
      places to you.

Gerunds after verbs like *appreciate, enjoy,
    avoid*

II. Special advice about the trip   Opening sentence of paragraph: mention the
  A. What to bring   subject, *advice*
    1. Clothes: kind and quantity   For the weather
        For recreational, touring activities

    2. Documents: passport, visa, etc.
  B. Precautions   What to avoid doing or saying
Conclusion: repeat the invitation and   Ask if and when your friend will come.
welcome your friend   Refer again to your friend's enjoyment of
      the country.
    Welcome him or her.

Closing of the letter: The closing begins at the left margin.
Choices: Sincerely,   Use a comma after the closing.
      Your friend,   Use an initial capital only for the first word.
      Yours,   These closings reveal degrees of friendship.
      With kind/warm regards,   *Sincerely* is used for someone who is
      Affectionately,   not so well known. *Affectionately* and
      Love,   *Love* are used for a relative or a very good
    friend (more likely to be used by a
    woman).

213

2. Composition (to be done before or after the grammar practice)

A. Organizing the Composition

Before writing your composition, fill in the required information on this organizational work sheet. The work sheet follows the preliminary outline used for the discussion. Guidance for writing each paragraph is given at the right side of this work sheet. The pages of the discussion outline provide additional help for the composition.

You may use phrases on this work sheet except where it calls for full sentences.

Organizational Work Sheet
(Preliminary notes for the composition)

Title of the composition _____
(Do not use quotation marks or a period for a title at the top of the page. Use initial capital letters for the first word of the title and for all other words except articles, prepositions, and coordinate conjunctions *[and, or, but]*.)

(Street address) _____   Single line spaces (on the computer)

(City) _____

(Date) _____   The information goes at the top left side of the paper.

(Opening of the letter)

Dear _____ ,   Four line spaces down from the date (on the computer)

Opening begins at the left hand margin.

A comma is used with the opening of an informal or personal letter.

Introduction: greeting
Opening sentence of paragraph _____   Two line spaces down (on the computer)

_____

_____

_____

_____

Transitional lead-in from the greeting in the introduction to the visit you are suggesting

_____

_____

_____

_____

_____

Same paragraph as the introduction, or a new one

Include an invitation to be with you.

I. Tell why your friend would enjoy visiting the country.
   Opening sentence of paragraph _____

_____

_____

_____

_____

New paragraph

Mention the subject, *enjoyment of the country.* (Point I may be more than one paragraph.)

   Reasons for enjoyment
   A. The people _____

_____

_____

   B. The attractions_____

_____

_____

_____

_____

Start giving the kinds of attractions and where they are found in the country.

II. Special advice about the trip
    Opening sentence of paragraph _____

_____

_____

_____

_____

_____

_____

New paragraph

Mention the subject, *advice.* (Point II may be more than one paragraph.)

A. What to bring _____

_____

_____

_____

_____

_____

B. Precautions _____

_____

_____

_____

_____

_____

Conclusion: repeat the invitation and welcome your
friend. _____   New paragraph

_____

_____

_____

_____

_____

(Closing of the letter)

_____   Use a comma after the
closing.
Use an initial capital letter
only for the first word.

B. Writing a 400/500-Word Composition

Write the composition based on your notes on the organizational work sheet. Be careful of your paragraphing. Use separate paragraphs for your introduction and your conclusion. (Long paragraphs may be broken in two at appropriate places, but single-sentence paragraphs should be avoided.)

Below is the form for a personal letter or email that is printed on a computer. Follow this form whether your letter is done on a computer or handwritten. Use double line spacing in the body (contents) of the letter to allow room for corrections.

(Leave space for a top margin.)

(your street address) _____ (Use single line spaces for the address.)

(city) _____

(date) _____

(Allow a few blank lines between the date and the greeting.)

Dear _____,

(Enter contents of the letter here.)

        Your friend,

or Sincerely,

or Yours,

or Affectionately,

or Love,

C. Correcting/Rewriting the Composition (peer review)

When you bring your composition to class, you will be asked to exchange it with that of another student.

First check the other student's development of the composition, then check the items listed under Editing.

1. Development of the Composition
Introduction and Conclusion
Transitional lead-in
Paragraphs—opening sentences and supporting details
Are these well done, or can you suggest ways to improve them? Write your
    comments on the student's composition.

2. Editing
Grammar
Usage (spelling and punctuation)
Vocabulary
For grammar and usage, the information under Symbol Chart for Correction
    of Compositions in the Appendix can be helpful.

When the peer review is over, hand in your composition to your teacher, who will return it to you later with additional comments and correction symbols used for the mistakes. Then you will be asked to rewrite the composition, taking into account what your fellow student and what your teacher suggested for the improvement of the composition.

After you have revised your composition, hand it in to your teacher together with your first draft.

☑ Grammar Practice

Exercise 1: Participles in Main Verbs— *-ing* and *-ed*

The *-ing*, *-ed* participial forms of verbs are used with auxiliaries from be (*is, are, was, were*, etc.) to express action in progress or passive action.

> *-ing* participle: expresses action *in progress*
>> They are *loading* the boat now.

> *-ed* participle: expresses *passive* action
>> The boat was *loaded* yesterday.
>> (active: They loaded the boat yesterday.)

With irregular verbs, the third principal part (find, found, *found*) corresponds to the *-ed* participle.

> Many types of tropical plants are *found* in our forests.

If the verb expresses both progressive and passive action, the word *being* comes before the *-ed* participle.

> The boat is *being loaded* now.
> (active: They are loading the boat now.)

Use the correct form of the verb in parentheses. Remember that with the auxiliary *be:* (1) the *-ing* participle expresses action in progress; (2) the *-ed* participle expresses passive action.

1. Our tourist guide is (take) _taking_ care of everything.

2. You are (invite) _invited_ to stay at my home when you visit my city.

3. While you are (prepare) _____ for your trip, read the travel brochures I sent you.

4. We will be (spend) _____ several days at this beautiful beach.

5. You will be (impress) _____ by the handiwork of these people.

6. In a few days we will be (stroll) _____ along the Pacific shore.

7. Many colorful birds can be (see) _____ in our jungles.

8. You will be (interest) _____ in our ancient architecture.

9. A lot of money is (be) _____ (spend) _____ by my country to improve our roads.

10. The buildings were once (destroy) _____ by an earthquake and were (rebuild) _____ many years ago.

11. A sweater or coat must be (wear) _____ when you go up this mountain.

12. A subway was (be) _____ (construct) _____, but the work was (stop) _____ for lack of money.

13. Our government has been (try) _____ for a long time to attract more tourists.

Exercise 2: Participles as Adjectives

The *-ing* and *-ed* participles may also be used as *adjectives.* Thus, from the sentence:

The dances *excited* the spectators.

We derive:

the *exciting* dances   *-ing* is used with the *subject* and tells
(active)   who or what is *causing* the action

the *excited* spectators   *-ed* is used with the *object* and tells who
(passive)   or what is *receiving* the action

Use the correct *-ing* or *-ed* adjectives based on the verb in each sentence.

1. Our mountains have always *astonished* tourists.
   our _____*astonishing*_____ mountains   _____*astonished*_____ tourists

2. The customs of these people *interest* visitors.
   the _____ customs   _____ visitors
   of these people

3. The cathedral *amazed* the sightseers.
   the _____ sightseers   the _____ cathedral

4. The walk usually *tires* the hikers.

the _____ walk   the _____ hikers

5. The experience *satisfied* the travelers.

the _____ experience   the _____ travelers

6. The poverty of the people *shocked* the tour group.

the _____ tour group   the _____ poverty
                                        of the people

7. The visit of the tourists *surprised* the villagers.

the _____ villagers   the _____ visit of
                                        the tourists

Exercise 3: Participles in Reduced Adjective and Adverbial Clauses

A. Verbs in some clauses may be reduced to *-ing* or *-ed* forms. The subject and a form of *be* may be omitted with a progressive or passive verb in an adjective or adverbial clause.

Adjective Clause:	*progressive:* **The people (who are) living in this region are very friendly.** *passive:* **The pottery (which is) made in this town is of very fine quality.**
Adverbial Clause:	*progressive:* **While (they were) traveling in the East, they bought some antique jewelry.** *passive:* **Although (they were) warned about the dangers of the trip, they decided to go to the jungle anyway.**

Reduce the adjective clauses or adverbial clauses by omitting their subject and a form of *be*.

1. The sights which are waiting for you in Alaska will astound you.

   The sights waiting for you in Alaska will astound you.

2. While they were wandering through the town, they were entertained by several mariachi bands.

   While wandering through the town, they were entertained by several mariachi bands.

3. This hotel offers gracious hospitality which is unmatched anywhere in the country.

   _____

4. Although they were advised to check most of their money with the hotel, they took a large sum of money with them when they went shopping.

   _____

5. Anyone who is looking for a chance to gamble will find lots of casinos in Las Vegas.

   _____

6. While you are eating dinner, you will enjoy a fantastic floor show.

   _____

7. The local people who are strolling along the beach will greet you pleasantly.

   _____

8. The cliffs which are located along the coast are very steep.

   _____

9. If you are given the opportunity, you should certainly make a side trip to see our famous rain forest.

   _____

B. The -*ing* reduction may also be made with active verbs that do not use the auxiliary *be*.

| Adjective Clause: | Anyone visiting (from *who visits*) our country will want to return. |
| Adverbial Clause: | Before coming (from *you come*) to our country, you should look over the travel brochures. |

Change the words in parentheses into a reduced adjective clause or a reduced adverbial clause.

1. Near San Francisco, you will visit a modern castle (it, contain, many works of art).

   Near San Francisco, you will visit a modern castle containing many works of art.

2. While (you, visit, New York), you must be sure to go to a performance at the Lincoln Center for the Performing Arts.

   While visiting New York, you must be sure to go to a performance at the Lincoln Center for the Performing Arts.

3. After (you, see, amazing, sights, that, our town, offer), you will enjoy a fabulous dinner in your hotel.

   _____

4. Since (they, discover, wonderful, marketplace, outside the town), they have bought many handsome things from the local artisans.

   _____

5. Anyone (the person, not wish, take, the side trip, to the canyon) should inform the tour director.

   _____

6. Before (they, leave, for, their trip), they got as much information as possible about the countries they were visiting.

   _____

7. Until (I, come, New York), I had never been to a circus.

   _____

223

8. While (I, watch, clowns, acrobats, aerialists, animals, perform), I realized how much enjoyment I had been missing in my life.

_____

9. Although (they, not stay, that hotel), the visiting couple took advantage of all its facilities.

_____

10. Some of the people (they, collect, tickets, in, this off-Broadway theater) are also the performers in the play.

_____

Exercise 4: Gerunds after Verbs

Some verbs may be followed by the *-ing* form (gerund) of other verbs.
When you come to this country you should *avoid discussing* politics.

The more common verbs of this type are:

anticipate	miss
appreciate	postpone
avoid	practice
consider (meaning keep	put off
in mind, think	recommend
favorably about)	regret (for the past)*
delay	remember (for the past)†
enjoy	risk
finish	stop
look forward to	suggest
mind	

These verbs also take simple noun objects.

When you come to this country, you should avoid *any discussion* about politics.

---

* *Regret* is followed by the infinitive when it does not refer to past time: We regret to inform you that the trip has been canceled.
† *Remember* is followed by the infinitive when it means "remind oneself about something in the future": We must remember to buy tickets for the ballet once we arrive in town.

A. Change the italicized noun objects to *-ing* objects after the verbs.

1. You may risk *the loss of your money* if you do not keep it in a safe place.

    You may risk losing your money if you do not keep it in a safe place.

2. I am greatly anticipating *your travel with me*. (keep *your*)

    _____

3. I hope you will consider *a stay with me* in my favorite town for a while.

    _____

4. You must not delay *your phone reservation*. (add *make*)

    _____

5. I recommend *traveler's checks*. (add *bring*)

    _____

6. After you practice *the use of the surfboard*, you will enjoy *the ride on the waves*.

    _____

7. The archaeological expedition stopped *the exploration of these ruins* for a while.

    _____

8. I suggest *an evening flight*. (add *take*)

    _____

9. Do you mind *a late arrival at our hotel*?

    _____

10. They finished *the construction of this highway* a short time ago.

    _____

11. I'll always remember *the sight of the sunset at Waikiki Beach*. (Use *see* for the verb.)

    _____

B. Complete the following sentences using *-ing* verbs after the italicized verbs. Use real sentences about a visit to the country you selected.

1. In this country a visitor should *avoid* _____ *talking about politics* _____.

   or

   _____ *walking in the streets at night* _____.

2. When you visit _____, you should *consider* (= think favorably about)

   _____.

3. When you are preparing to come to _____, I *suggest* _____

   _____.

4. When you get there, you will *appreciate* _____

   _____.

5. To avoid getting sick while you are traveling, I *recommend* _____

   _____.

6. In this country, you will *enjoy* _____

   _____.

7. You can relax in my favorite town. You can *stop*_____

   _____.

8. While you are there, you must not *miss* _____

   _____.

9. The weather is very nice now. Don't *postpone* _____

   _____.

Exercise 5: *would rather* vs. *had better*

Auxiliaries that are sometimes confused are *would rather* and *had better*. Keep in mind that *would rather* means *prefer*, and *had better* means *should* in the sense of advisability. The contraction for both *had* and *would* as auxiliaries is *'d*.

would rather	If you'd rather come by train than by plane, then leave a day earlier.
(= prefer)	(*Choices* are involved; the second choice often begins with *than*.)
had better *(= should)*	You'd better bring warm clothes with you if you want to be comfortable in the mountains. (*advice*, sometimes a warning)

Note that these auxiliaries are followed by the infinitive forms without *to*. *Would rather* has a past time, *would rather have*.

I would rather have gone to the mountains than to the beach.

(My preference was for the mountains, but I went to the beach instead.)

Had better has no past time.

Both auxiliaries are made negative by placing *not* right after them.

I'd rather not take a long trip at this time.

You'd better not take a long trip at this time.

A. Use *had better, would rather,* or *would rather have* with the words in parentheses. Do not use *to* after these auxiliaries.

1. If you (take) <u>would rather take</u> a cruise than go swimming, I'll make a reservation on the boat for you.

2. You (telephone) <u>had better telephone</u> me when you arrive in my country.

3. I'm sure you (have) _____ someone reliable go with you to the marketplace than go alone.

4. You (take) _____ a first aid kit with you.

5. I (relax-*past*) _____ more than rushed around seeing so many things.

227

6. We (take) _____ a taxi if we don't want to miss our plane.

7. I (take) _____ a taxi than a bus to get to the airport.

8. You (not bring) _____ much luggage if you plan to go camping.

9. If you (not go) _____ sightseeing in the city, then bring only sports clothes with you.

10. You (not go) _____ boating if the weather is bad.

11. I (stay) _____ at a hotel than inconvenience your family by staying at your home.

12. You (come) _____ next month when I can be with you.

13. Yesterday, I (visit-past) _____ Versailles than stayed in Paris.

B. Use five sentences for each of the following.

1. Tell what a person *had better do* if he or she comes to the selected country as a visitor.

    Anyone who visits _____ had better get a visa.

2. Tell what you *would rather do* if you visit another country.

    If I visit another country, I would rather see the impressive architectural sights than the cities and towns.

Exercise 6: Word Forms

Use the correct form of the word in parentheses, and complete the unfinished words.

1. My (suggest) _suggestion_ is that you come by plane.

2. Check the plane schedules (careful) _____ for the times of (depart) _____ and (arrive) _____ of your plane.

3. My (recommend) _____ is that you take as little lug-_____ as possible.

4. If you follow my advi-_____ you'll be able to see some very (beauty) _____ (nature) _____ (scene) _____.

5. The people are very hospit-_____, (friend) _____, and (honesty) _____. They will help make your trip very (comfort) _____ and (enjoy) _____.

6. You'll find a good (describe) _____ of this cathedral in the travel folder. It also gives an (explain) _____ of its (religion) _____ and (history) _____ significance.

7. In this region you'll see many (architecture) _____ remains of an ancient (civil) _____.

8. Water (ski) _____ and (surf) _____ are very popular sports at this beach.

9. You will be greatly impressed by the (tropic) _____ (plants) in the country.

10. From the top of this mountain you will get a (panorama) _____ view that is breathtak-_____.

11. In that market, you can buy some very (color) _____ carpets and ceram-_____.

12. We will go dancing in a club that accommo- _____ 500 people.

13. Some regions that are good for our (recreate) _____ activities are too (mountain) _____ for (farm) _____.

Exercise 7: Sentence Review

Make full sentences from the word groups below and complete the unfinished words. Make whatever changes or additions are needed, but do not change the word order. Use commas, semicolons, or periods wherever necessary. Use the tense given at the beginning of each word group.

1. (present) Our beaches / consider / most beautiful / continent.

    Our beaches are considered the most beautiful on the continent.

2. (present) Many color- / birds / can see / our jungles.

    _____

3. (present) A lot of money / spend / now / improve / our roads.

    _____

4. (present) You / may see / all kinds / interest- / sights / this village.

    _____

5. (future) While / eat / dinner / you enjoy / fantastic / floor show.

_____

6. (present) Cliffs / locate / along / coast / be / very steep.

_____

7. (present) Before / come / the country / you / should look over / travel brochures.

_____

8. (future) Near / San Francisco / you visit / modern / castle / contain / many works of art.

_____

9. (present) Anyone / not wish / take / side trip / should inform / tour director.

_____

10. (past) After / delay / two hours / train / finally / pull / into / station.

_____

11. (past) Before / go / into / desert / they / never / realize / how / beautiful / it / can be.

_____

12. (present) You / may risk / lose / your money / if / you / not keep / it / safe place.

_____

13. (present) I / suggest / you / visit / ruins / castle. (give 2 possibilities)

_____

14. (present) It / recommended / tourists / not drink / water in the small villages.

_____

15. (future) You / be / greatly / impress- / by / tropic- / plants / the country.

_____

▷ Extra Speaking and Writing Practice

Exercise 8: Spelling—Doubling Final Consonants before Added Vowels

A final consonant is doubled if:

   (1) a syllable beginning with a *vowel* is added; and

   (2) the word originally ends in *one* consonant preceded by *one* vowel; and

   (3) the stress is on the syllable where the doubling of the consonant might occur.

      Examples: *plánned, rúnning, occúrred*

Do not double the consonant if:

   (1) a syllable beginning with a *consonant* is added: *develop + ment = development;* or

   (2) the original word ends in a *vowel: dine + ing = dining;* or

   (3) the original word ends in *two consonants* or has *two vowels:*

        bend + ing = bending,

        rain + ing = raining; or

   (4) the stress is not on the syllable where the doubling of the consonant might occur.

        develop + ed = devéloped

Note: For this spellling rule, *y* is regarded as a vowel.

Rewrite the words, adding the required endings.

pót + ery	*pottery*	bénefit + ed	
begín + er		bíg + est	
drúg + ist		múd + y	
súffer + ing		ráin + ing	
shíp + ed		equíp + ed	
occúr + ence		equíp + ment	
shín + ing		márvel + ous	
límit + ed		cáncel + ed	
wráp + ed		díagram + ing	
sún + y		wórship + er	

Note: British usage doubles some *l*'s, *p*'s, or *m*'s before added vowels.

Exercise 9: Business Letter to a Tourist Office

You would like to travel to a particular foreign country for your vacation. Write or email a letter to the tourist office to get information for your trip.

Some of the things you might ask about are:

- interesting places to visit (tourist offices usually have brochures that describe such places)

- the airlines that go to that country

- the travel regulations (inoculations, what you may bring in or take out of the country, etc.)

- the currency of the country

Thank the tourist office for the information you are requesting.

Business correspondence should be typed. Follow this basic format for a typed letter. If you use email, you may need to modify the form.

Your street address   (Use single line spacing for the address.)
Your city, state, zip code
(Country, if needed)
Date

(skip a few lines)

Name of tourist office
Street address (make one up)
New York, NY 10003
USA (if needed)

(skip a line)

Dear Sir or Madam:

(skip a line)

_____

_____

_____

(Use single line spacing within the body of a business letter. Leave a two-line space between paragraphs.)

Very truly yours,

(skip a few lines)

(sign your name in this space)
(type your name.)

Exercise 10: Composition with Descriptive Paragraphs

Write two separate paragraphs describing the same scene of nature. *Each paragraph should be written from only your own particular viewpoint as you witness the scene.* The first paragraph should be an objective description, the second paragraph a subjective one that includes your feelings.

1. Objective Description. In this paragraph tell only what you see as you walk or drive along. For example, for mountains, note whether they are high or low, whether they are covered with vegetation or are bare of vegetation. For lower land, note whether it is a valley, whether it is flat or rolling land, or whether it is hilly or rocky land. Note the kind of vegetation (trees, flowers), farmland, buildings, and animals. For bodies of water (rivers, lakes, oceans), note the size (large or small, narrow or wide). You might mention the kind of movement of the water (waves, current) and the color of the water. You might also describe what is on the water (boats, canoes) and what is on the shores.

2. Subjective Description. In this paragraph describe the same scene of nature in a more colorful way. Your words should express your emotional reaction to the scene.

Here are some terms from travel brochures that can be helpful to you with a subjective description. However, do not use too many of them, since an overuse of such emotionally charged words will make your description sound exaggerated or insincere.

Adjectives: spectacular, breathtaking, unique, picturesque, splendid, exciting, enchanting, fantastic, thrilling, majestic, delightful

Adjectives plus Nouns: scenic view, colorful landscape, sun-drenched beaches, sparkling lakes, quaint villages, unspoiled natural beauty, panoramic view, indescribable beauty

Exercise 11: Journal Writing

Write a journal entry on the following subject. Write freely since you are the only one who will see this entry.

Write about some place in your country or in another country that you would like to visit. Consider the natural beauty, cultural attractions, and historic significance.

Now use your journal entry as the basis for a more careful letter to friend. This letter is to be handed in to your teacher.

◎ Listening-Writing Practice

Exercise 12: Dictation

Your teacher will dictate the paragraph three times. The first time is for listening only, the second time is for writing, and the third time is for checking what you have written.

Immediately after you give your teacher the dictation you have written, check the dictation in the book for any problems you had in writing it.

> New Orleans, located in southern Louisiana, near the mouth of the Mississippi River, attracts more than one million tourists a year. Especially appealing to visitors is the French Quarter, where the houses still retain their Old World charm. New Orleans has a reputation for excellent food, with many restaurants, some world famous, serving seafood from nearby waters. The greatest number of tourists come to New Orleans to join in the merrymaking that takes place on Mardi Gras. For about a week in February the streets overflow with people, many in masks and costumes. People dance in the streets to music that is everywhere. They witness spectacular parades with elaborate floats that are accompanied by bands. Another great attraction for tourists is New Orleans jazz, which originated in the late 19th century and has become world famous.

Exercise 13: Dicto-comp

Take notes as your teacher reads the dicto-comp to you several times. Then reconstruct the dicto-comp from your notes. The dicto-comp does not need to be written exactly as you heard it, but it should be grammatically correct.

Before you write the dicto-comp, your teacher may ask the class to get together in groups to check with each other on what you heard.

Immediately after you give your teacher the dicto-comp you have written, check the dicto-comp in the book for any problems you had in writing it.

> Dear Teresa,
>
> How wonderful to get your letter yesterday with the good news that you'll be able to visit me in New York City this summer. There are so many great things to see and do here. It's true, as they say, that the city never sleeps.
>
> One thing we must do is get to the Times Square area to see some Broadway plays. Our city has tried very hard to improve this area, and it is now much safer than it used to be.
>
> We'll also go to some performances at Lincoln Center—maybe a ballet, the opera, or a concert. The Center itself is very beautiful. The buildings surround a splendid fountain, where we can sit and admire the fantastic Chagall murals of the Metropolitan Opera House.

Another opportunity we mustn't miss is a visit to the world-famous Metropolitan Museum. It's so large and grand that we could spend days there.

I also want you to enjoy some of our natural attractions. We'll go rowing in the big lake in Central Park, right in the heart of Manhattan. We'll even take the subway to Brooklyn to visit our beautiful Botanical Gardens, and if you like we'll take a swim at the beach of our fabulous Coney Island.

One day when the weather is good, we can go to see the famous Statue of Liberty. From the ferry that takes us there, we can get a wonderful view of downtown Manhattan.

There's so much more to see and do, but I'll tell you about them when I see you.

Since you're coming in the summer, bring lightweight, casual clothes. Don't bring too much, because you can buy almost anything you would like in New York—cheaper clothes in discount stores or more expensive ones in the large, upscale stores.

Of course you can stay with me. I have a comfortable sleeper-sofa in the living room. I'm very close to the subway so we can get around the city easily.

Let me know exactly when you're coming. I'm really looking forward to your visit.

With warm regards,
Anna

 # Reading-Writing Practice (summary: "Travel in Hawaii")

You are going to write a one to three paragraph summary of a reading selection. A summary is a restatement, in shortened form, of the main ideas of a selection.

In preparation for the summary, skim through the selection quickly to determine the way the ideas are developed (through comparison, contrast, listing, time, space, or example). Then reread the selection carefully, underlining the important points that should be included in the summary. (Do not underline too much.)

In writing the summary, use your own words as much as possible. You may include the important words from the reading selection, but use quotation marks around whole phrases taken directly from the selection.

Devote more attention to the main points than to their supporting details. Omit examples unless they are important to the development of the ideas. Do *not* give your own ideas in a summary.

The selection to be summarized might have been written by a travel agency to invite tourists to vacation in Hawaii.

Travel in Hawaii

When winter comes, with its cold and snow, why not come to beautiful Hawaii, where the sun shines all year round. Our beaches are world famous, and you will be delighted by the **lush vegetation,** the breathtaking waterfalls, and the high volcanic peaks of the islands. You will see why Hawaii is truly the "**Paradise** of the Pacific."

Immediately on your arrival at the Honolulu International Airport, you will feel not only the warmth of the sun but the warmth of the people. In true **"aloha"** spirit you will be greeted with a flower **lei** and a drink from the pineapple juice fountain.

Honolulu is on the island of Oahu, where four-fifths of the Hawaiian population live. Most tourists like to spend some time at the famous Waikiki Beach in Honolulu. Waikiki has great hotels that provide many **amenities** to make your stay comfortable and enjoyable. You can spend your days on the beach sunning and swimming. At night you can have all kinds of entertainment, but you mustn't miss a **luau** on the beach. Under a splendid setting sun and fanned by delicious **balmy** breezes, you will feast on fish or roast pig, **savor** the taste of Hawaiian **poi,** and **relish** the fresh fruits of the island. You will be entertained by Hawaiian music and dance. You will get to see hula dancing, with grass-skirted dancers **rotating** their hips gracefully while telling a story with their hands. You may even be invited to join in the dancing.

The island of Oahu has other great places to see. One is the Pearl Harbor memorial to those who died during the Japanese attack that brought the United States into World War II. Another is the Honolulu campus of the University of Hawaii, with its famous East-West Center, created in 1960 to promote cultural and technical exchange. Also not to be missed is the Polynesian Cultural Center on the other side of the island. There you will be thrilled by talented performers from different parts of the South Sea Islands.

While you are in the state of Hawaii, you will certainly want to go to some of the other islands. A great favorite is the largest island, also called Hawaii or the Big Island. On this island is the Hawaii **Volcanoes** National Park, where you can view two of the most active volcanoes in the world sending up flaming curtains of lava. This park also has giant fern forests.

Another island well worth a visit is Maui. The picturesque old whaling port of Lahaina is on the west coast. This island also has the Haleakala **Crater,** the largest **dormant** volcano in the world.

The island of Molakai also attracts many visitors. Its coast rises in a series of steep **cliffs,** and there are enormously high waterfalls. The island is known in history because it once was a refuge of **lepers.**

One more island worth seeing is Kauai, called the Garden Isle because of its spectacular vegetation. A great scenic view here is the extraordinary Waimea **Canyon,** which has a steep descent of 3,000 feet.

So be sure to come to Hawaii. Come for the fun in the sun. Come for the thrilling views. Come for a great cultural experience. You will leave with unforgettable memories of your vacation in the "Paradise of the Pacific."

Vocabulary

1. **lush**—rich, abundant, luxuriant
2. **vegetation**—plant life
3. **paradise**—a place or state of great happiness
4. **aloha**—a Hawaiian word meaning love and good will. It is used as both a greeting and a farewell.
5. **lei**—a wreath of flowers and leaves, generally worn around the neck
6. **amenity**—anything that adds to one's comfort; convenience
7. **luau**—a Hawaiian feast, usually with entertainment
8. **balmy**—mild, pleasant
9. **savor**—taste or smell with enjoyment
10. **poi**—a Hawaiian food made of taro root mixed with water, cooked, and pounded into a paste
11. **relish**—enjoy the taste
12. **rotate**—make a circling movement
13. **volcano**—a vent (opening) in the earth's crust through which molten rock (lava), rock fragments, gases, ashes erupt from the earth's interior
14. **crater**—a bowl-shaped opening of a volcano
15. **dormant**—inactive
16. **cliff**—a high, steep face of rock
17. **leper**—a person with leprosy, an infectious disease that caused great deformities. Before medication became available to treat leprosy, lepers were isolated in separate communities.
18. **canyon**—a long, narrow valley between high cliffs, often with a stream flowing through it

FYI **For Your Information**
(letter written about a vacation in Japan)

This is a letter that the author wrote to a colleague in the United States while visiting in Japan. The author had been invited to visit Japan for a month by a former Japanese student who had become a friend.

___

Dear Julia,

My Japanese friend has been unbelievably kind to me during my visit with her in Japan. You wouldn't believe the many places I've been to and the many customs I've adopted. I've learned to sleep on a futon and to take my shoes off before I enter a home. I've even learned how to put on a kimono. (I have photos to prove it.)

My friend has taken me to lots of shrines and temples, with extremely beautiful gardens and ponds, many gods (big and little) and Buddhas. In front of one of the shrines in Kyoto was a huge flea market with a large section of antiques, some of which were exquisitely beautiful and very expensive. I bought a lovely Imari bowl, and I probably would have bought more if it hadn't started to rain very hard.

I was surprised to find so many of our American fast-food restaurants everywhere. I saw Wendy's, Arby's, Kentucky Fried Chicken, and McDonald's restaurants. There was a McDonald's right on the street in the Ginza, the fashionable shopping area in Tokyo. Customers were being served by girls wearing cute outfits and straw hats.

Most of the restaurants I saw displayed very realistic replicas of each dish they served. The Japanese dishes I ordered were very tastefully arranged on the plate. But the Western dishes served in some restaurants were a horror. When the food was served, exactly as in the replica, the meat was swimming in sauce, and everything looked as though it had just been slopped on the plate.

I loved one Japanese restaurant in Okayama where my friend took me for lunch. We were in one of the private rooms arranged around a rock garden in the center. The waitresses were dressed in kimonos, and the ordering was done by telephone. All these extras made the already good food taste better.

In one restaurant I had eel for the first time. I was surprised at how good it was. In another restaurant, in Kyoto, we had dinner country-style. The whole restaurant was filled with smoke coming from the stove where all the dishes were being prepared right in the seating area of the restaurant. The dishes kept coming very fast, one after the other, all washed down with the excellent beer of Japan.

We also visited some big department stores. I was quite surprised that they had food shops at the bottom level. All the food was beautifully arranged—the fresh meat, fish and produce, and the sweets. Young people were hawking their wares, and when a sale was made, the salesperson ran, not walked, to get the package wrapped and to get the change. (I also saw this kind of running by gas station attendants and by a hairdresser.) Also, in the stores there were young girls at the top and foot of the escalators telling customers to be careful, to watch their step. I was told that the employees were trained to take pride in their contribution to the company, no matter how low their position.

The Bon Festival was taking place while I was in Japan. When we were in Odawara we watched a spectacular display of fireworks. I was told that during the time of this three-day festival, the spirits of the dead come to visit relatives, and then are sent back with the fireworks. When we went to Hamamatsu, I finally got my wish to see a bon dance. Women, mostly older ones and wearing the same style of kimonos, were slowly dancing around in a circle. (A few men were also in the circle.) The children were dancing in their own inner circle. On a raised platform in the center were the musician and four dancers. A lady showed me how to dance (I was the only foreigner there), and she praised me when I got the steps right. When I left I was given boxes of crackers and two cloths with the symbols of the city.

In Hamamatsu, I was also taken to visit a Marriage Plaza. (We stopped there because I was intrigued to see that the name was in English.) Everything that was needed for an elaborate wedding was on display there. There were Western-style wedding gowns, gowns for the bridesmaids, luxurious kimonos, and all kinds of accessories—all for rent at very high prices. I also saw replicas of kinds of food to be served at a wedding, jewelry, and presents to be given to the guests. I think a fortune could be spent for weddings in Japan.

During the times we stayed in hotels, I found that no matter how expensive a hotel was, there were certain similarities. One was that the rooms were all quite small. Another was that they all provided certain amenities—a kimono, bed slippers, a toothbrush, toothpaste, and a disposable razor. There were also facilities to make tea. What they differed in was the elegance and costliness of the kimonos and the slippers.

There is much, much more I could tell you about, but I'll wait until I see you back home. I'll conclude with a story that was told to me in Japan about McDonald's. A Japanese couple took their youngster to the United States for the first time, and they went to eat at a McDonald's restaurant. The child was surprised. "Oh," he said, "they have McDonald's here, too."

With warm regards,
Marcella

Appendix

Symbol Chart for Correction of Compositions

*agree   *agreement.* Make the verb singular or plural according to the main word in the subject.

> The architecture of these buildings *is* very interesting.

If *each* or *every* is part of the subject, the verb must be singular.

> *Everybody is coming* to the party.

*ap   *apostrophe.* An apostrophe has been incorrectly added or omitted. Apostrophes are used for contractions with auxiliaries *(who's = who is)* or possessives of nouns *(the girl's hat)* but not for the possessive of pronouns *(its function, whose book)*.

*art   *article.* The article *(a, an, the)* is incorrect or omitted. Use an article with a singular countable noun. Do not use an article with a noncountable noun that stands alone *(I am studying history)*. Use *the* if the noncountable noun is followed by a modifier *(the* history *of the United States)*.

*C   *capital letter.* Correct for capitalization. Use an initial capital letter for a word referring to nationality or religion *(an Italian custom; the Catholic religion)*, a day of the week, a month, a holiday, a geographic name.

*⌢   *close up.* Join together as one word—them⌢selves.

*comp   *comparison.* Use the correct word form, preposition, pronoun, or auxiliary required in a comparison.

concl   *conclusion.* Add a conclusion, or rewrite a weak conclusion.

con   *connection.* Use an appropriate connection within a paragraph.

coor   *coordination.* Too many short sentences have been written separately or joined by *and*. Subordinate some of the sentences.

dangl   *dangling.* Correct the *-ing* or *-ed* phrase that has no subject to be attached to.

Dangling:	While *watching* TV, *her dinner* was burning on the stove.
Correction:	While she was watching TV, she didn't notice that her dinner was burning on the stove.
Or:	While she was watching TV, her dinner was burning on the stove.

*frag   *fragment.* Do not cut off a part of a sentence from the rest.

Fragment:	She has many hobbies. *For example, tennis and dancing.*
Correction	She has many hobbies, for example, tennis and dancing.
Or:	She has many hobbies. Among them are tennis and dancing.

From *Writer's Companion* by Marcella Frank, Prentice-Hall, 1983.
Note: Starred symbols indicate more elementary types of faults.

*H *hyphen.* Correct or add a hyphen within a word or at the end of a line. Do not use a hyphen at the beginning of a line.

inform *informal.* Change the informal expression to one that is more appropriate for formal English.

intro *introduction.* Add an introduction, or rewrite a weak introduction.

*neg *negative.* Avoid the use of a double negative.

Double Negative:	There isn't nobody here.
Correction:	There isn't anybody here.
Or:	There's nobody here.

*N *number (of nouns and adjectives).* Use the correct singular or plural form for a noun. Adjectives do not have any plural form except for *this* (plural *these*), *that* (plural *those*), *much* (plural *many*), *little* (plural *few*).

par *paragraph development.* The paragraph does not develop one main point, or it includes more than one point, or its main point is not sufficiently developed.

¶ *new paragraph.* This paragraph is too long, or the wording suggests that you are turning to another aspect of the point you are developing, or a new point is being made.

no ¶ *no new paragraph.* The paragraph is very closely related to the one that precedes it. Avoid single sentence paragraphs.

// *parallelism.* Use the same grammatical form for word groups connected by words like *and, or, than.*

Fault in Parallelism:	The girl promised to stay home that week and that she would study for her tests.
Correction:	The girl promised to stay home that week and to study for her tests.

prep *preposition.* Correct the preposition fault.

*pro *pronoun.* Correct the pronoun fault. The fault may be:
1. an incorrect form of the pronoun
2. a confusion between *it* and *there*
3. a vague or unclear reference of a pronoun
4. a change in pronoun number (singular or plural)
5. a shift in person *(we, you, one)* in a general statement
6. an unnecessary pronoun

*p *punctuation.* Correct the punctuation. Watch especially for a comma or a semicolon that has been added or omitted. Correct a run-on sentence (two sentences incorrectly joined into one by a comma or no punctuation) by using a period or a semicolon.

Run-on:	I will have to read more in college, consequently I will improve my reading skill.
Correction:	I will have to read more in college; consequently I will improve my reading skill.

repet	*repetitious.* Cut out the unnecessary expressions or ideas that repeat what has already been said.
***SS**	*sentence structure.* Supply the missing subject, verb, or object. Or correct the form of a phrase used as a subject or an object.
***sp**	*spelling.* Use the correct spelling. Observe the rules for doubling final consonants, keeping or dropping final *e,* changing *y* to *i,* combining the letters *i* and *e.*
***trans**	*transition.* Rewrite the opening sentence of the paragraph so that it connects with the preceding paragraph or so that it makes the point of the paragraph clear.
	lead-in transition. Add a connection, or rewrite a weak connection between the general statements of the introduction and the beginning of the specific topic of the composition.
vague	*vague.* Make the expression or the statement more specific in relation to the point being made.
***V**	*verb.* Use the correct verb tense, verb form, or auxiliary.

Form: be + _____ -*ing* (progressive)   will
             be + _____ -*ed* (passive)   do
             have + _____ -*ed* (perfect tenses)   may + _____ -(no ending)
                                              must
                                              can
                                              should

	Use the *-ing* form of a verb after a preposition.
***WF**	*word form.* Use the correct ending for the word (determined by the word's part of speech function in the sentence).
***WO**	*word order.* use the correct word order for: questions and indirect questions, adverbials, adjectives.
	Do not separate a verb and its object.
	Reverse the word order.
wordy	*wordy.* Remove the excessive wording that has been used for the idea being expressed
***WW**	*wrong word.* Choose the exact word for the intended meaning.

Punctuation Rules

1. Commas in sentences with introductory or final grammatical elements

A comma is generally used after an introductory element, especially if this element is long or if the writer would normally pause at this point in speech. A comma after a short introductory element is optional.

Words: *Finally*(,)[*] they were able to take their trip around the world.

Phrases: *As a matter of fact,* they went on the trip sooner than they had expected.

Clauses: *Before they left,*[†] their friends gave them a big party.

There are some types of introductory phrases that require commas.

Hoping to see as much as possible, they planned their itinerary carefully. (participial phrase)

Happy to be leaving at last, they boarded the plane with great anticipation. (adjective phrase)

The weather causing no problems, they had a comfortable flight. (absolute construction)

Final elements are less likely to be set off by commas, especially those indicating time. However, as with introductory elements, a pause in speech determines whether a comma will be used.

Words: They realized their dream *unexpectedly.*

Phrases: They realized their dream *in an unexpected manner.*

Clauses: Their wish came true *when they unexpectedly inherited some money.*

The same elements that require commas at the beginning of the sentence also require commas when they appear at the end of the sentence.

They planned their itinerary carefully, *hoping to see as much as possible.* (participial phrase)

They boarded the plane with great anticipation, *happy to be leaving at last.* (adjective phrase)

They had a comfortable flight, *the weather causing no problems.* (absolute construction)

From *Writer's Companion* by Marcella Frank, Prentice-Hall, 1983.

[*] The parentheses around a mark of punctuation indicate that the punctuation is optional.

[†] The comma is required after the short introductory element in this sentence to avoid a temporary misreading as "Before they left their friends."

2. Commas in sentences with interrupting elements

Since interrupting elements are regarded as parenthetic, commas are placed on *both sides* of the elements.

A. Adverbial elements

Words: His father, *fortunately,* was very rich.

Phrases: His father, *as a matter of fact,* was very rich.

Clauses: His father, *as I've been told,* was very rich.

If a short word or phrase is felt to be closely related to the rest of the sentence, the commas may be omitted.

Their wish *finally* came true.

B. Nonrestrictive structures

An adjective structure that follows a noun may either narrow down (that is, restrict) the reference of the noun, or it may only add more information about the noun without identifying it further. *Those structures that do not identify their nouns are considered nonrestrictive and require commas.*

Note the difference in punctuation in the following sentences.

Restrictive—No Commas
Land which is surrounded by water is an island. (The noun *land* is a general (class) word. It is identified by *which is surrounded by water.*)

Nonrestrictive—Commas on Both Sides
Manhattan, which is surrounded by water, is an island. (The noun *Manhattan* is already identified by name, so *which is surrounded by water* does not limit its identity further.)

The same punctuation rule applies to participial phrases, which may be considered shortened forms of *who* or *which* clauses.

Restrictive: Land *surrounded by water* is an island.

Nonrestrictive: Manhattan, *surrounded by water,* is an island.

Other shortened forms of nonrestrictive *who* or *which* clauses also require commas if the nouns they refer to are already identified by name.

The Palace, *a very expensive restaurant,* serves only the best food.

The Palace, *famous for its fine food,* is a very expensive restaurant.

The nonrestrictive phrase can also be moved to the beginning of the sentence.

Surrounded by water, Manhattan is an island.

3. Commas and semicolons in combined independent sentences

A. Comma

The boy was sick, *so* he didn't go to school.	When connectives like *so, and, but,* and *or* (coordinate conjunctions) join sentences, a comma is used. The comma may be omitted if both sentences are short.

B. Semicolon

The boy was sick; he didn't go to school.	No connective joins the sentences.
The boy was sick; *therefore*(,) he didn't go to school.	Adverbials like *therefore, however, otherwise, moreover* (conjunctive adverbs) can connect the sentences. These adverbials may take other positions in the second part of the sentence, but *the semicolon remains in the position where the period might have been written.*

4. Commas and quotation marks in direct speech

Quotation marks are used around the words of direct speech, and commas separate these words from phrases like *he said, they asked.*

> Someone in the audience shouted, "That's a crazy idea."

> She asked her husband, "Why can't we move to a better neighborhood?"

Note the following:

- the comma after *shouted* and *husband;*
- the position of the quotation marks—both the opening and closing quotes are near the top of the letters;
- the position of the final period and the question mark—these are *inside* the closing quotation mark;
- the use of a capital letter for the first word of the direct speech.

Phrases like *he said* and *they asked* are also set off with commas where they appear in the middle or at the end of the quoted speech.

> "Why," she asked, "can't we move to a better neighborhood?"

> "That's a crazy idea," someone in the audience shouted.

5. Unacceptable commas

A. A comma should not be placed between the subject-verb-complement center of the sentence.

(1) Between a subject and a predicate

Unacceptable: The fact that there are a few exceptions, does not disprove his theory.

Such an unnecessary comma often appears at the end of a restrictive adjective clause, which should not be punctuated with commas at all.

Unacceptable: People who love their freedom, are willing to fight for it.

(2) Between a verb and its complement

The most common fault here is to place a comma between the verb and the word that introduces a noun clause object.

Unacceptable: Everyone in the same room said, that he was guilty.
I don't know, why he did it.

B. An interrupting adverbial element that has a comma on one side should have a comma on the other side as well.

Unacceptable: Astrology as everyone knows, deals with the influence of the heavenly bodies on human lives. (This sentence requires another comma before *as*.)

C. A comma should not be used between two sentences that have been joined into one with either no connecting word or with an adverbial such as *therefore, however, for example, in other words.* Such unacceptable sentences are called *run-on* sentences.

Run-on Sentence: The people in my country are friendly and honest, a visitor doesn't have to be afraid of anything.

I will have to read more in college, consequently I will improve my reading skill.

Sometimes even the comma is omitted in a combined sentence.

Run-on Sentence: Manhattan is an unusual island it's close enough to the

East Coast to be connected by several bridges.

Run-on sentences can be corrected by placing a semicolon or a period where the two sentences come together.

D. A comma should not be put after a subordinate conjunction.

Unacceptable: I do not believe in astrology although, I find it very interesting.

6. Unacceptable semicolons

Most unacceptable semicolons cut off a part of a sentence instead of joining two sentences into one. Such faults can be corrected by *changing the semicolon to a comma.*

The following are examples of the most common types of final elements that are unacceptably cut off with semicolons instead of commas.

> His secretary has worked overtime for several days; hoping to finish all the work she has to do.

> The transit workers in the city went on strike; the result being that many people could not get to their places of employment.

> Some people get most of their news from the newspapers; while (or whereas) others

> get their information mainly from television.

> I want an education that will broaden my outlook on life; an education that will help me face the world in a more mature way.

Sometimes the same final elements that are cut off unacceptably with semicolons are separated even more sharply from their sentences with periods. The final part that has been cut off and placed in another sentence is usually labeled a *fragment.*

Spelling Rules

1. Spelling rules for *ie* and *ei* words

A. Use *ie* when the letters have the sound of *ee* (as in *eat*).

        achievement, piece, chief, belief

    Exceptions: 1.   after *c*, use *ei:* receive, deceit

                  2.   seize, (n)either, leisure, weird

B. Use *ei* when the letters have other sounds than *ee*.

        weight, height, foreign, their

    Exception: friend

2. Spelling rules for adding final elements

A. Adding -*es* rather than -*s*.

    (1) Add -*es* to nouns and verbs ending in sibilant sounds—*s, z, ch, sh, x*.
         glasses, buzzes, teaches, dishes, mixes

    (2) Add -*es* to nouns and verbs ending in *y* preceded by a consonant;
         the *y* changes to *i*.
         babies, carries

But: enjoys, monkeys (*y* is preceded by a vowel)

    (3) Add -*es* to some nouns ending in *o*.
         heroes, potatoes
         Other nouns ending in *o* may take either -*s* or -*es*.
         cargoes *or* cargos, volcanoes *or* volcanos
         (Check the dictionary if you are not sure whether -*s* or -*es* is required
         with such nouns.)

B. Doubling final consonants before added syllables *beginning with vowels*.

    Double the consonant if:

        the syllable ends in *one* consonant preceded by *one* vowel and the
        stress is on the syllable where the doubling might take place.

    One-syllable word   plán + ed = plánned
                     hót + er = hótter

    Two-syllable word   omít + ing = omítting
                     occúr + ence = occúrrence
              but: prefér + ence = préference (the stress shifts
                     to the first syllable)

In British usage, a final *l, p,* or *m*, is doubled even if the stress is not the final syllable—cáncelled, kídnapper, díagramming.

C. Dropping or keeping silent *e* before added syllables.

From *Writer's Companion* by Marcella Frank, Prentice-Hall, 1983.

    (1) Drop the *e* before a vowel.

        advertise + ing = advertising
        arrive + al = arrival
        noise + y = noisy (for this rule, the adjective ending *y* is treated as a vowel)

        Exception: When adjective suffixes beginning with *a, o, u* are added to words ending in *ce* or *ge,* the *e* is kept in order to prevent a change in pronunciation.

        noticeable, changeable

    (2) Keep the *e* before a consonant.

        advertise + ment = advertisement
        care + ful = careful
        entire + ly = entirely

        Exceptions: (a) In a few nouns ending in *-ment,* the *e* is dropped.[*]
                      judgment, abridgment
                  (b) The *e* is dropped before *th.*
                      width, ninth, fifth
                  (c) In words ending in *-ple, -ble,* or *-tle* the *le* is dropped before *ly.*
                      simply, possibly, subtly

D. Changing final *i* to *y* before added syllables.

    (1) Change *y* to *i* before a vowel.
        mystery + ous = mysterious
        marry + age = marriage
        easy + er = easier

    (2) Change *y* to *i* before a consonant.
        happy + ness = happiness
        glory + fy = glorify
        beauty + ful = beautiful
        easy + ly = easily

3. Spelling changes in prefixes before certain letters

AD = *to, at, toward*

ac + c	accelerate, accidental, accommodate
ac + q	acquaint, acquire, acquisition
af + f	affectation, affidavit, affiliate
ag + g	aggrandize, aggregate, aggressor
al + l	allegiance, allergy, alleviate
an + n	annex, annihilate, announcement

---

[*] British English keeps the *e* before the *-ment* suffix—judgement, abridgement.

ap + p	appreciate, approximate, applause
ar + r	arrangement, arrest, arrival, arrears
as + s	assignment, assistance, association
at + t	attempt, attorney, attraction

COM or CON = *with, together;* also an intensifier (from Latin *cum*)
(usually *con,* except before *m, p, b, r, l*)

com + m	commemorate, commercial, committee
com + p	compensate, competition, complicate
com + b	combat, combination, combustible
cor + r	correction, correspond, corrupt
col + l	collaborate, collapse, collateral

DIS = *away, apart, deprive of, cause to be the opposite of*

| dif + f | difference, difficulty, diffuse |

IN = *in, not;* also an intensifier

im + p	impartial, impractical, improvise
ir + r	irrational, irregular, irrelevant
il + l	illegal, illegible, illiterate
im + m	immature, immigrant, immobile
im + b	imbalance, imbecile, imbibe

OB = *toward, for, about, before*

oc + c	occasion, occupation, occurrence
op + p	opponent, opportunity, opposite
of + f	offensive, offer, official

SUB = *under, below*

suc + c	successful, succinct, succumb
suf + f	suffer, suffice, sufficient
sug + g	suggestion, suggestive
sum + m	summarize, summit, summon
sup + p	supplement, supplier, support, suppose

Irregular Verbs

Simple Form of the Verb	Past Tense	Past Participle
arise	arose	arisen
awake	awoke (*sometimes* awaked)	awaked (*Brit.* awoke, awoken)
be	was	been
bear	bore	borne (*meaning* carry)
		born (*meaning* have children)
beat	beat	beaten (*sometimes* beat)
become	became	become
begin	began	begun
bend	bent	bent
bet	bet (*sometimes* betted)	bet (*sometimes* betted)
bid (*meaning* offer money at an auction)	bid	bid
bid (*meaning* ask someone to do something)	bade (*or* bid)	bidden (*or* bid)
bind	bound	bound
bite	bit	bitten (*or* bit)
bleed	bled	bled
blow	blew	blown
break	broke	broken
breed	bred	bred
bring	brought	brought
broadcast	broadcast (*sometimes* broadcasted)	broadcast (*sometimes* broadcasted)
build	built	built
burst	burst	burst
buy	bought	bought
cast	cast	cast
catch	caught	caught
choose	chose	chosen
cling	clung	clung
come	came	come
cost	cost	cost
creep	crept	crept
dig	dug	dug
dive	dived (*or* dove)	dived
do	did	done

Adapted from *Modern English: Exercises for Non-native Speakers,* Part 1, *Parts of Speech,* 2d ed., by Marcella Frank, Prentice-Hall Regents, 1986, pages 233–36.

draw	drew	drawn
dream	dreamt (*more often* dreamed)	dreamt (*more often* dreamed)
drink	drank	drunk
drive	drove	driven
eat	ate	eaten
fall	fell	fallen
feed	fed	fed
feel	felt	felt
fight	fought	fought
find	found	found
flee	fled	fled
fling	flung	flung
fly	flew	flown
forbid	forbade (*or* forbad)	forbidden
forget	forgot	forgotten (*Brit.* forgot)
forsake	forsook	forsaken
freeze	froze	frozen
get	got	gotten (*Brit.* got)
give	gave	given
go	went	gone
grind	ground	ground
grow	grew	grown
hang	hung	hung
	hanged (*meaning* suspended by the neck)	hanged (*meaning* suspended by the neck)
have	had	had
hear	heard	heard
hide	hid	hidden (*or* hid)
hit	hit	hit
hold	held	held
hurt	hurt	hurt
keep	kept	kept
kneel	knelt (*or* kneeled)	knelt (*or* kneeled)
knit	knit (*or* knitted)	knit (*or* knitted)
know	knew	known
lay	laid	laid
lead	led	led
leap	leapt (*more often* leaped)	leapt (*more often* leaped)
leave	left	left
lend	lent	lent
let	let	let

lie	lay	lain
light	lit (*more often* lighted)	lit (*more often* lighted)
lose	lost	lost
make	made	made
mean	meant	meant
meet	met	met
mislay	mislaid	mislaid
mistake	mistook	mistaken
overcome	overcame	overcome
pay	paid	paid
put	put	put
read	read	read
rid	rid	rid
ride	rode	ridden
ring	rang	rung
rise	rose	risen
run	ran	run
say	said	said
see	saw	seen
seek	sought	sought
sell	sold	sold
send	sent	sent
set	set	set
sew	sewed	sewn (*or* sewed)
shake	shook	shaken
shed	shed	shed
shine (*intrans.*)	shone	shone
shoot	shot	shot
show	showed	shown (*or* showed)
shrink	shrank (*also* shrunk)	shrunk
shut	shut	shut
sing	sang	sung
sink	sank (*also* sunk)	sunk
sit	sat	sat
sleep	slept	slept
slide	slid	slid
slit	slit	slit
speak	spoke	spoken
speed	sped (*or* speeded)	sped (*or* speeded)
spend	spent	spent
spin	spun	spun
spit	spit (*sometimes* spat)	spit (*sometimes* spat)
split	split	split

spread	spread	spread
spring	sprang (*also* sprung)	sprung
stand	stood	stood
steal	stole	stolen
stick	stuck	stuck
sting	stung	stung
stink	stank (*also* stunk)	stunk
stride	strode	stridden
string	strung	strung
strive	strove (*also* strived)	striven (*also* strived)
swear	swore	sworn
sweep	swept	swept
swim	swam	swum
swing	swung	swung
take	took	taken
teach	taught	taught
tear	tore	torn
tell	told	told
think	thought	thought
thrive	throve (*or* thrived)	thriven (*or* thrived)
throw	threw	thrown
thrust	thrust	thrust
undergo	underwent	undergone
understand	understood	understood
wake	woke (*sometimes* waked)	waked (*Brit.* woke, woken)
wear	wore	worn
weave	wove	woven
weep	wept	wept
win	won	won
wind	wound	wound
withdraw	withdrew	withdrawn
withhold	withheld	withheld
withstand	withstood	withstood
wring	wrung	wrung
write	wrote	written

Answer Key

Unit 1. Traveling to Another Country

Exercise 1

4. very, 5. very, 6. so, 7. very, too, 8. so, very, 9. so, 10. so, 11. too, very,
12. so, 13. very, 14. very, too.

Exercise 2

A.2. left, got, put, 3. left, began, gone, 4. felt, felt, 5. ate, drank, eaten, drunk,
  6. thought, had, 7. knew, understood, 8. came, come, 9. written, told,
  10. said, hit, stolen, 11. seen, heard.

B.2. It had been made for me by my girlfriend.
  3. Such a wallet cannot be bought in this country.
  4. It was found by a customs inspector.
  5. It was given back to me by him.
  6. I was told by him to be very careful with money.
  7. All my money has already been spent.
  8. More money will be sent (to) me right away by my mother (or by my mother right
    away).
  9. Some bills will be paid with this money.
  10. The rest will be put in the bank.

Exercise 3

4. change, 5. to allow, to take, 6. preparing, 7. buying, getting, 8. make,
9. gather, 10. pack or to pack, 11. check, 12. looking, 13. to think, 14. beating,
15. being, 16. having, 17. thinking, 18. making.

Exercise 4

A.3. After I made, after making,
  4. After I purchased, After purchasing,
  5. After I received, After receiving,
  6. Before I left, Before leaving,
  7. Before I boarded, Before boarding,
  8. After the flight attendants served, After serving,
  9. After I arrived, After arriving,
  10. Before I was able, Before being able.

Exercise 5

A.3. (in order) to learn,

  4. (in order) to withdraw money, for money,

  5. (in order) to pick up my plane ticket, for my plane ticket,

  6. (in order) to get a shot, for a shot,

  7. in order not to be tired,

  8. in order not to be hungry,

  9. (in order) to claim my suitcases, for my suitcases,

 10. (in order) to have it.

B.3. for,   4. (in order) to,   5. (in order) to,   6. for,   7. (in order) to,   8. for,   9. for, 10. (in order) to.

Exercise 6

3. There was,   4. There were,   5. It was,   6. There was,   7. There was,   8. It was,   9. There was,   10. There was,   11. It was,   12. There were.

Exercise 7

2. objections, approval,   3. preparations,   4. anxiety,   5. withdrawal, purchased,   6. departure, tearful,   7. flight, comfortable, attentive, helpful,   8. passengers,   9. arrival, inspection,   10. nervous, frightened.

Exercise 8

2. a (doctor), medicine,   3. a lawyer,   4. a physicist,   5. an (economist), economics,   6. a psychiatrist,   7. an (accountant), accounting,   8. a chemist,   9. a (financier), finance,   10. a mathematician,   11. a (photographer), photography,   12. an engineer,   13. a psychologist,   14. a (nurse), nursing.

Exercise 9

2. Last month I flew to New York. (or ;) I had never flown on such a large airplane before.

3. My parents objected to my going away because I was not (or wasn't) used to living alone.

4. I had my tailor make some new clothes.

5. My heart almost stopped beating from fear and excitement.

6. I applied (for) a visa after getting (or I got) my passport.

7. I checked my luggage; (or .) then I boarded the plane for New York.

8. I went to the doctor to get a shot.

9. I worked hard for the money to come to this country.

10. There were many things that had to be done (or that I had to do) before I could leave.

11. It was very cold and windy when I arrived at Kennedy Airport.

12. There was a pretty girl sitting next to me.

13. I made a withdrawal from the bank; (or .) then I purchased my plane ticket.

14. When the day of departure arrived, I bid a tearful goodbye to my family and friends.

15. The flight was very comfortable; (or .) the flight attendants were attentive and helpful.

Exercise 10

A. carried, flies, delaying, journeys, hurried, accompanied, travel agencies, difficulties, studying, worried, enjoying, parties, annoying, delayed, employed.

B. loneliness, employee, enjoyment, luckily, librarian, friendlier, employment, variety, beautiful, mysterious, payment.

Unit 2. Geography

Exercise 1

1. (b) To the east of Italy is the Adriatic Sea,   (c) To the south of Italy is the Mediterranean Sea,   (d) To the west of Italy is the Mediterranean Sea.
2. (b) France is bordered on the south by the Mediterranean Sea and Spain,   (c) France is bordered on the west by the Atlantic Ocean.
3. (b) Paris is located in the northern part of France,   (c) Lisbon is located in the western part of Portugal,   (d) Madrid is located in the central (or north central) part of Spain,   (e) Rome is located in the western part of Italy,   (f) Berlin is located in the eastern part of Germany.

Exercise 2

2. —, —   3. the,   4. The, the, —,   5. —, —,   6. The, —,   7. The, —, —,   8. —, the,   9. The, —, the, the,   10. The, —, —,   11. The,   12. the.

Exercise 3

2. is surrounded, is attached,   3. are found,   4. are situated,   5. are grown,   6. are caught,   7. are raised,   8. is produced,   9. are manufactured,   10. are cultivated,   are raised,   11. are trapped,   12. are made.

Exercise 4

vegetables, beets, potatoes, grapes, coconuts, bananas, oats, oysters, pearls, eggs, feathers, cows, pigs, goats, textiles, chemicals, handicrafts, fertilizers.

meaning "kinds of"; fruits,   cheeses,   wools,   fishes,   wines

Exercise 6

3. Mexico City, (which is) the biggest city in my country, is located . . . ,
4. Two other big rivers in Italy flow into the Adriatic Sea, the Adige and the Piave.
5. The Amazon, (which is) the largest river system in the world, drains . . . ,
6. Africa, (which is) a great plateau, is about . . . ,
7. My country, Malaysia, . . .

Exercise 7

2. Saudi Arabia has two capitals, Riyadh and Mecca.
3. Europe, (which is) a huge peninsula, is subdivided . . .
4. Rising from great depths of the sea, the islands of Japan are mostly mountainous. (or The islands of Japan, rising from great depths of the sea, are mostly mountainous.)
5. In the northern part of Argentina is the Gran Chaco, a land of forests, lakes and swamps.
6. Once famous for its precious metals, Peru today produces . . . (or Peru, once famous . . .)
7. Alaska, the largest of the fifty states, has a variety . . . (or The largest of the fifty states, Alaska has a variety . . .)

Exercise 8

A.2. Scandinavia, which consists of (or consisting of) Norway, Sweden, and Denmark, is in the northern part of Europe.
3. New Delhi, (which is) the capital of India, is thickly populated.
4. Holland, which lacks (or lacking) natural resources, has been a nation of sailors for centuries.
5. South America, (which is) roughly triangular in shape, is joined to . . .
6. Chile, (which is) sometimes called the "Shoestring Republic," stretches along . . .
7. Israel, which lies (or lying) between Egypt and Jordan on the eastern shores of the Mediterranean, is a hot and arid land.

Exercise 9

2. (comma fault) We already have small industries, one of the largest of which is the textile industry.
3. There are also many other small islands, some of which are gathered in small archipelago fashion.
4. There are many rivers in Venezuela, the most important of which . . .
5. (comma fault) Most of Denmark is farm land, about half of which is used for grazing.
6. Island groups off the Asian mainland are Japan, the Philippines, and Indonesia, all of which have become . . .
7. (comma fault) Asia is very rich in natural resources, many of which have not been developed.

Exercise 10

2. Among the many metals in this area of the continent are gold and silver.

3. At the northern shore of Morocco is the Strait of Gibraltar.

4. Situated near the Persian Gulf are Iran's rich oil fields.

5. In the eastern part of South America are two broad plateaus.

6. Located in the Elburz Mountains is Demavend, Iran's highest peak.

7. Lying in the western Pacific is Micronesia, or "little islands."

Exercise 11

2. mining,   3. farms, farmers,   4. cultivation, rocky,   5. raising, grazing,
6. production,   7. boundary,   8. central,   9. Lying,
10. agricultural, manufactured,   produced,   11. developing, industrialized,
12. commercial, industrial,   13. economy, development, economic.

Exercise 12

2. The United States is bounded on the north by Canada and the Great Lakes.

3. London is located in the southeastern part of England.

4. The Suez Canal separates Africa from Asia.

5. North America and South America are situated in the Western Hemisphere.

6. Dairy products are made from milk.

7. Cultivating crops (or The cultivation of crops) is very difficult in rocky regions.

8. Manhattan is an island (which is) surrounded on all sides by water.

9. Lima, (which is) the capital of Peru, is situated on the west coast.

10. Mexico City, (which is) the biggest city in my country, is located in the central part of the Republic of Mexico.

11. The Pacific Ocean is the largest ocean in the world.

12. The Sahara Desert extends from the Atlantic Ocean to the Nile River.

13. My country has two important rivers, both of which (or Both of them) make a great contribution to the economy of the nation.

Unit 3. Biography

Exercise 1

2. in, (on),   3. from, to/until,   4. at,   5. —, in, from,   6. (on),   7. from, until,
8. at,   9. in,   10. on,   11. in, (on),   12. during.

Exercise 2

2. My friend has been visiting (or has visited) me since January (or for three months). My friend came to visit me two months ago.

3. Dimitri has been married since July 5 (or for one month). Dimitri got married one month ago.

4. Anabel has been a lawyer since February (or for ten months). Anabel became a lawyer ten months ago.

5. My older sister has been in the United States since 1976 (or for 20 years). My older sister arrived in the United States 20 years ago.

6. Georgia has been studying medicine since 1995 (or for three years). Georgia began to study medicine three years ago.

(In the above sentences the word *for* may be omitted.)

Exercise 3

A.3. it, which (or that) gave me (the) most trouble,

   4. there, where my brother went,

   5. she, who was teaching this subject,

   6. they, who came to say good-bye to me,

   7. there, where I was born,

   8. he, who encouraged me to go to the university,

   9. he, who helped me (to) learn the English language,

  10. they, which (or that), were taught in my school,

  11. there, where I studied (for) four years.

(*That* may be used instead of *who* in sentences 5, 6, 8, 9.)

B.2. it, which (or that) I had (for) a long time,

   3. it, which (or that) I received in high school,

   4. them, who(m) (or that) I met in elementary school,

   5. it, which (or that) I had to fill out,

   6. it, which (or that) I attended,

   7. him, whom (or that) I ever had,

   8. it, which (or that) I liked the best.

C. *Whom, which,* or *that* may be omitted from all the sentences in B.

D. 2. teacher, of whom I was most fond,

   3. street, on which I used to live,

   4. teacher, for whom I had the most respect,

   5. person in whom I had confidence,

   6. thing about which I could think,

   7. school to which I went,

   8. town from which I came (or come).

E.2. I was most fond of,   3. I used to live on,   4. I had the most respect for,

   5. I had confidence in,   6. I could think about,   7. I went to,

   8. I came (or come) from.

Exercise 4

3. The subject which (or that) gave me (the) most trouble in high school was English.
4. English, which gave me (the) most trouble in high school, is now . . .
5. Everyone on the block is helping the family whose house burned down yesterday.
6. The Johnsons, whose house burned down yesterday . . .
7. I would like to visit again the street on which I used to live (or where I used to live), or that I used to live on.
8. Everyone would enjoy visiting Tokyo, where I grew up.
9. My parents, who loved me very much, gave me everything I needed.
10. A boy whose parents had money could afford to go abroad to study.
11. My best friend, whose parents had money,   could . . .
12. The children with whom I used to play (or whom, who, that I used to play with, or I used to play with) all lived on the same block where I lived.

Exercise 5

2. , considered the founder of modern psychoanalysis,
3. , the first woman in Europe to earn her doctorate,
4. , the originator of the theory of evolution,
5. , shocked by the corruption of the Catholic Church,
6. , a patriot who wanted to see Italy made strong,

Exercise 6

2. infantile,   3. was born, died,   4. married, marriage, death,
5. was engaged, engagement, died,   6. biographer,   7. engaged, married,
8. births, deaths,   9. neighborhood,   10. occupation,   11. married,
12. birth, marriage, death.

Exercise 7

2. Albert Camus went to public schools in Algiers; (or .) then he entered the University of Algiers.
3. William Shakespeare, the famous playwright, was married to Anne Hathaway. He had three children.
4. The Prime Minister of England usually resides at 10 Downing Street in London.
5. Abraham Lincoln was born in 1809 in Kentucky. He was assassinated in Washington (on) April 15, 1865.
6. Mahatma Gandhi became engaged at the age of seven. (or ;) He married when he was fourteen years.
7. Sigmund Freud, (who is-was) the founder of modern psychoanalysis, had a great influence on modern thought.
8. Edgar Allan Poe married a young cousin of his in 1836. The marriage lasted until her death in 1847.
9. The teacher who taught me English was very strict.

10. Everyone would enjoy visiting the town where I come from (or which, that I come from, or I come from).

11. The Garzas, whose house burned down yesterday, are being helped by everyone on the block.

Unit 4. Instructions (how to make or do something)

Exercise 1

A.3. The seeds are planted in even rows.

  4. The table should be sandpapered before it is painted.

  5. The tennis ball is thrown high in the air and (it is) served . . .

  6. The oven should be preheated before the cake is put in it.

  7. Plenty of fluids should be drunk if you have a cold.

  8. A screwdriver is used to loosen the screws.

  9. The air in the tires should be checked before . . .

  10. All the dry ingredients are mixed and (are) added to the others.

  11. These exercises should be done regularly every morning.

Exercise 2

A.2. Your health would improve if you did these exercises.

  3. You would learn faster if you practiced every day.

  4. The piano would sound better if you had it tuned.

  5. The garden would look better if you watered the plants every day.

  6. The car could last a long time if you took good care of it.

  7. You could save money if you bought food in season.

  8. If you took some driving lessons, you would learn to park the car.

  9. If you followed these instructions carefully, you would have no trouble.

B.2. would have improved, had done,

  3. would have learned, had practiced,

  4. would have sounded better, had had,

  5. would have looked, had watered,

  6. could have lasted, had taken,

  7. could have saved, had bought,

  8. had taken, would have learned,

  9. had followed, would have had.

C.2. If you practiced a lot, you would be an excellent pianist.

  3. If you studied hard, you would become a good student.

  4. If you shopped wisely, you would save money.

  5. If you watched the road carefully, you would become a better driver.

  6. If you didn't look down at the keyboard keys, your keyboarding speed would improve.

  7. If you went outside, your work wouldn't get done.

D.2. had practiced, would have been,

　3. had studied, would have become,

　4. had shopped, would have saved,

　5. had watched, would have become,

　6. hadn't looked, would have improved,

　7. hadn't gone, would have got (ten).

Exercise 3

3. Pin (or you must pin) the pieces of material together carefully; otherwise the dress won't come out right.

4. Tune (or you should, must tune) the piano regularly; otherwise it won't sound right.

5. Hold (or you must hold) your fingers in the right position over the keyboard keys; otherwise you will make mistakes.

6. Follow the instructions carefully; otherwise you won't get your new computer to work.

7. Turn on (or you must turn on) the ignition in the car with your key; otherwise the car won't start.

8. Serve (or you must serve) the ball diagonally across into the box of your opponent; otherwise the serve doesn't count.

9. Learn (or you should, must learn) to skim in reading; otherwise you will never become a fast, efficient reader.

Exercise 4

3. don't have to put,　4. mustn't do,　5. mustn't leave,　6. don't have to take,

7. mustn't drive,　8. mustn't go,　9. don't have to do,　10. mustn't pick,

11. don't have to be.

Exercise 5

A.2. the pharmacist fill my prescription, my prescription filled,

　3. the bank teller cash my check, my check cashed,

　4. the lawyer draw up my will, my will drawn up,

　5. the administrative assistant make the travel arrangements, the travel arrangements made,

　6. the shoemaker repair my shoes, my shoes repaired,

　7. the auto mechanic change the rear tires, the rear tires changed,

　8. the painter paint the whole house, the whole house painted,

　9. the tailor lengthen my skirt, my skirt lengthened,

　10. the carpenter build some bookcases for me, some bookcases built for me,

　11. the gardener trim the hedges, the hedges trimmed,

　12. the handyman replace the furnace filters, the furnace filters replaced.

Exercise 6

2. Once the chicken is cooked, add the sautéed mushrooms.
3. Leave the pan on a low flame for 30 to 40 minutes.
4. After you hem the dress, the last step is ironing it.
5. correct,
6. When doing this dance step, place your arms on your partner's hips. (or When you do this dance step, your arms . . .)
7. If you construct and finish the table carefully, no one will know that you made the table yourself.
8. correct,
9. correct.

Exercise 7

2. that we show respect . . . , 3. that we never tell . . . , 4. that we let . . . ,
5. that we try . . . , 6. that we be . . . , 7. that we call attention . . . ,

Exercise 8

2. practical, 3. simple, 4. attractive, 5. delicious, 6. enjoyable, 7. nutritious,
8. sautéed, 9. simmered, 10. precaution, 11. incentive, 12. ingredient,
13. activity, 14. accomplishment, 15. alteration.

Exercise 9

2. A screwdriver is used to loosen the screws.
3. The piano would sound better if you had it tuned.
4. The car would last a long time if you took care of it.
5. If you had practiced every day, you would have learned faster.
6. Your illness would have got(ten) better if you had stayed in bed.
7. You should (or must) learn to skim in reading; otherwise you will never become a fast, efficient reader.
8. You must turn on the ignition in the car; otherwise the car won't (will not) start.
9. You mustn't add much turpentine if you want the paint to cover the wood completely.
10. Dale Carnegie advised that we (should) make the other person feel important.
11. I had the gardener trim the hedges.
12. I will or I'll have some bookcases built by the carpenter.

Unit 5. Holidays

Exercise 1

A.2. on,   3. (on),   4. at,   5. in,   6. On, in,   7. in, in,   8. On, at, at,   9. (on),
10. on, (on).

Exercise 2

3. (the) sixteenth,   4. the,   5. the, —,   6. (the) first,   7. the,   8. the third,
9. (the) twenty-fifth,   10. the, the.

Exercise 3

A.3. the enjoyment of holidays by children or children's enjoyment of holidays,
    4. the celebration of the good harvest of 1621 by the Pilgrims or the Pilgrims'
      celebration of . . .
    5. the election of government officials,
    6. the Declaration of Independence,
    7. the exchange of gifts,
    8. the observation of Memorial Day by Americans or Americans' observation of
      Memorial Day.

B. 5. electing government officials,
    7. exchanging gifts.

Exercise 4

2. honors, were,   3. wears, has,   4. have, takes,   5. is,   6. enjoy,   7. is, marks,
8. are, do,   9. gets, is,   10. are,   11. depends, has, cares,   12. is,   13. gets.

Exercise 5

2. Flowers for those who died in service to their country are bought on Memorial
   Day.
3. New clothes are sometimes worn on Easter Sunday.
4. Turkey is eaten on Thanksgiving Day.
5. Many holidays are observed on Mondays.
6. Store windows are decorated for . . .
7. A lot of money is sometimes spent to . . .
8. Horns are blown on New Year's Eve.
9. A wreath is put on . . .
10. Christmas carols are sung . . .
11. The flag is displayed . . .
12. New Year's resolutions are made . . .

Exercise 6

2. few,   3. many,   4. much,   5. a few,   6. much,   7. few,   8. a little,   9. a little,
10. little,   11. few,   12. much, little.

Exercise 7

2. customary, 3. death, 4. religious, 5. decorated, festive, 6. appearance,
7. enjoyment, 8. pride, heritage or inheritance, 9. merriment,
10. commemorates, 11. festivities or festivals, 12. symbolizes,
13. originally, birth, celebration, widened, enjoyable, activities,
14. basically, generally, especially, national.

Exercise 8

2. Mother's Day is observed in May, Father's Day in June.
3. Many holidays occurring (or that occur) on Sunday are celebrated (on) the following Monday.
4. It is customary for families to eat Thanksgiving dinner together.
5. The exchange of (or Exchanging) gifts adds enjoyment to (the) Christmas holidays.
6. Memorial Day is observed (on) the last Monday in May.
7. The decoration of (or Decorating) their homes takes some people a long time.
8. Everybody likes to have a holiday from work.
9. There are few people who do not enjoy holidays.
10. Few people came to the parade because of the heat.
11. In the United States, Election Day occurs (on) the first Tuesday after the first Monday in November.
12. There is a lot of noise (on) New Year's Eve.
13. Each of their children gets (or got, will get) a handmade gift for the holiday.
14. A lot of (or Lots of) money is (or was, will be) spent (in) preparing for the (or a) holiday.
15. Some holidays are basically religious, (or ;) others are generally observed by everyone in the country.

Exercise 10

2. Boxes, sweethearts, 3. buses or busses, beaches, 4. leaves, trees,
5. days, dishes, 6. beliefs, 7. churches, prayers, blessings,
8. parties, costumes, games, 9. classes, businesses, 10. witches, symbols,
11. wishes, 12. cemeteries, wreaths, graves, 13. speeches, parades.

Unit 6. Telling Stories

Exercise 1

A.2. Chicken Little told Ducky-Lucky that the sky was falling and that they had to tell the king.
  3. Rumpelstiltskin told the maiden that he would spin the gold if she would give him her firstborn child.

4. The Beast told Beauty that she had forgotten (informal—forgot) her promise, and so he decided to die, for he could not live without her.

5. The giant said that he smelled the blood of an Englishman.

6. The wolf told the little pig that he would huff and puff and blow his house in.

7. Bluebeard told his wife that she would die at once because she had disobeyed him.

8. Father Bear told Mother Bear that someone had been sleeping in his bed.

B.2. They said, "Clothes made of this cloth are invisible to a stupid person."

3. The emperor said, "If I wear such clothes I can distinguish the clever people from the stupid."

4. The emperor said, "I have to have this cloth woven for me immediately."

5. The people who saw the emperor in the procession said, "He looks marvelous in his new clothes."

6. A little child said, "The emperor has nothing on at all."

7. All the people finally said, "The emperor is not wearing any clothes at all."

Exercise 2

2. Cinderella asked her stepsisters whether (or if) they had enjoyed themselves at the ball.

3. The genie of the lamp asked Aladdin what his wish was.

4. Bluebeard asked his wife why there was blood on the key.

5. The two thieves asked the emperor whether (or if) it wasn't a beautiful piece of cloth.

6. The emperor asked whether (or if) his suit didn't fit him marvelously.

7. A little child who was watching the procession asked why the emperor wasn't wearing any clothes.

8. At the ball, all the people asked who that beautiful girl was.

Exercise 3

1. c. What big legs you have.   d. How strangely you are behaving.

2. a. What a nice cottage this is   b. How small the beds look   c. How good this food tastes.   d. How tired and sleepy I am.   e. How very far I have gone.

3. a. How lucky I am to see such a beautiful girl.   b. How beautiful she is.
   c. What a beautiful girl she is.

4. a. What a beautiful color the cloth is.   b. How well the clothes fit.
   c. How magnificent your new clothes are.

Exercise 4

2. A fable is a fictitious narrative intended to teach some moral truth in which animals act like human beings.

3. A legend is an oral narrative about some wonderful event handed down for generations among a people and popularly believed to have a historical basis. 4. A myth is

a traditional story about gods and heroes, serving to explain some natural phenom-
enon, the origin of man, or the customs and institutions of a people.

5. An epic is a long narrative poem in very dignified style celebrating episodes of a
people's heroic tradition.

Exercise 5

2. found, beginning,
3. diminutive, rarely, harmful, mischievous,
4. finally, heroine, strength, cleverness, assistance,
5. attractive, appearance, lovely, virtuous princess,
6. caused, jealousy, wicked,
7. favorite,
8. purity, innocence,
9. beautiful, immediately,
10. abandoned,
11. disobedience, forbidden,
12. Chinese, magician.

Exercise 6

2. Cinderella said to her stepsisters, "I will help you (to) get ready for the ball."
3. Little Red Riding Hood said to the wolf, "Grandmother, what big teeth you have."
4. The weavers said (that) they could weave the finest cloth in the world.
5. All the people finally said (that) the emperor was not wearing any clothes at all.
6. Bluebeard asked his wife, "Why is there blood on the key?"
7. The genie asked Aladdin, "What is your wish?"
8. The sultan asked his minister whether (or if) he had ever seen such precious jewels.
9. Aladdin asked the magician why they had come to the cave.
10. When Hansel touched the house he cried, "Gretel, it is good enough to eat!"
11. The queen asked the magic mirror, "Who is the most beautiful woman?"
12. Cinderella asked how she could get to the ball.

Exercise 7

Meanings are given earlier in the exercise.

Exercise 8

A. confusion, engagement, advertisement, ninety, arrival, excitement, observance, immediately, shining, useful, dining, accurately, shiny, invitation, fortunately, continuing, practicing, safety, natural, completely, nervous, noisy, entirely, announcement,
judgment, (*Brit.* judgement), argument, (*Brit.* arguement), lovely, financial, writing.

B. noticeable, advantageous, twelfth, changeable, ninth, courageous, fifth.

Unit 7. Superstitious Beliefs

Exercise 1

3. If a woman wants to have a baby boy, she will wear blue colors during her pregnancy.
4. The groom will carry his bride . . . if he wants to avoid . . .
5. If your left hand itches, you will receive money.
6. You will give away money if your right hand itches.

(*Note:* In nos. 3 and 4, the verb in the main clause may be in the present tense.)

Exercise 2

2. If you walk under a ladder, you will have bad luck. Walking under a ladder will bring you bad luck.
3. If a black cat crosses your path, . . . A black cat's crossing your path . . .
4. If you spill salt on the table, . . . spilling salt . . .
5. If you find a four-leaf clover, . . . Finding a four-leaf clover . . .
6. If you find a penny, . . . Finding a penny . . .
7. If you open an umbrella in the house, . . . Opening an umbrella . . .
8. If you break off the bigger end of the wishbone, . . . Breaking off . . .

Exercise 3

A.2. gave, would put, 3. tried, would get, 4. decided, would not have,
5. got, would wear, 6. gave, would give, 7. stepped, would say.

B.2. had given, would have put, 3. had tried, would have got (ten),
4. had decided, would not have had, 5. had got (ten), would have worn,
6. had given, would have given, 7. had stepped, would have said.

Exercise 4

4. ; therefore, 5. ; otherwise, 6. ; however, 7. ; therefore, 8. ; however,
9. ; therefore, 10. ; otherwise.

Exercise 5

A.3. A-The, a, —, 4. —, the, 5. a-the, —, —, 6. The, —, 7. —, a, —, —,
8. a, —, 9. A, a.

B.2. a, —, the, the —. 3. the, —, the, 4. an, the, —. 5. a, the, a,
6. a, a, The, a.

C.2. A, the, 3. The-a, the, the, 4. —, an, 5. —, an, the, 6. the, the, the, —, —, 7.
An-the, —, —, 8. —, the.

(*Note:* Sometimes *the* is used before the word *number,* as could be done in sentences 4 and 8.)

Exercise 6

4. most of the,   5. most,   6. the most,   7. most,   8. most of the,   9. most of the,
10. most,   11. most of the,   12. most.

Exercise 7

2. superstition, unreasonable, belief, supernatural,
3. originates, ignorance, natural, causes.
4. —, —, mysterious,
5. signs, omens, symbolize, —, —.
6. unlucky,
7. Seeing, signal, death,
8. Misfortune, breaking.

Exercise 8

2. If a black cat crosses your path, you will be unlucky.
3. Breaking a mirror will bring you bad luck.
4. If a bridesmaid had caught the bridal bouquet, she would have become a bride herself within the following year.
5. If someone sneezed, I would say, "God bless you."
6. If I had decided to get married, I would not have had the wedding on Friday 13 (or the thirteenth).
7. He was worried because the-a mirror had fallen (informal-fell) off the wall in the bedroom.
8. Superstition is the result of fear of the unknown.
9. The house where he used to live is (was) haunted by ghosts.
10. Tradition has preserved many superstitions.
11. There was once a belief that gold could be made by man.
12. Seeing a crow is a sign of death.

Exercise 10

1. orderly, cautious, self-confidence, planner.
2. friendly, unpredictable, good humor, objectivity, intimacy, nonconformist.
3. imaginative, changeable, disorganized, subtlety, security, reality.
4. courageous, impulsive, aggressiveness, initiative, patience, persistence.
5. determined, conservative, vitality.
6. talkative, adaptable, versatility, warmth.
7. possessive, changeable, intuition, security.
8. cheerful, dictatorial, arrogance, generosity.
9. modest, diligent, fanatic.
10. hesitant, intellectual, emotional, commitment.
11. suspicious, determination, loyalty.
12. friendly, enthusiastic, persistence.

Unit 8. Rules of Etiquette (politeness)

Exercise 1

2. bring up, grow up,   3. call up,   4. takes off, comes into,   5. bring up,
6. eat in, eat out,   7. take off,   8. make up,   9. gets (stands) up, comes into,
10. picked up,   11. turn up.   12. put out

Exercise 2

3. turned it down,

4. put it off,

5. didn't bring him up, are not bringing him up, will not bring him up,

6. get over it,

7. pick them out, does not try them on,

8. call them up,

9. take it off,

10. call for her, takes her out,

11. call it off.

Exercise 3

2. . . . Then we start . . . ,

3. (use all we's or all you's),

4. . . . Finally we eat some dessert.

5. When you are . . .

6. (use all we's or all you's),

7. (use all one's or all you's).

Exercise 4

2. disobedient, misbehave,

3. impolite, disrespectful,

4. inconsiderate, indecent, disapproval,

5. unaccustomed, unacceptable, impropriety,

6. immodest,

7. inappropriate, improper,

8. unable, inability,

9. disapprove, disregards.

Exercise 5

2. medieval, chivalrous,   3. well-mannered, ill-mannered,   4. well-bred, ill-bred,
5. behavior, courteous, impolite,   6. courtesy, consideration, behaves, propriety, decency.
7. socially, customary,   8. permissive, politeness, courtesy,   9. obedient, respectful,
permission,   10. lying,   11. promptly, invitation,   12. punctually, invited.

Exercise 6

A.2. Parents should bring up their children to have good manners, so that when the children grow up, they will be well-bred.

3. The date of-on this invitation is illegible. (or;) I can't make it out.

4. They are worried about their son. They are afraid they have not brought him up or (didn't bring him up, are not bringing him up, will not bring him up) well.

5. He never wears clothes that suit the occasion. He doesn't know how to pick them out.

6. She is wearing (or was wearing, wore) a beautiful dress, but nothing else that she has (or had) on goes (or went) with it.

B.1. It is impolite to be disrespectful to one's elders.

2. A person who is unable to like other people often has the inability to be polite to them.

3. It is unpleasant to be with people who are discourteous.

4. They have disobedient children who misbehave.

5. Rules of etiquette tell us what kind of behavior is courteous and considerate.

6. You should arrive punctually when you are invited to dinner.

Unit 9. Vacations

Exercise 1

3. preparing, 4. spending, 5. impressed, 6. strolling, 7. seen, 8. interested,
9. being spent, 10. destroyed, rebuilt, 11. worn, 12. being constructed, stopped,
13. trying.

Exercise 2

2. interesting, interested, 3. amazed, amazing, 4. tiring, tired,
5. satisfying, satisfied, 6. shocked, shocking, 7. surprised, surprising.

Exercise 3

A. 3. hospitality unmatched anywhere . . . ,

4. Although advised to check . . . ,

5. Anyone looking for . . . ,

6. While eating dinner . . . ,

7. people strolling along . . . ,

8. . . . located along . . . ,

9. If given the opportunity . . .

B. 3. seeing the amazing sights that our town offers,

4. discovering a-the wonderful marketplace outside the town,

5. not wishing to take the side trip to the canyon,

6. before leaving for their trip,
7. coming to New York,
8. watching the clowns, acrobats, aerialists and animals perform (or performing),
9. not staying at that hotel,
10. collecting tickets in this off-Broadway theater.

Exercise 4

A.2. your traveling with me,
3. staying with me,
4. making your phone reservation,
5. bringing traveler's checks,
6. using the surfboard, riding (on) the waves,
7. exploring these ruins,
8. taking an evening flight,
9. arriving late at our hotel,
10. constructing this highway,
11. seeing the sunset at Waikiki Beach.

Exercise 5

A.3. would rather have,   4. had better take,   5. would rather have relaxed,
6. had better take,   7. would rather take,   8. had better not bring,
9. would rather not go,   10. had better not go,   11. would rather stay,
12. had better come,   13. would rather have visited.

Exercise 6

2. carefully, departure, arrival,
3. recommendation, luggage,
4. advice, beautiful natural scenery,
5. hospitable, friendly, honest, comfortable, enjoyable,
6. description, explanation, religious, historic(al),
7. architectural, civilization,
8. skiing, surfing,
9. tropical,
10. panoramic, breathtaking,
11. colorful, ceramics,
12. accommodates,
13. recreational, mountainous, farming.

Exercise 7

2. Many colorful birds can be seen in our jungles.
3. A lot of money is being spent now to improve (or for the improvement of) our roads.

4. You may see all kinds of interesting sights in this village.

5. While eating (or you eat) dinner, you will enjoy a fantastic floor show.

6. The cliffs located (or that are located) along the coast are very steep.

7. Before coming (or you come) to the country, you should look over the travel brochures.

8. Near San Francisco you will visit a modern castle containing (or that contains) many works of art.

9. Anyone not wishing (or who does not wish) to take the side trip should inform the tour director.

10. After being delayed (or it was delayed) two hours (or a delay of two hours), the train finally pulled into the station.

11. Before having gone (or going) or Before they had gone (or went) into the desert, they never realized (or had realized) how beautiful it could be.

12. You may risk losing your money if you do not (or don't) keep it in a safe place.

13. I suggest that you visit (or your visiting) the ruins of the castle.

14. It is recommended that tourists not drink the water in the small villages.

15. You will be greatly impressed by the tropical plants in (or of) the country.

Exercise 8

beginner, druggist, suffering, shipped, occurrence, shining, limited, wrapped, sunny, benefited, biggest, muddy, raining, equipped, equipment, marvelous (*Brit.* marvellous), canceled (*Brit.* cancelled), diagraming (*Brit.* diagramming), worshiper (*Brit.* worshipper).